FIGHT ANOTHER DAY

FIGHT ANOTHER DAY

Christopher Langley

May 2013

LT COLONEL J.M. LANGLEY, MBE, MC

WITH AN INTRODUCTION BY AIREY NEAVE, DSO, MC, MP

Pen & Sword
MILITARY

First published in Great Britain in 1974 by
William Collins Sons & Co Ltd

Reprinted in this format in 2013 by
Pen & Sword Military
An imprint of
Pen & Sword Books Ltd
47 Church Street
Barnsley
South Yorkshire
S70 2AS

ISBN 978 1 78159 253 3

A CIP catalogue record for this book is
available from the British Library

Typeset in Sabon by Phoenix Typesetting, Auldgirth, Dumfriesshire

Printed and bound in England
By CPI Group (UK) Ltd, Croydon, CR0 4YY

Pen & Sword Books Ltd incorporates the Imprints of Pen & Sword Aviation,
Pen & Sword Family History, Pen & Sword Maritime, Pen & Sword Military,
Pen & Sword Discovery, Pen & Sword Politics, Pen & Sword Archaeology,
Pen & Sword Atlas, Wharncliffe Local History, Wharncliffe True Crime,
Wharncliffe Transport, Pen & Sword Select, Pen & Sword Military Classics,
Leo Cooper, The Praetorian Press, Claymore Press, Remember When,
Seaforth Publishing and Frontline Publishing

For a complete list of Pen & Sword titles please contact
PEN & SWORD BOOKS LIMITED
47 Church Street, Barnsley, South Yorkshire, S70 2AS, England
E-mail: enquiries@pen-and-sword.co.uk
Website: www.pen-and-sword.co.uk

This book is dedicated to my five children
in the hope that they will never have
to fight another day

Author's Note:

Although all the events described in this book are true I have in certain cases changed the names of some of the people involved.

Contents

Illustrations and Maps

Illustrations

The drawings throughout the text are by John Western

Maps

Introduction

by Airey Neave, DSO, MC, MP

During the Second World War the organization of secret escape routes broke fresh ground in military intelligence, and Jimmy Langley, the author, was one of the first in the field. His half-humorous style, ignoring his own sacrifice, epitomizes the spirit of those days. Despite the loss of his arm in France in 1940, he not only escaped from France but for the rest of the war was concerned in helping others to safety.

We are now able, 30 years afterwards, to judge the contribution to the Allied victory of all those who worked to get back to fight another day. As this book illustrates, the highest tribute must be to those who constantly risked their lives in German-occupied territory. Thanks to them, over 3000 Allied airmen and several hundred soldiers evaded capture. The balance of sacrifice was tragic. We know that 500 men and women were executed or died in concentration camps. A far greater number succumbed to their ill-treatment after Europe was liberated from the Nazis. It may well be, as Jimmy Langley suggests, that for every man who got back a Belgian, Dutch or French patriot died.

This is something we, who did not endure occupation, must never forget. It is part of the history of this century that from the first dark hours of German invasion there were always men and women from ordinary homes ready to hide helpless British soldiers. They showed a sense of human values that we badly need today. Those who are still alive seek no publicity. Their memorial lies in the great achievements of the underground escape movement in saving lives. They acted in the name of charity and freedom. Unlike the men they rescued, who were protected by the Geneva Convention on prisoners of war, they were civilians exposed to brutal treatment by the Nazi counter-espionage Services.

These brave people came from every side. Communists and priests combined in what they believed to be a great human cause. It inspired doctors, nurses, artists and poets, but the majority came from simple cafés and farms in every corner of North-West Europe. They wished to play their part, however humble, in the Allied struggle. At the end of the war it was known that several thousand had each in some way influenced the return of a fighting man.

Such a movement, however spontaneous, could not have succeeded without leaders. There were four great pioneers who worked largely without any aid from England. Colonel Ian Garrow, Louis Nouveau, Andrée de Jongh (Dedée) and General Albert Guerisse (Pat O'Leary). Jimmy Langley describes their wonderful careers and the obstacles and dangers which they overcame to create the first escape routes to neutral Spain. Without them we could have done little. They all possessed the quality of true leadership. There were others who followed their example, so that by the end of the war the member of an aircrew, if he were shot down, had more than an even chance of getting home—one young pilot was back within a week.

It was the sudden reappearance of airmen reported lost, at RAF Stations, that had so deep an impact. When the great raids on Germany began, and losses began to mount, these miraculous returns from the unknown encouraged the whole RAF. They knew that, even if wounded, they had a chance of avoiding capture. The lectures and escape aids of MI 9 increased their confidence. More than once we took an airman back to his Station after one of our successful operations by sea from Brittany. The joy with which he was greeted made all our efforts worth while.

There were more hard-headed calculations. These trained aircrew were of vital importance. Sadly, many of them were killed on later operations.

By 1942, most flying men had come to realize the value of our work, even if the Air Ministry were slow to back Room 900. In October of that year I took the colourful Mary Lindell, Comtesse de Milleville, to RAF Tangmere for her flight by

Lysander to France. (It was she who organized the return of the two surviving 'cockleshell heroes' after the Commando raid on Bordeaux.) Out of the moonlight came a very young pilot, a Battle of Britain type, wearing the DSO and DFC. No one who knew those men can ever forget them as they were. A slight figure, he took both her hands in his: 'I just wanted to thank you for going over there.'

No study of the escape organizations would be complete without a note on the essential significance in their operation of women guides and couriers. Quite young girls took on the responsibility of escorting parties of airmen who knew no French from Brussels or Paris by train to the Spanish Frontier. They had to face controls and perhaps interrogation and keep their heads in dangerous moments. Among the most courageous was Peggy van Lier, Jimmy Langley's wife, who narrowly survived. These young girls were ideal for the dangerous task of guide, but they ran enormous risks. By the end of 1942 the Germans were infiltrating the lines with their own agents disguised as 'Americans'. They also made devastating use of the British traitor, Harold Cole.

Helping evaders to safety was a role particularly suited to women. Airmen were often ill or wounded, and needed nursing in secret for weeks on end. Then there was the problem of hiding and feeding them in a chain of 'safe' houses until they could be guided to the frontier or sometimes be taken off by sea. Belonging to an escape organization was distinguished from espionage and sabotage as humanitarian or even 'Red Cross' work. Inevitably, the different missions became entangled, much to the fury of the redoubtable Sir Claude Dansey of the Secret Intelligence Service at Broadway Buildings in Westminster. He had his priorities. But what patriot would refuse to help an Allied airman on the run?

The strange organization known as 'Room 900', which Jimmy Langley vividly describes, had no real precedent, though there have been many famous escape routes in history. I mention two. The Giffards of Chillington, the Pendrells, the Lanes and other brave families smuggled Charles II to

France in 1651. In October 1915 Nurse Edith Cavell was shot by the Germans for hiding British soldiers in her clinic in Brussels and helping them to neutral territory in Holland. Three centuries ago men were ready to die for their king and the Catholic faith. At the beginning of our own century Edith Cavell did what she believed to be morally right—to give aid to helpless British soldiers—and she explained as much to the Germans. During the Second World War hers was the example. It was her legend which brought a human touch to the escape movement and helped to distinguish 'Room 900' (an accommodation address at the War Office) from the regular Secret Intelligence Service of which it formed a tiny part.

Jimmy Langley has described the eccentric and frustrating set-up at Broadway and the attitude of the Secret Intelligence Service towards escaping in general. In fact, it was due to his perseverance that Room 900 got any results. I remember at my first meeting with 'Uncle Claude'. He gave me such a freezing glance that I wondered if I had been wise to escape from Colditz in January 1942. 1942 was a tremendous year for me, arriving at Broadway Buildings on the second anniversary of my capture by the Germans and, in December, marrying a direct descendant of the Giffards of Chillington who had saved Charles II. Like Jimmy Langley, I was practically and emotionally involved in the whole business of escape and its organizations.

In this book the reader will find many anecdotes of wartime intelligence giving it a special flavour. From 1941, when, despite his terrible wound, he escaped from Lille, Jimmy Langley's career was one of devotion to the escape lines. I know that he experienced much disappointment. He was accused by the sarcastic Dansey of 'loving his agents'. Those of us who had experience of the escape lines disliked this cynical attitude. By the end of the war Jimmy Langley's one-man section mysteriously entitled 'IV Z', was manned by other escapers, including Ian Garrow. We were all young and we made several blunders. Perhaps, as Jimmy Langley says, we were 'too little and too late'. If there had been a separate organization from the Secret Intelligence Service much more might have been achieved.

We were supported throughout our battles with 'Uncle Claude' by the remarkable soldier who first founded this novel branch of secret intelligence. Brigadier Norman Crockatt was the creator of MI 9—his work in training the armed forces to evade capture deserves a separate and important book. It was he who persuaded the Secret Intelligence Service to accept responsibility for building an underground escape system in Occupied Territory. This meant that Room 900 remained 'small beer' throughout the war. (But it was intimate and amusing. With our fellow operators, 'Monday' at the British Embassy in Madrid, and Donald Darling, 'Sunday', at Gibraltar, we tried to give encouragement and aid to our own people in the field.

I hope that all who read this fascinating and honest account by Jimmy Langley will sense the sorrow and elation, the triumph and tragedy of the escape lines. He has made through this book his own unique contribution to a moving chapter in the history of war.

I. HE WHO FIGHTS

Dunkirk

1

Build Up for Battle

'I do not know what you will do in life but at all costs avoid becoming a club or pub bore,' my father would often say, adding, 'the worst are those who talk or write about themselves.' It is largely due to the insistence of my children, who assure me I have a good tale to tell about how I passed the wartime years, that I have disregarded this excellent advice. It was my good fortune to be associated with a large number of men and women whose patriotism and courage went far beyond the call of duty and much of what I have written is a small token of my appreciation for all that they did.

War, as I saw it, was largely courage, suffering bravely borne, dogged determination to carry on in the face of disaster, and triumphs over the well nigh impossible. However, there were other less pleasing aspects – incredible blunders, muddled and confused thinking, treachery and betrayal. I believe my experiences represent a fair balance between men's achievements and their failures; further, for good measure, it is leavened with humour which so often brightened even the darkest hour.

During the inter-war years a distinguished, if stupid, soldier of renown achieved notoriety by his oft-repeated statement, 'I recommended my servant for the VC because he followed me wherever I went.' I do not fall into that category, though I must confess I thought that when I 'escaped' from the Germans the whole business of getting back to England would be a matter of some congratulation; but I never imagined it would be regarded as an epic of courage and endurance, as it was by many. At the time it was useless to point out that as the Germans had acquired half Europe they had more problems on their plate than trying to catch one junior army officer, that running away hardly came into the category of bravery, and that travelling by train and hiding in hotels did not call for much endurance. I hold this view today, and indeed when I was asked if I would accept an offer to represent the escapers of the last war in the Association of POWs of the 1914–18 War I refused, solely on the ground that I was not a genuine escaper.

My activities in the second half of the war in helping escapers, or perhaps more accurately 'evaders', to return from enemy-occupied territory was more in my blood. At the outbreak of the First World War my father had given up a promising career at the Bar to join the South Staffordshire Regiment. He was wounded, and on recovering was appointed Assistant Military Attaché in Berne. This, as I discovered many years later, was a cover for his work as a member of the British Intelligence Service. I doubt if he ever expected his son to follow in the same career.

I was in fact one of the 'war babies', and made my own small personal contribution by very nearly becoming a casualty on the home front a few weeks after my birth. A minor stomach operation was bungled by a young and inexperienced surgeon, and those in authority made the necessary arrangements for what they considered was inevitable. However, my mother took a different view and moved herself into the nursing home to what she called 'take charge'.

I have never been able to obtain a clear and unbiased account of the subsequent battle with the matron. My mother would never go further than saying 'At least I saved your life', the look on her face and the tone of her voice indicating that the cost was high. Apart from survival, my souvenir of this event was a stomach scar which truly fitted a 'war baby', and through the years ahead excited the interest and admiration of doctors.

Early in 1918 the family joined my father in Switzerland, where we all remained for the rest of the war. When peace came we all returned to England. My father was full of confidence that he could take up where he had left off five years before; after all, the 'War to end all Wars' had been

A CAREER.

(The Right Man in the Right Place.)

You should see our son James!
You should just see our James!
As bright as a button, as sharp as a knife!
My wife says to me and I say to my wife,
"You 'll never have seen such a son in your life
As our jammy son, James."

He is now three years old;
He 's a good three years old;
When the fellow was two you could see by his brow
(At the age of a year, you could guess by the row)
That this was a coming celebrity. Now
He 's a stout three-year-old.

Question: What shall he be?
Tell us, what shall he be?
Shall he follow his father and go to the Bar,
Where, passing his father, he 's bound to go far?
"But one knows," says his mother, "what barristers are.
Something else he must be!"

Do you fancy a Haig?
Shall our James be a Haig?
The War Office tell me he 's late for this war,
Have the honour to add there won't be any more
Since that 's what the League of the Nations is for;
So it 's off about Haig.

But his mother sees light
(Mothers always see light).
"This League of the Nations we mentioned above,
With the motto, 'Be Quiet,' the trade-mark, a Dove,
Will be wanting a President, won't it, my love?"
Jimmy's mother sees light.

Yes, that could be arranged;
Nay, it must be arranged.
In the matter of years Master Jimmy would meet
Presidential requirements. What age can compete,
In avoiding the gawdy, achieving the neat,
With forty to fifty? Thus, forty-five be 't.
Given forty-two years, he 'll be finding his feet
And the Treaty of Peace should be getting complete . . .
And so that 's all arranged.

HENRY.

won, and did not the greatest politician of the age talk of 'Homes for Heroes'? Alas, as two generations of men and women who fought for Britain now know only too well, the nation's gratitude is very short lived, and 'God is forgotten and the soldier slighted' with the most astonishing rapidity.

My father was probably better off than a million or more others, since as a contributor to *Punch* he had achieved considerable success with his 'Watchdog' series of humorous despatches from the trenches. He also wrote a number of amusing poems, one of which, 'A Career', was to prove over optimistic!

However, the next six years was a hard, relentless struggle to rebuild a shattered career, and it was not until 1925 that he was on the road to success and able to launch me on the educational programme as accepted by the professional classes of the time: preparatory and public schools followed by university.

My particular preparatory school, Aldeburgh Lodge, was situated at Aldeburgh in Suffolk, later to become famous for its Festival. The school had the simple aim of training boys for the public schools from which, it was confidently assumed, they would go on to be leaders within the British Empire. The theme was service to God, King and Country, which required unquestioning obedience to those in authority, a stiff upper lip and a goodly measure of 'play up, play up and play the game.' Discipline was strict but just and the only thing I really disliked was the food.

It is, however, an ill wind that blows nobody any good as the following conversation in 1946 with a colleague who had survived three years on the Burma railway as a Japanese POW shows.

'It was absolutely bloody, I suppose. You're lucky to be alive.'

'Yes, I owe my survival largely to Aldeburgh Lodge.'

'How come?'

'The Jap food was better. I used to say to myself every day – you survived Aldeburgh Lodge food and therefore you will not have much difficulty in surviving here.'

All in all I look back with gratitude to my four years at

Aldeburgh Lodge, where, though never happy, I received a training that was to prove of immense value in life ahead, and a sense of pride in one's country. Empire Day was a whole holiday and our heroes were Captains Scott and Oates, Admiral Nelson and Nurse Edith Cavell; our poetry 'The Charge of the Light Brigade' and 'How Horatius held the Bridge'; our music 'Land of Hope and Glory' and 'Onward Christian Soldiers'. Better than film stars, footballers and pop music? I still think so! Tough and active both physically and mentally, the headmaster expected the same from others. 'You must do something in life. In the churchyard over one grave there is the following epitaph – "He did no harm, neither did he good" – What a miserable life. Do something, if you only kill your mother at least you will have done something. But do not tell your mother my advice!' Strong medicine for the young.

In the autumn of 1929 I went on to Father's old school, Uppingham, and then in 1934 I left for Cambridge destined for my father's old college, Gonville and Caius. However, there was a change in plan when, in reply to a letter from him requesting I be allocated his old rooms, the bursar stated it would first be necessary for me to pass the college entrance examination. To this intolerable interference with the laws of nepotism my father stiffly replied that if this was the case he would wish me to go to the best college, and in due course I was accepted for Trinity Hall.

I started off studying history, until the boredom of reading about Europe in the Middle Ages drove me to economics. The Americans have a delightful word for use by an individual when he is completely at sea, 'CAIK', standing for 'Christ am I Konfused'. When the uninitiated point out that 'confused' is not spelt with a 'K' they are roughly informed that this stresses just how confused the speaker is. Towards the end of my second year I was well and truly in the 'CAIK' class as far as my studies of economics were concerned and I could see little hope of extracting myself. Convinced anyway that war with Germany was inevitable, I decided to leave Cambridge and join the army. My father, who put himself in charge of selecting the most suitable regiment, chose the Coldstream Guards, the tradition and history of which I knew nothing, in preference to the South Staffordshire Regiment, with which he had served in France. Years later I asked him why.

'No problem. For some months I was in close association with a battalion of the Rifle Brigade, the Greenjackets, near Ypres in 1915. One evening there was a discussion in the mess as to the fighting qualities of the regiments which go to make up the British Army. Opinion differed so the commanding officer proposed that every officer should write on a slip of paper the name of the regiment he would wish to have on his flanks in attack or retreat. The results were in favour of the Brigade of Guards with the Coldstream one vote ahead of the Grenadiers.'

I could not resist asking why he had not selected the Rifle Brigade.

'You have not sufficient intelligence to live happily day after day with Wykehamists.'

My interview with Colonel Arthur Smith, commanding the Regiment, was not an easy one. After inviting me to be seated, he looked at me in silence for a few moments and then said 'Why do you want to join the army and why this regiment?' I had expected an interrogation about my career to date, so these questions took me by surprise.

'I think there will be a war in a year or two, sir, and my father said he wished me to join the best regiment in the British Army.'

'Two good reasons. Now what do you usually eat at breakfast?'

I could not for the life of me see how what I ate at breakfast could have anything to do with joining the regiment, but mine not to reason why.

'Eggs and bacon, or kippers – toast, butter and marmalade, sir.'

'Butter *and* marmalade?'

'Yes, sir.'

'Well, you should not have both. If ever you have breakfast with me you will be offered butter *or* marmalade.'

I made a mental note to confine myself to dry toast should ever we breakfast together.

'Are you frightened of me?'

I had been warned that Colonel Arthur detested any bluff or half truths. 'Yes, sir.'

'Why?'

'I do not know, sir.'

'Well, you need not be. Do you ever read?'

'Yes, sir.'

'What books?'

It was rumoured that Colonel Arthur was deeply religious, so I tried to think of the titles of some good and improving books but only heard a small voice saying 'The stories of Bulldog Drummond and Edgar Wallace, sir.'

That's torn it, I thought – butter *and* marmalade, and now cheap crime novels. There was a long silence and I prepared myself for peremptory dismissal.

'All right, there is a vacancy for you in the regiment. The Adjutant will tell you when and where to report. Goodbye and good luck.'

It would be at least three months before I would be commissioned and posted to a battalion, so my father, who had friends who were high court judges, arranged for me to go on circuit as Judge's Marshal.

The Marshal is the judge's ADC, and his main duty is to protect him from assassination, an unlikely occurrence in pre-war years. Knowing nothing of the law I found most of the cases very interesting and was lucky to serve Lord Goddard, later Lord Chief Justice, and Lord Oaksey, who was to preside after the war at the Nuremberg Trials of the German War Criminals.

In August 1936 I received orders to report to the 1st Battalion Coldstream Guards, then stationed at Windsor Barracks, and in a highly nervous state I made myself known to the picquet officer in the mess on a Sunday evening in September.

I had been warned that newly joined ensigns were not

usually spoken to for the first three or four weeks except in connection with their duties. It was no surprise when the picquet officer merely told me to report to the Adjutant at eight o'clock, and instructed one of the mess servants to get hold of the orderly I had been allocated and see that he unpacked and put out my uniform, etc. Later I was told that the reason for not speaking to new officers was that should they prove unsatisfactory it made it much easier to get rid of them if they had not been 'accepted'. However, my probationary period was of short duration, as after two weeks the battalion moved out for field training where, of necessity, much of the formality of life in barracks had to be abandoned.

Pre-war annual manœuvres were inevitably repetitious, the only variant being the weather and the area. In 1936 they were in Sussex and largely memorable for the number of times we clambered up and down Chanctonbury Ring. I was posted to No 3 Company, the 'Coal Box Company' as it is always known, since it is usually made up of the shortest officers, NCOs and guardsmen who, tradition has it, are small enough to be buried in coal boxes if coffins are not available. The company commander, who had served with the regiment in the Great War, regarded manœuvres with amused tolerance, but nonetheless made certain that the company treated them with the utmost seriousness. Young officers were kept hard at work.

After three months' service with a battalion, if one so wished and the regiment were agreeable, it was possible to change to a regular commission. Discreet enquiries elicited the information that my application would be approved, and I asked my father to give me an allowance of £500 per year, which was considered to be the minimum required by an officer in peace time. Alas, this sum would have stretched the family finances to breaking point, and instead my father arranged for me to be taken on by a firm in the City. In February 1937 I joined, as a very junior clerk, the merchant banking house of Helbert Wagg & Co, Ltd, returning annually to the regiment for two weeks' field training.

Initially I enjoyed working in the City, but after the Munich crisis life became intolerably boring, and I shall never forget the feeling of relief and inexpressible joy I felt one May evening in 1939 on receiving orders to report to the 2nd Battalion at Albuera Barracks, Aldershot, for three months' concentrated training. Less encouraging was a typed slip from the Adjutant instructing me to bring my own pistol and field glasses – such were the deficiencies of the army in 1939 – and to have some knowledge of the art of riding a motor cycle.

Life with the 2nd Battalion was fun and the imminence of war added spice to the intensive training. I was posted to No 3 Company commanded by Major Angus McCorquodale but, as I joined a training squad for young officers I saw little of him until late August, the day after general mobilization had been declared, when he summoned me to the company office. He was a man of few words and there were no preliminaries. 'In the event of war I would like you to command No 15 Platoon. John Pigott Brown is junior to you in rank but he has been to Sandhurst and will be my second-in-command. We shall be three officers with the other two platoons commanded by platoon sergeant-majors.' Several other officers had been posted to the company all senior to me and with far greater experience. I could hardly believe my luck as I stammered out my thanks.

On the evening of Saturday, 2 September, the single code word 'Mussolini' came over the telephone, the warning that the declaration of war was imminent. On Sunday, 3 September, at 10.45 a.m., Colonel Bootle Wilbraham (the late Lord Skelmersdale) who commanded the battalion, summoned all officers to the mess to hear the Prime Minister, Neville Chamberlain, speak on the radio.

It was a memorable gathering. Few had any doubts but that war was only a few minutes away, but despite that there were no takers when someone offered the odds of a bottle of champagne against a case that there would be no war. Such is eternal optimism. The older officers who had been in the First World War were silent, lost in their own thoughts.

Neville Chamberlain spoke and we were officially at war. There was a short silence as we digested the fact and I think many of us expected a couple of armed Germans to invade the mess. A friend of mine, Bob Combe, well known for his irrepressible sense of humour then spoke up.

'The people I am sorry for are the Germans,' he announced to all and sundry. No one said anything, though I saw Colonel Bootle smile.

'You see,' continued Bob 'they already know they have lost. You cannot beat us – it simply is not on.' Colonel Bootle moved towards the door, indicating that it was time to return to our duties. However, the last words were Bob's. 'Of course, none of us will, I much doubt, ever mount guard again.' It was evident that the wholesale killing of us all did not meet with general approval. 'I mean,' Bob hastily continued, 'that I do not think there will be any ceremonial parades after the war.' He glanced at Colonel Bootle, and added 'If there are, I only hope Regimental Headquarters do not try experimenting again with goat skins instead of bear skins. I am told the smell was unbearable.'

Outside there was no indication that we were at war. No 15 Platoon, stripped to the waist in the hot September sun, were completing slit trenches alongside the London–Aldershot road and occasionally glancing at a procession of large black Daimlers. 'Loonies from London' I overheard one guardsman comment. 'What the hell is the use of evacuating those poor bastards?' came the reply. My platoon sergeant took up the running. 'Stop chattering about what is not your business and get on with your work.' Yes, nothing had changed.

Then, suddenly, everything did change. Three guardsmen passed by carrying an open ground sheet filled with live small arms ammunition. 'For the anti-aircraft Bren on the tennis court of the Officers' Club,' they explained. There was an awed silence. We had none of us ever seen live ammunition in such profusion and handled with such careless abandon. From that point on we knew we were at war.

At dawn on 17 September the battalion entrained at Aldershot for Southampton and that night crossed the Channel on the *Maid of Orleans* to Cherbourg, arriving at the British Expeditionary Force's staging area near Le Mans on 19 September. Three days later we moved to the north of France and during the autumn and winter worked on the defence positions along the Franco–Belgian frontier around the village of Bachy.

In late January 1940 the whole battalion moved down to the Saar, where the French were in contact with the Germans. However, we soon returned to the north of France, where we were stationed at Pont à Marc, a small village on the main Lille–Paris road, and, with improvement in the weather, field training became the order of the day. Whenever Angus had his way, which was frequently, this consisted of retreat and rear-guard exercises. His doctrine was simple, 'We always start a war with a major retreat – Corunna – Mons – to quote only two. What makes you think it will be different this time?'

Spring also brought a spate of lecturers from England, including one who spoke on 'Escaping from a POW Camp'. The only talk that No 15 Platoon really enjoyed and looked forward to with keen anticipation was the battalion medical officer, Pip Blacker, on 'Venereal Disease – Its Dangers and Consequences'. Not even Pip at his best could, however, curb the amatory ambitions of No 15 Platoon, as I had in some embarrassment to inform Colonel Bootle one Friday afternoon in April. I had just taken pay parade and was walking back to my billet when he drew up in his car. 'I did not know, Jimmy, that No 3 Company were having a cross-country run this afternoon.' Nor did I, and my face must have showed it.

'I have just come back from Brigade Headquarters and have passed most of the company running in the general direction of Templeuve' – a village some three miles away – 'No 15 Platoon was well in the lead. You might find out and let me know what it is all about.'

I was fully aware of the attractions that were to be found

in Templeuve, and suddenly understood why my platoon were so grateful when I paid them first. Colonel Bootle laughed when I told him. 'A pity Templeuve is not farther away, but I must say No 15 Platoon appeared remarkably fit, they were setting an absolutely cracking pace.'

Early in May I was summoned by Colonel Bootle who informed me that he had agreed to my appointment as an instructor at a new sniping school in England. He added that my posting should arrive in some three weeks.

It did, on 10 May – too late, for at dawn that same day Hitler solved the problem of what I should do with my life.

2

Up Guards and at Them

'Good morning, sir. Here is your tea. Your bath is ready. It is a fine morning. The Germans invaded France, Belgium and Holland at dawn. Major McCorquodale has cancelled today's training programme and there will be a meeting of all officers and platoon commanders at 8.15 in the company office.'

Thus Guardsman Birks, my servant, announced the end of the Phoney War, the move from Sitzkrieg to Blitzkrieg. Relief that at last the test had come – fear of the unknown – little time for contemplation.

Allied strategy had decreed that the BEF would take up a defensive position on the River Dyle, north-east of Brussels. As part of the brigade in reserve we did not move forward until the evening of 12 May. Leaving France was sad and depressing, not least as one had had time to contemplate the possible unpleasantness ahead. However, morale rose considerably as we marched through Templeuve to the cheers and good wishes of the girls from 'the café at the corner' who got quite out of hand when 15 Platoon appeared and I was devoutly thankful that Colonel Bootle was a long way ahead.

It was a text-book introduction to war with little to make the two night marches differ from manœuvres, and by midday on 14 May the battalion were 'digging in' on the outskirts of the village of Leefdael, midway between Brussels and Louvain, in soil so soft that it made trenching a pleasure. The first rude awakening was a truck-load of retreating Belgians careering through the main village street shouting 'Gas! Gas!'

There was a moment of near panic and even 34 years later I blush with shame at my actions when I realized I had not got my gas mask. I moved at a very fast pace uphill and out of the village to get clear of the gas, only to realize that I was increasing rather than decreasing the distance from that momentarily most desirable piece of military equipment. A rapid change of course followed in the vague hope that I might get through the contaminated area to where I had left my gas mask without having to draw breath. Doctors maintain it is impossible to suffocate oneself voluntarily. They may be right but I was within an ace of achieving it before Guardsman Birks arrived carrying my mask.

The most dismal and depressing sight of all was the civilian evacuation of Leefdael, on the orders of the mayor. Some packed up carefully, buried or loaded their valuable possessions on a vehicle and freed their animals. Others just threw the first objects that came to hand into a car, cart or wheelbarrow, giving no thought to the future of chickens, cows, rabbits, dogs and cats, and leaving fires burning and lights on. All, however, joined the pitiable stream moving slowly along the road to Brussels. Little could be done to alleviate animal suffering except milk the cows and loose all the other animals to fend for themselves. Orders were to shoot the dogs as in most cases they would not permit anyone to let them off their chains.

It was early morning of 16 May that the really dramatic moment came. Angus and I were watching the evasive action of a British Lysander reconnaissance plane and admiring the pilot's courage and skill in avoiding the German anti-aircraft fire. It seemed impossible that he would survive as he weaved in and out of the clumps of smoke from the shells and each time we were sure it must be the end. When at last he turned for home we switched our glasses to Louvain where shells could be seen bursting and then to convoys on the road back to Brussels. Suddenly Angus said in a quiet voice 'What do you make of that returning convoy of 15-cwt trucks?' I looked at it. Yes, there was no doubt. The trucks were full with the covering tarpaulins in place. This was withdrawal – retreat – call it what you like. Once again the British Army was starting a campaign with a retreat.

'I expect we shall receive official confirmation shortly' remarked Angus and at 11 p.m. the company withdrew to the battalion rendezvous on the Brussels–Louvain road. As we left our position we passed a battery of guns firing away. 'Got to use up our ammunition – cannot take it with us,' shouted a voice out of the dark. A moment later a salvo of shells landed behind us. The retreat was on and the Germans were not so far away. Angus had been right.

My diary for that first few days of the retreat records the long marches by day and by night along roads cluttered with refugees and the time spent digging trenches which we abandoned after a few hours as the withdrawal continued. Twice 15 Platoon came under shell and machine-gun fire, but we never saw a live German. Yet the enemy was never very far behind us. Once I left my walking stick behind during the 'ten minutes in the hour' halt. A despatch rider who volunteered to retrieve it returned with a bullet through the petrol tank of his motor cycle.

Late one afternoon, after we had been marching for some eight hours, the confusion on the road was such that 15 Platoon became separated from the rest of the company. I decided to have a ten-minute halt at a cross-roads where the military police were doing magnificent work sorting out and re-grouping units. Close by was a large brewery, which I proposed to inspect in the hope of being able to refill our water bottles, most of which were empty. Leaving the sergeant in charge I started to look for a tap without, however, any success, and was just giving up when I heard a shot which seemed to come from the house in the courtyard. The front door was open so I walked into the hall and then into the first big room, which appeared to be the owner's study. Standing by the large desk was an officer endeavouring to force the roll top of the desk. Failing so to do he drew his revolver and fired what I presume was a second shot into the lock. This time he was successful, and was soon opening the drawers and going through their contents. I must have made some noise as he turned round and faced me.

'What the hell do you want?' he shouted.

'Water,' I replied nervously.

'Well, there isn't any here and the sooner you get out the better.'

I complied and I suppose an older and wiser man would have left it at that but I was tired, hot and angry at his rudeness so I reported the facts to the sergeant in charge of the military police on the cross-roads. He acted with astonishing speed and a few minutes later the officer – a captain – was led out of the brewery by two military police, one carrying his revolver.

'What will happen now?' I asked the sergeant.

'My orders are explicit. Shoot looters on the spot. But there are some officers over there' he replied, pointing to a group nearby 'And I shall request the senior to confirm these orders.' A little later Angus arrived in his truck and we were on our way again – this time to the village of Pecq.

'I am putting you in charge of the bridge over the Escaut,' Angus informed me. 'You will order the RE officer to blow it the moment you think there is the faintest chance of a German attack. Do not however destroy it with half the BEF still on the other side.'

'There is a section from company headquarters with two Bren guns about 50 yards beyond the bridge with orders to let refugees through one at a time and well spaced out, also to search all wagons. If they are in any doubt as to the *bona fides* of the refugees or see any enemy they are to fire first and ask questions afterwards. There is a second section at the end of the bridge with similar orders. Both will withdraw over the bridge, not however before closing the gap in the barbed wire fences. The moment there is any alarm or on hearing three long blasts on a whistle, indicating that you are going to blow the bridge, No 13 Platoon is ready to take over what is left of the bridge on this side. Any questions?'

I had unpleasant visions of a large farm cart full of Germans hidden under hay trundling on to the bridge.

'Do I have to let farm carts through?'

'That is up to you. Right, if there are no more questions I will give Sergeant Smith his instructions.'

I only knew Sergeant Smith by sight as a member of the Headquarter's Company Signals Platoon and assumed his

activities would be limited to looking after the field telephone. I could not have been more wrong.

'Sergeant Smith, have you got a revolver?'

'No, sir.'

'Can you use one?'

'Yes, sir.'

'Right. Take mine, it is loaded, and listen carefully. The

moment Mr Langley tries to sit or lie down, you are to shoot him, do you understand?'

The implications of this order may not have been immediately clear to Sergeant Smith, who looked somewhat startled, but they were to me and I began to protest.

'Shut up, Jimmy. Surely you realize that the moment you sit or lie down you will go to sleep and *that* you are not going to do. Repeat my order, Sergeant Smith.'

'The moment Mr Langley tries to sit or lie down I am to shoot him.'

'Right, If I find Mr Langley alive and asleep you will know what to expect. Good luck!'

On night manœuvres there is always a slight relaxing of the formal relationship between officers and NCOs and a tendency to indulge in friendly gossip, all brought about by the discomforts mutually shared. Such an atmosphere was noticeably absent on the bridge over the Escaut during that May night. Angus's orders had been heard by all present who, after ruminating on them, could not but wonder who else he might have ordered to shoot whom. Even the signaller who would normally have been sitting, crouching, or lying by his set, found it more relaxing to arrange things so that he could carry out his duties standing. I did not even dare to go near the sides of the bridge in case Sergeant Smith should consider this the first move to sit on one of them.

As the night wore on the stream of refugees dwindled and soon ceased altogether, a fact which both the RE officer and I considered alarming as we felt that the Germans would clear the roads before attempting any rush to capture the bridge. To add to our worries a mist started to rise and soon visibility was down to less than 50 yards. Finally an aircraft arrived and, circling overhead, dropped parachute flares lighting up the whole area.

In his account of the 2nd Battalion's activities during 1939–40* Colonel Bootle Wilbraham states that the RE officer persuaded me to agree to the destruction of the bridge. That is not strictly correct. I was much too frightened of Angus's

* *No Dishonourable Name*, David Quilter, S.R. Publishers, 1972.

wrath if I blew the bridge too early without adequate reasons. I simply felt that under cover of the mist a determined attack had a high chance of success. At 1 a.m. I gave the order and the bridge was blown.

It was not till noon the next day that I was reunited with 15 Platoon who had done an excellent job digging themselves in below the river bank some 100 yards from the remains of the bridge.

Further, the platoon area contained one feature of immense defensive value, namely a small château with a walled garden which ran down to the river bank. Initially both Angus and I failed to appreciate its potential having in mind General Alexander's dictum that 'to hold a canal or river you must be on it, not behind it.' However, when going over it in search of water we found that the window in an upstairs bedroom overlooked not only most of 15 Platoon area but also all the ground in front of the company on our right flank.

It did not require much military knowledge to realize that a machine gun or two Bren guns firing from the window would make any attack by day if not impossible at least very hazardous. That the enemy might come to the same conclusion and destroy the château by shellfire before attacking was, of course, a possibility, but one we considered remote and a justifiable risk. Suppressing our joint dislike of separating the Bren guns from their sections, two were mounted in the bedroom, leaving the platoon lining the river bank with one Bren gun. Around 1 a.m. firing broke out near the bridge but after about 15 minutes it died away and from then on the night passed quietly. There were sounds of movement the other side of the river, however, and the possibility of a dawn attack seemed high. 'Stand to' passed off without incident and it was not until I was half way back to the platoon HQ in the château, having supervised distribution of breakfast to the sections on the river bank, that someone from the far bank shouted 'Hi! Can any of you fellows over there swim? I am not very good at it and I have a wounded man with me who must be helped.'

If the Germans had waited three seconds more before opening fire I think they would have wiped out the platoon. As it was they fired as soon as the first three men had climbed out of the slit trenches on to the top of the bank, killing one and wounding the other two, but warning all the rest of the trap.

Completely taken in I had also turned back to go to the help of the non-swimmer but fortunately had decided to climb the bank nearer the place from where the shout had come. To describe 15 Platoon as disorganized would be an understatement. If they had scrambled out of the trenches up the bank fast, without, of course, their rifles, it was nothing to the speed with which they tumbled back, momentarily shocked and unnerved. However, one man kept his head, Volkes, a Norfolk farmer's son, the Bren gunner. I had not covered the few remaining yards back to the trenches before he had the gun in action sweeping the farther bank, silencing the German fire and giving the rest of the platoon time to sort themselves out.

While our trenches bore little resemblance to those of the 1914–18 war, being little more than a series of shallow pits linked by a slit trench, we had had time to construct two small camouflaged observation posts which gave us an immense advantage as the enemy had to expose himself in order to look over the river. It was from one of these posts that the sentry on duty first saw the German helmet slowly rising over the river bank. Each time he fired the helmet would disappear only to reappear a few moments later. However, with his fourth shot he was luckier, knocking the helmet off the bayonet on which it was being raised and lowered. His success was acclaimed by clapping and laughter from the Germans but I was furious. Was there no trap we were not going to fall into!

The firing had brought John Pigott-Brown down from company HQ to find out how we were faring and it was as he was returning that we came upon the body of one of my men lying at the bottom of a pit where he had been the sole occupant. It did not take a moment to find out how he had been killed – a bullet between the eyes. 'A sniper,' said John, raising his Zeiss field glasses and looking over the bank. I scarcely heard the shot only seeing John on his knees at the bottom of the trench, blood pouring from under his steel helmet which had a hole on both sides just above the rim.

I never for a moment thought that he was anything but dead and was very surprised when he said 'What has happened?' I told him and he replied, 'Well, I have a hell of a headache.' I advised him to lie still for a while and then I removed his steel helmet – to find that the bullet had gone round his head cutting a path through his scalp. 'Can you deal with the sniper?' he queried. 'I don't know, but I'll try.'

It was my lucky day and I can only assume that having had two 'kills' at the same spot the sniper did not think anyone would be fool enough to offer him a third. I had thought he would be some way back possibly in a barn 200 yards off, and had he not moved I doubt if I would ever have spotted him. Far from being in the barn he was lying on the top of the bank in a clump of nettles not 50 yards away, with his field glasses slowly sweeping our lines. Even with the naked eye his rifle and telescopic sight were clearly visible. Once I had seen him the rest was comparatively easy, but nonetheless I was violently sick when it was over.

John said he felt all right though he did not look it and I went as far as the château with him on the way to company HQ. He was evacuated to England and I never saw him again as he was killed at Longstop Hill in Tunisia in 1942.

From the window in the château there was at first little to be seen as even from there the Germans below the river bank were out of sight. However, we did not have long to wait before things began to happen. From a small copse in front of the company on our right flank four pairs of Germans emerged, each pair carrying what appeared to be a stretcher over which was draped a Red Cross flag. The party was led by two Germans neither of whom had rifles and I assumed they were going out to recover their dead and wounded and told the Bren gunners not to fire.

When they were about a hundred yards from the river bank

and still well within our view they stopped and started to unload whatever was on the stretchers under the Red Cross flags. As there were only 10 of them and they all seemed to be unarmed our interest was largely due to the fact that they were the first Germans we could observe at leisure. It therefore came as a complete surprise when what I had thought was a ground sheet suddenly started to swell and emerged as a fully inflated black rubber boat to be followed a moment later by a second and then a third. It did not need much wit to guess what the rest of the equipment was, or what they intended doing.

It has frequently been said that a major fault of the Bren gun is that all the shots from a burst of fire tend to fall too close together. Be that as it may it is an admirable fault when it comes to destroying rubber assault boats and a minute after both guns opened fire everything was flat, boats and men. Twice during the morning the Germans attempted to rush fully inflated boats across the open ground but they never had a chance. During the second attempt we came under machine-gun fire, one of the Bren gunners was wounded, and we knew we had been spotted.

I did not think they would make a fourth attempt until they were fairly certain they had knocked us out and so rather than wait for the inevitable I sent the Bren gunners back to their section and moved platoon HQ to the cellar. For once we were not caught out. One of the very first shells burst in the bathroom leading off the bedroom which had served us so well and a few minutes later the whole first floor was cut off when the only staircase was destroyed.

All in all it had been a most successful morning and although we had made such fools of ourselves at first I felt Angus would forgive our errors. At dusk a stretcher party arrived to carry away our dead, whom we had laid out behind the slit trenches. I was removing their equipment and ammunition when to my horror and surprise one of them, who had the point of a bullet sticking out of his forehead just above his nose, suddenly opened his eyes and asked if I had any whisky. Thoroughly ashamed at my carelessness in not making certain he was dead I complied with his request though I later learnt he died the next day.

Except for considerable sounds of movement the night passed quietly and it was not till mid-morning that the Germans started the same game of raising steel helmets on the end of bayonets. This time they were three in number, but on my orders nobody fired and each time the helmets appeared they were raised a fraction higher remaining a few seconds before being lowered. Sergeant Pickles and I simultaneously spoke our thoughts. 'One of those three helmets has a Hun head inside it.'

'Right, Sergeant. Tell the men who have the helmets in their sights to fire the next time they appear after I give the signal by waving my steel helmet in the air.'

The results were most gratifying in the form of loud shouts of consternation and a half dozen stick grenades, none of which caused any damage. Throughout the day there was desultory shelling which had no effect but to kill and wound a number of sheep, horses and cows that were wandering round in the fields behind us. One of the latter, maddened with pain, leapt into the moat surrounding the château and swam round it, mooing in a most mournful and depressing manner until I finished her off with my rifle.

In the afternoon I was summoned to company HQ where Angus gave orders to make preparations to withdraw under cover of darkness.

I had few worries about withdrawing, except from the area next to the bridge where, for the second time, we had called for artillery support as there were indications that the Germans were bringing up bridging material. Platoon Sergeant-Major Robinson, whose platoon was on the actual bridge-end, and I decided we had better imitate Beau Geste at Fort Zinderneuf, and as the last section slipped away in the darkness he and his platoon sergeant ran up and down the tow path firing Bren guns from the hip. This was far beyond my physical capacity and all I could do was fire my rifle standing up. The Germans did not reply and we were not followed.

The next three days in the trenches dug by the BEF during the winter of 1939 were, as far as I was concerned, without any significant event. But we were under constant pressure.

3

Destination Dunkirk

Even his best friend would not have given Angus high marks in the art of being dramatic, but he certainly rose to the occasion at the evening company conference on Monday, 27 May 1940. 'We are going home,' he announced, 'by way of Dunkirk.' No one said anything.

'Platoons will withdraw as quietly as possible at 22.00 hours and form up on the main road to Lille. There are no maps but I will lead the company and I have route cards made out by battalion HQ which I will give you and all your section commanders. There will be no halting for the first 30 miles. Final destination the harbour at Dunkirk for embarkation to England. Any questions?'

'How far is it to Dunkirk?'

'About 60 miles.'

There was a long silence while we all digested this information. Finally we were dismissed, and that night another long march duly began.

At dawn there was a marked change in the weather. The clear blue sky and blazing sun which seemed so much part of the retreat were replaced by banks of low grey cloud and frequent heavy showers, superb marching conditions and unsuitable, so we persuaded ourselves, for attacks by Stuka dive-bombers or low-flying fighters.

While the weather may have been conducive to making good marching time, the conditions on the roads rapidly deteriorated as more men, lorries of every description, guns and, last but by no means least, a mass of French horse-drawn vehicles joined the retreating columns. On the outskirts of Poperinge the chaos and confusion were such that I began to doubt if we would ever get through, even individually, let alone as a fighting unit. However someone – I later learnt it was Colonel Bootle – had arranged a diversion with guides to indicate the new route. These were Belgian Boy Scouts who, immaculately dressed, carrying their staves and, smiling and laughing, cheerfully pointed out the way. Why and how a troop of Belgian scouts was on parade in the swirling mass of men, guns and horses that choked the debris littered street of Poperinge on that May afternoon is beyond my comprehension. In common with many of my friends I had always regarded the Scout movement with derision and not infrequently cracked a joke at their expense. I have not done so since.

Once clear of Poperinge we were ordered to halt to rest and allow stragglers to catch up. Suddenly Brigadier Beckwith Smith, ('Becky' to all), who commanded the 1st Guards Brigade, of which we were part, drove up in his car.

'Marvellous news, Jimmy' he shouted. 'The best ever!' Short of the German army deciding to call it a day, which seemed improbable, I could think of no news deserving the qualifications of 'marvellous' and the 'best ever!'

'It is splendid, absolutely splendid. We have been given the supreme honour of being the rearguard at Dunkirk. Tell your platoon, Jimmy – come on, tell them the good news.'

After all the months together I knew 15 Platoon very well, and had not the slightest doubt that they would accept this information with the usual tolerance and good humour they displayed in all the vicissitudes of life 'on active service' or 'in action'. However, I did not think they would class it as 'marvellous' and the 'best ever'.

'I think it would come better from you, sir.'

'Right, right', he replied as he strode across, and after telling them to remain seated, made known to them the change in plan.

Then, to my delight, since I had never heard this from him direct, he recalled his earlier instruction, which had become a by-word during the retreat, as to how to deal with Stuka dive-bombers.

'Stand up to them. Shoot at them with a Bren gun from the shoulder. Take them like a high pheasant. Give them plenty of lead. Remember, five pounds to any man who brings one down. I have already paid out ten pounds.'

High spirits and optimism are very infectious, especially when they are not forced. Becky genuinely regarded the task as a supreme honour and I could see that much of his enthusiasm was shared by 15 Platoon.

A meal in the morning, the superb example of 'keeping

your head when all about are losing theirs', so courageously displayed by the Belgian Boy Scouts in Poperinge, and Becky's words did much to help 15 Platoon through the next 24 hours which it took to cover the remaining 20 miles to our last fighting line on the Bergues-Hondschoote Canal.

The cottage which was to be the king pin of No 3 Company's defence position still stands today and would, I suppose, be described by an estate agent as 'a fine example of a Flemish farm cottage standing in its own land overlooking the canal with a superb view over the fields both towards the sea and inland. Three downstair rooms – attic. Boat available. Outhouses. Ideal for conversion to holiday home. Fishing.' All this was basically true but what he would not add was that the water comes from, and tastes strongly of, the canal and that the lack of 'mod cons' has left its mark. However, the view over the fields is superb as the Germans were to learn to their cost.

As in the case of the château at Pecq, neither Angus nor I had the slightest illusion what the enemy would do when they discovered how we were using the cottage. But the chances were that they would again attack first rather than systematically destroy every building that might be a strong-point; and so it proved. However, an adequate trench system was highly desirable and the work was put in hand without delay. Throughout the campaign we had always had the best possible soil for trenching, soft, easy to dig with no rocks or chalk, but never so sandy that it caved in and needed revetting. Once again we were in luck and by the evening we were well entrenched though there were ominous signs that we had reached the water level and, when the sluice gates of the canals were opened to flood the country, the water slowly rose, though never high enough to make occupation impossible.

All through the day there was a continuous stream of British and French troops, who crossed the canal by the bridge on our right. They varied from two platoons of the Welsh Guards, who had been fighting near Arras – though they looked as though they had performed nothing more arduous than a day's peace-time manœuvring – to a bedraggled, leaderless rabble.

I also came across some outstanding individuals. One, a corporal in the Royal East Kents (Buffs), particularly excited my admiration. Barely five feet tall, wearing socks, boots and trousers held up by string, he had a Bren gun slung on each shoulder with a rifle slung across their barrels. The slings of the Bren guns had cut deep into his shoulders, his back and chest were caked in blood and I could see part of both his collar bones. I offered him a mug of tea and ordered him to drop the Bren guns as I would be needing them. He looked me up and down.

'I would rather take them with me, sir.' I told him to obey orders but he still made no effort to comply. Instead, in a tired utterly unemotional voice, gazing over my shoulder, he spoke his mind. 'My major's dead somewhere back there. His last words were "Get those guns back to England, they will be needing them soon." ' He looked me straight in the eyes. 'And begging your pardon, sir, I am going to.' I put a generous measure of whisky in his tea, a first-aid dressing between the slings and his shoulders and wished him the best of luck.

I yield to no one in my admiration of the French. In the years to come I was to owe them debts of gratitude which I can never hope to repay but they were not at their best on that hot day in May 1940. Delighted to find themselves under British protection they infuriated me by throwing all their weapons in the canal. When I remonstrated they merely shrugged their shoulders and said that as France had lost the war the sooner they could surrender without the chances of being shot the better. The officers were worse than the men, since they frequently added what stupid fools we were to go on fighting.

The night passed without incident, and the next day was occupied in strengthening our defences and collecting weapons, ammunition, food and clothing from the lorries and trucks immobilized on the road running along the enemy side of the canal. We made a splendid haul and the 'fire power' of the company, now only 37 men strong, was most promising as the following list from my diary shows: Twelve Bren guns, three Lewis guns, one Boyes anti-tank rifle, 30,000 rounds of small arms ammunition and 22 Mills grenades.

The old soldiers in the platoon were especially delighted with two Lewis guns, weapons which they had spent much of their army career using, as they regarded the new-fangled Bren gun as infinitely inferior. I acquired a new and very much needed battle-dress, a large artillery officer's compass – quite useless under the circumstances, but a splendid toy – a portable battery-powered radio and 500 cigarettes.

The living room–kitchen in the cottage took on the, appearance of a small country grocer's shop with stacks of bully beef, tinned milk, vegetables (the cabbage was one of the nastiest foods I have ever tried to eat) and stew, but best of all marmalade and Wiltshire bacon. To add to our home comforts there were plenty of chickens around the farm, the odd cow, while some genius found two cases of white wine, *très ordinaire* but nonetheless very drinkable, and a couple of crates of beer. Angus turned up in the afternoon, having spent the day trying, without success, to find some men who had somehow been misdirected to Dunkirk. He brought with him a bottle of whisky and two bottles of sherry, so we were well supplied with the necessities and some luxuries of life.

During most of the day we had watched spectacular aerial 'dog fights' over Dunkirk and saw more than one German bomber go down in flames. The only aircraft which came anywhere near was a British Lysander flying very low along the canal. We had been ordered to treat all low-flying aircraft as enemy, regardless of the markings. I happened to be standing by a Bren on anti-aircraft mountings and got in a good burst, without success I am pleased to say, as I was later informed that it contained Lord Gort who was having a last look at the final line of the BEF.

Angus packed me off to bed on a straw mattress on the floor of one of the small back rooms, the company's forward headquarters, the main HQ being in a trench some 50 yards back from the cottage and farm, and as far as I was concerned the night passed quietly.

In the classic phrase 'the day of the game dawned fine and, clear' – the Glorious First of June – but it started badly for me. At about 2 a.m. I found one of my section commanders had got at the rum ration which I had foolishly issued in jars to each section the evening before, as I had felt that we might have other more pressing business at dawn. There was nothing to do except hope that he would sleep it off and that Angus would not be too angry. To add to my anxiety a lone shell – obviously from our own side – crashed into the wall of a small barn where some men were sleeping. We were lucky to get away with only two killed. This was not an auspicious start but from then on things looked up.

The top room of the cottage was an attic used for storage, but there were also some pieces of old furniture and several crates of empty beer bottles. With the help of these we were able to construct two excellent Bren-gun nests. Careful removal of the roof tiles gave the gunners good observation, and I much doubted if the muzzles of the guns would be spotted even by the keenest Hun eye. The partial removal of two more tiles supplied observation posts of sufficient size to permit the use of field glasses. The only drawback was that neither the roof nor the end walls appeared strong enough to offer protection against enemy fire, and we had no sand bags. However, evacuation to the ground floor or the slit trenches would be only a matter of seconds. Two buckets of cold water, for the dual purpose of cooling the wine, the beer and the Bren-gun barrels, completed our preparations as we 'stood to' awaiting the dawn.

At first light the fields in front were covered with a thick mist. This rapidly disappeared as the sun rose and revealed, to our utter astonishment, some hundred or so Germans standing in groups about 600 yards away in a field of green corn. A quick glance through the glasses revealed that they had no rifles – only spades – though the lack of piles of earth in the corn seemed to indicate they had not made much progress with their digging. They appeared utterly unconcerned and were gathering up their equipment in a lackadaisical way, presumably preparing to move off.

The section commander was very much quicker than I was and as we had all seen the enemy his orders were easy. 'No 1 gun 600. No 2 gun 800. Fire!' I could see the spray as the burst from No 1 gun cut through the dew-covered corn – about 50 yards short. 'Both guns 700!' I shouted above the din. I cannot say that the resulting massacre – it was not much less – gave me any pleasure. Rather, I felt slightly sick. The corn was high enough to conceal a man till he started to crawl but that did not really matter as we simply sprayed the whole area for a couple of minutes till nothing moved.

Then we had another surprise. From a group of buildings about 1000 yards away, a group of figures emerged, formed themselves into a rough line and started to advance. As they approached I saw that they were civilians, mainly women, with the odd German here and there carrying a stretcher on his shoulder. Their object was clear. Collecting up anyone they could lay hands on the Germans were using the civilians as protection and to carry back the wounded, relying on the fact that we would not fire on women and old men. Their assumption was correct, but good use of a rifle accounted for three of the enemy, who, once they thought they were protected, got up from the corn and started to walk back on their own.

Around midday the Germans showed signs of frenzied activity despite our efforts to discourage them, and mounted an attack on the area where the bridge across the canal had been blown. This was partially held by No 1 Company, under Evan Gibbs, on our right and partially by a company of a regiment from the north of England, the road leading back from the bridgehead to Dunkirk being the boundary line. We had an excellent view of what was happening and made good use of the Brens until the inevitable occurred.

We had seen the Germans rush up what looked like an anti-tank gun on wheels and watched with interest as it was pointed our way and fired. Nothing happened and we turned a Bren gun on to it. Then there was the most awful crash and a brightly lit object whizzed round the attic, finally coming to rest at the foot of the brick chimney stack. One glance was enough – it was an incendiary anti-tank shell. Our exit, Bren guns and all, coincided with the arrival of Angus's orders to get out. He had seen the first shell pass over the roof and the second go in. The Germans put four more shells into the attic and then desisted. After a decent interval we went back, but the enemy were out of sight in the houses of the small hamlet on their side of the bridge.

I rejoined Angus partly to find out whether he had any further instructions and partly to pass him the gist of a splendid interview with the last man out of Dunkirk which we had heard over the portable radio. The impression he had managed to convey that he had held back the advancing Germans single-handed until jumping into a boat excited our keenest enjoyment.

Our gossip was interrupted by a visitor who introduced himself as the captain commanding the company on No 1 Company's right, and said that he had been sent over by Evan Gibbs. He informed us that the Germans were massing for an attack on the bridgehead, that his men were exhausted and that he proposed to withdraw while the going was good. Angus merely said 'I order you to stay put and fight it out.'

'You cannot do that. I have over-riding orders from my colonel to withdraw when I think fit,' came the reply. Angus did not beat about the bush. 'You see that big poplar tree on the road with the white mile stone beside it? The moment you or any of your men go back beyond that tree we will shoot you.' The captain started to expostulate but Angus cut him short. 'Get back or I will shoot you now and send one of my officers to take command,' and his hand moved towards his revolver. The captain departed without further words.

'Get a rifle,' Angus ordered me, picking up one that was lying nearby. When I returned with mine he said 'Sights at 250. You will shoot to kill the moment he passes that tree. Are you clear?'

'Yes.'

We had not long to wait before the captain appeared, followed by two men. They stood for a long time by the tree and then the captain walked on. Both our rifles went off simultaneously: he dropped out of sight and the two men ran back. Some minutes later the German artillery opened up on the bridgehead, all along the canal bank including our positions, and then the attack went in. The Germans eventually stopped on the road near the tree where the captain had stood. The firing died away. To our delight Bob Combe and Pop Wyatt, commanding No 2 Company on our left, suddenly appeared on the excuse of 'seeing if we were all right'. Angus called for his servant who was squatting in the trench nearby. 'Go into the cottage and in the little room on the left you will see two bottles, some glasses and a small table. Bring them all here.'

'Sherry?' he said to Pop. 'Whisky if you prefer it, though I think we ought to save that as we may need it later.'

We all accepted sherry and Angus looked over towards the Germans on the road who were sauntering up and down apparently without a care in the world. Even the distant guns were quiet and it seemed just like pre-war manœuvres.

Angus raised his glass, 'To a very gallant and competent enemy.'

We all followed suit and then exchanged news until some big guns a long way back opened up on a farm some way behind us. The shells were landing in the flooded fields and we watched with fascination the great columns of water they sent up, reminding me of pictures I had seen of the Battle of Jutland.

'Time to go back,' said Angus and off Pop and Bob went.

Three out of the four of us were to be killed within the next 24 hours.

It was much later in the afternoon when firing had recommenced that Angus sent me over to see how Evan Gibbs was faring. Evan was grey with fatigue and very worried because one of his Bren guns was unmanned. The gunner had been killed, and he felt that the Germans might capture it. Despite all I could do he insisted on trying to recover it. He did not get very far, and though a guardsman very bravely ran out and brought him in he died soon afterwards.

I returned to report that the only officer left was Ronnie Speed who had only joined the battalion a few weeks earlier and that he proposed to withdraw on to us. Angus replied quietly 'Is your flask full?' I told him it was nearly empty. 'Take mine and make Ronnie drink all of it. If he won't or still talks of retiring, shoot him and take command of the company. They are not to retire.'

Ronnie was looking miserable, standing in a ditch up to his waist in water and shivering. I offered him Angus's flask and advised him to drink it, which he did. 'You are not to retire. Do you understand?' He nodded, but was killed half an hour later when the enemy attacked and drove what was left of No 1 Company back on to us.

My memory of the next few hours is disjointed. Someone cooked a delicious chicken stew over a fire behind one of the outhouses and I can remember wolfing it down with white wine. The Germans tried to bring up some guns in front of us but they were knocked out by the Boyes anti-tank rifle. An old woman suddenly appeared asking for shelter and I told her to go to hell. Then I felt deeply ashamed, called her back and apologized, offering her shelter in one of the rooms at the back of the cottage. One of my section commanders asked what he should do with all the unopened tins and I was engulfed by a wave of hatred for the Germans. Why should these bloody bastards invade other people's countries, destroy their homes, villages and towns, machine-gun and bomb them on the roads, and take what did not belong to them? Well, they were not going to get any of our food. 'Destroy them.' 'How?' came the query .'Stick a bayonet into every tin.' We indulged in an orgy of destruction. If the Huns were not going to eat our food they were not going to cook their own. In a rage I smashed the cooking stove with a hammer.

We got the Brens back in the attic and dealt with the Germans who were advancing along the canal road. We managed to set three lorries on fire, which effectively blocked the road. Later – how much later I do not know – I went down to see how Angus was. He was lying on the top of the trench, half curled up, still in 'service dress', Sam Browne breeches, green stockings and brown shoes but he no longer wore his famous papier mâché steel helmet. A dead guardsman was lying beside him. I told him I thought we could hold the enemy from the cottage but I am not sure he understood. 'I am tired, so very tired,' he said and then, with a half smile, he rallied and gave me his last order. 'Get back to the cottage, Jimmy, and carry on.'

The Germans got into a cottage on the other side of the canal where part of the roof and front had been blown away. They poked a machine-gun through the tiles, but we saw it and blasted them away with a Bren gun before they could fire.

In one Bren gun the firing pin had melted rendering it useless and when the firing died away I ordered the other gun downstairs where it would be more effective if the enemy tried to swim the canal and rush the cottage. I doubted if they would do this, but to show them we were still very much alive I started my favourite sport of sniping with a rifle at anything that moved. I had just fired five most satisfactory shots and, convinced I had chalked up another 'kill', was kneeling, pushing another clip into the rifle, when there was a most frightful crash and a great wave of heat, dust and debris knocked me over. A shell had burst on the roof.

There was a long silence and I heard a small voice saying 'I've been hit,' which I suddenly realised was mine. That couldn't be right; so I called out, 'Anybody been hit?' A reply from behind – 'No, sir, we are all right.'

'Well,' I replied more firmly, 'I have.' No pain, just a useless left arm, which looked very silly, and blood all over my battle-dress. A stretcher bearer arrived and put a field dressing on my arm, removed my watch, which he later sent to my parents in England, and bandaged my head. I remember being half carried, half helped down from the loft and some time later being put into a wheel barrow. Later splints made out of a broken wooden box were tied round my arm and I was put into an ambulance, then off we went to the beaches. No pain, only a terrible thirst. I shouted for water, but no one heard me over the noise of the engine. For what seemed hours we bumped along, continually stopping and starting. The man above me must have been bleeding badly as the blood began to drip on to my face and I had to keep wiping it off with the edge of my blanket.

At last the door was opened. My stretcher was pulled out, a water bottle was held to my mouth. In the half light of dawn I could see sand dunes and a voice said 'This way. The beach is about two hundred yards ahead of you.'

A grey life boat lay at the water's edge with a man in a long dark blue naval overcoat standing by it. He came over.

'Can you get off your stretcher?'

'No, I do not think so.'

'Well, I am very sorry we cannot take you. Your stretcher would occupy the places of four men. Orders are only those who can stand or sit up.' I said nothing. I was just too damned tired to sit up, stand up or argue.

Back to the ambulance and – oh joy – more water. A bombed building in Dunkirk, water again, this time mixed with orange juice. Back in the ambulance, a short drive and then a new face and a gruff hard voice. 'Have you had your anti-tetanus injection and when?'

'Never.'

'Just like you bloody officers. Avoid anything unpleasant. I hope this kills you!'

A large syringe, more suitable for a horse than a man, full of grey liquid, was pushed into my right arm.

'Water, please.' A bottle was produced, the other four stretchers were removed, and I was left to my own devices.

A cheery voice. 'What, you still here. I am very sorry, you got overlooked. I am Phillip Newman, the surgeon in charge of the casualty clearing station. You're Langley, aren't you?'

'Yes, what time is it?'

'Eight o'clock in the morning. Breakfast time.'

I must have slept for more than sixteen hours. Except for a dull throbbing in my arm I felt fine, hungry and, of course, thirsty.

'Hey, corporal,' shouted Newman. 'Help me with this stretcher.'

Thus I arrived in the 'Chapeau Rouge', a vast nineteenth-century house, on the outskirts of Dunkirk, which had obviously got its name from the strange hat-like roof over the tower and which was the temporary abode of the 12th Casualty Clearing Station.

'No eggs or bacon I'm afraid,' said Newman. 'But plenty of bread, marmalade, butter and tea.' Butter *or* marmalade I thought as I worked my way through a whole pot of marmalade, a quarter of a pound of butter and great chunks of bread.

Newman came over. 'I am very sorry about last night. All the walking wounded were evacuated but I completely forgot about you in the ambulance.' I told him I doubted if I could have walked.

'It was only about a hundred yards across the sands and anyhow you would have been helped. However, it is too late now. I will have a look at that arm of yours as soon as we can get through the badly wounded,' he replied.

Not long after my arm was set in plaster of paris and Newman handed me a fragment of shell about the size of a cigarette butt. 'We dug it out of your head. Pure wood I think it must be to stop that,' he said laughing.

Inside the house it was unpleasantly hot, with the air reeking of ether and the smell of unwashed bodies, and buzzing with flies and blue bottles. I asked if I could be moved outside and provided with some form of fly whisk. Hardly had I been installed in the position of my choosing, at the top of the granite steps which led up to the huge wood and glass double-fronted door, and provided with the branch of a tree to keep off the flies, than the shelling started.

The first three shells landed on the lawn which bordered the drive and the fourth in an ornamental lake. Just as I recovered from my surprise Phillip Newman and another doctor dashed by carrying two huge white glass jars full of ether. These they placed carefully in the shell holes and returned with a second load. No sooner were they back in the house when the next salvo arrived. The only shell that interested me was the one which hit the granite steps.

I was shielded by the angle of the steps, but not so the main doors which were blown off their hinges, one coming to rest some three feet from my stretcher. There was nothing to do except to await help and to continue warding off the flies.

It was very early next morning when an orderly rushed up the steps obviously very excited 'What's happening?' I queried.

'The Germans are at the gate and I do not know what to do,' he replied.

II. AND RUNS AWAY

ESCAPE AND RETURN

Author's route

Occupation Line

4

In the Bag

There had not been any question of taking prisoners during the retreat, but I knew that the general principle was 'no prisoners unless ordered' – a relic of the fierce trench fighting in the First World War. I was therefore extremely nervous about the German attitude to prisoners and was determined to ascertain the position without delay.

'Get another man and carry me out to meet them.'

Half way down the drive I asked them to put down my stretcher when I saw on the ground a little yellow book entitled in huge black letters *Fifty Filthy Facts about Hitler*. I got hold of it and pushed it as far down my trousers as possible.

If we were exhausted so were the Germans. The small section which wended its way up the drive was reeling with fatigue. Caked with dust, unshaven, two of them sank to the ground as they halted by the stretcher. I was surprised at the simplicity of their equipment: two small pouches, four toothpaste-like tubes, containing cheese, clipped to their belts, a gas mask, water bottle and machine-gun belts draped round their necks. My German was very limited so, pointing to the Red Cross flag flying over the house, I opened the conversation on what I felt would be the right note for the wounded. 'Wasser.'

The leader gave me a drink from his water bottle.

'Cigaretten' – this was a guess but one was handed to me and lit.

I felt I was 'giving too little and asking too much'.

'War sie wollen?'

'Marmaladen,' came the reply. Hoping there was a pot of marmalade left I sent off the orderly. There was no marmalade but a jar of jam seemed to give great pleasure and friendly relations were firmly established.

'Wo das Meer?' the leader asked. I had not the vaguest idea where the sea was but pointed in what I hoped to be the right direction.

He then said something I did not understand so I pulled out my cigarette case, which he took. Then I guessed what he wanted, and produced my silver flask, lighter, wallet and a large multiplex knife which I had acquired during the retreat. He pocketed the knife and cigarette lighter but handed back the rest.

'Offizier?' he queried.

'Ja,' I replied.

He called up his section, saluted, and set off towards the house. Only two of them made it; the rest reeled to right or left and sank to the ground at the first obstruction they encountered, but I was now a prisoner of war. We were not going to be massacred!

After 10 days the Germans decided to transfer some of the wounded to the BEF's base hospital Camières, near Calais, in France, and the remainder of us to Zuydcoote, between Dunkirk and La Panne, where there was a large hospital for tubercular children from Paris.

I had always understood that the Germans were highly efficient but they could hardly have made a greater mess of the move and several of us got lost. I spent the night with a group of French soldiers who were waiting, with ill-concealed anticipation, the surrender of France. They all had large stocks of food, much of it looted from the BEF dumps, and were only too pleased to give me a tin of 'singe', as the French bully beef is called, since, they informed me, it was made from Moroccan monkeys. The tin was date stamped 1919 but I found it delicious!

In the morning I was re-located by the Germans and carted off to the British ward at Zuydcoote, or rather to a ward half occupied by British wounded and half by French. I was rather sorry to leave my stretcher which had been my 'home' for fourteen days, but it was pleasant to take off my clothes, or rather what was left of them, and to sponge off the filfth, dirt and congealed blood. Removal of my trousers revealed

a flesh wound in my left leg into which the cloth had 'healed' and had to be cut away.

Re-clothed in French military hospital wear – a large sack-like night shirt – and lying in a comfortable bed, I took stock of my possessions. These were limited but useful: a tin of 50 Wills Gold Flake cigarettes, my silver cigarette case and flask, empty alas, and my wallet containing some £15 in French francs. The latter was largely No 3 Company's Imprest Account cash which Angus had divided into three during the retreat with orders to John and me to pay back our share when we reached England, which in due course I was able to do. A very dirty handkerchief, a pipe, an empty tobacco pouch and my diary, with a pencil, completed the inventory.

My neighbour on the left, a major in the Green Howards, informed me that my cash, flask and cigarette case would most certainly be stolen the moment I was asleep, so I had these strapped to my thighs with adhesive tape.

Life was pleasant enough except for the shortage of food and water. The drains in Dunkirk had been destroyed so all the water had to be boiled and was issued in the form of weak sugarless tea. A small compensation was the mug of white wine issued at lunch and supper. Theoretically we were on French army rations and if this was so I am not surprised that France collapsed. Breakfast was a thick slice of coarse grey-coloured bread and a cup of black sugared coffee. Lunch and supper consisted of a mug of greasy stew, half a potato, an inch square cube of meat and a slice of bread. As supper arrived at 5 in the afternoon and breakfast around 8 a.m. most of us kept the supper bread to ward off the pangs of hunger during the 13 hours without food. Someone discovered that the thick pads of skin that had formed on the soles of our feet during the retreat made an excellent form of chewing gum and many hours were happily passed carefully stripping this off. Unfortunately it did not re-grow.

I found I could walk so spent most of the day foraging for food in the hospital grounds. The supply of dandelion leaves rapidly gave out and the best hunting was amongst the remaining tubercular children and their nurses. The Germans kept them well supplied with cake, biscuits and chocolate, fragments of which they frequently dropped on the ground. The nurses were very sympathetic and any 'left overs' often arrived my way. I never found much during my scavenging but was optimistic when a private soldier, with badly burnt hands, asked me to open a tin of sardines he had picked up. I complied and asked him why he had not chosen someone with two good hands. 'Ah!' he replied, 'you are an officer and will not ask for the tin to lick out the oil!'

We saw little of the Germans though we were mildly interrogated by a somewhat supercilious young officer. As required I gave him my name, rank and number but refused to give my regiment. He smiled and wrote down 'Coldstream Guards' saying, 'You see, we know all about you.' I laughed and he moved on.

The most helpful visitor was a blonde American press reporter who took a liking to me which was heartily reciprocated when she gave me 100 cigarettes, a pound of chocolate, some sugar and a bag of apples. She told Phillip Newman that she thought he should operate on my arm again and said she would return in two days to see if he had done so. I asked her to bring me a razor, soap and shaving brush.

Phillip duly complied, though he said he could do little as the bones of both the upper and lower arm were nothing but a mass of splinters. He then asked for most of the cigarettes to give to the dying and those in great pain. Somewhat grudgingly I agreed, largely because the blonde had returned with my requirements and some more luxuries.

It was two days later, when sitting up in bed re-examining the soles of my feet for any skin I might have missed, that a spurt of blood from my arm hit me in the face. By incredible luck Philip Newman was talking to someone two beds away. He vaulted both and, using his hand, stopped the bleeding before applying a tourniquet.

'Your arm will have to come off,' he said.

'Must it?' I murmured.

'Yours is the choice. Dead in two days from gangrene or life without an arm.'

'When will you operate?'

'Now.' It was a bad moment as supper was just being served: food had become more important than recovery.

It was very little later when I woke up as my stretcher was

lifted. 'Where am I going?' I asked. 'Christ!' a voice replied, 'we were sent here to collect a couple of stiffs for burial. We thought you were one.' I hastily redirected them back to the ward. Shortly afterwards Phillip Newman passed by on his evening round. 'I've left you enough to tuck your evening paper under,' he said.

'Will I live?' I asked.

'I suppose you have a 25% chance – possibly less,' came the reply.

Years later I told him I did not think much of his idea of encouraging the sick. His reply was illuminating. 'My dear Jimmy, you were so damned pleased with yourself that I knew that with any further encouragement you would almost certainly have relaxed and made no further effort. I wanted to make you very angry and fight!' He did, and probably saved my life.

Next day I crawled the two hundred yards to the main gate and the German guard-house where visitors were admitted. It was a long laborious progress which took the best part of two hours, but I reaped a rich reward in food parcels from the local French who had come to visit the wounded. There were far too many for me to carry, but a German sentry took pity on me and sent me back with them on a stretcher.

Regretfully relations with the French wounded were not cordial. They complained bitterly that our morning bed-pan session always coincided with their short daily Mass. We replied that the calls of nature could not be denied and suggested they altered the time of their service. This the priest, who said he was very overworked, indignantly refused to do. They retaliated by playing a gramophone during our Sunday afternoon hymn-singing session – about the nearest we got to religion though once Phillip managed to persuade the French Protestant priest to take a Communion service in the operating theatre. It was a moving service but I was too young, stupid and disillusioned with all the misery and suffering I had seen to find any consolation in the agony of Christ.

While it is not for me to express any views on the Roman

Catholic religion, I still do not really understand why the Catholic priest refused to give absolution to a dying French captain, who asked me to perform the ceremony. He was alone in a little room apart which was reserved for the dying. He told me that after serving some years as a regular officer in the French Army he had retired, entered the priesthood and was the curé in a small village. On the outbreak of war he could have stayed on, but felt it his duty to rejoin his regiment. This was the reason why the priest, so he said, refused to have anything to do with him. I mildly pointed out that a Protestant British officer was hardly the right person to hear a confession and give absolution – even assuming, as he affirmed, it was permissible. He was quite adamant and so I listened to his confession, which became very incoherent towards the end, and prayed at his bedside until he died.

One day we were all spruced up for the visit of a German general and his entourage. Largely due to the shortage of water we had none of us shaved and I had yet to master the art of doing so with one hand and without a mirror. The General turned a fishy eye on me and coldly stated, in excellent English, that he had always understood Guards officers shaved every day. I replied that if he came back in a day or two he would find an improvement. Shaving in one's urine is painful and difficult. Every cut smarts and the soap will not lather properly. However, much to my surprise the general did make a return visit and after expressing satisfaction at my handiwork, asked if I wanted anything. I told him cigarettes and the ADC was ordered to give me all he had in his case.

One of the more pleasant features of life at Zuydcoote was that there was little hospital discipline. I never had my temperature taken while I was there and one did much as one liked. However, the arrival of some Belgian nurses, who were scandalized at the general free for all, led to the introduction of various routines, including daily massage of behinds to prevent bed sores. My masseuse was vast and her idea of massage was to treat my behind as though she was kneading bread, despite my vociferous protests. I nicknamed her 'The Elephant' on the grounds that I would prefer to have been stamped on by an elephant than massaged by her. Unfortunately she got to hear of this and in a spirit of helpful revenge she took charge of my bowels: an empty bed pan was the signal for a cold soap and water enema which was even more humiliating than the massage.

Oswald Normanby, an officer in the Green Howards, and I became friendly and spent many happy hours sitting in the sun talking about food and compiling menus. He chose Fuller's walnut cake as his first luxury on reaching England. I was more mundane and plumped for cold roast leg of lamb with mint sauce.

The fall of France was memorable in more ways than one. The Germans sent an interpreter round to announce the news and also that it was confidently expected that England would sue for peace in a few days. He also said we were to have a special celebration supper and a double issue of wine. We did, and it was delicious; sardines, hard-boiled eggs, lettuce and all the bread and potatoes we could eat. Most of the French cheered loudly at the news and we replied with 'There will always be an England', 'We're going to hang out our washing on the Siegfried Line' and 'Land of Hope and Glory'. All the French who could walk – they were mostly lightly wounded – got dressed and left, as they thought, for home. They were soon hustled back by the indignant Germans and we taunted them unmercifully about their new-found friends and their disloyalty to their ally. In all fairness I must say that there were some Frenchmen who cried bitterly and I think our demonstration, of somewhat dubious taste, was largely done to keep up our own spirits.

It was in August that the Germans decided to move all but the worst cases and one cold dawn we were packed into trucks for an unannounced destination. Phillip Newman did his utmost for our comfort, securing me a seat on the front of the lorry and giving everyone a blanket. I had by now acquired the top half of a Belgian despatch rider's uniform, a pair of battledress trousers and some felt slippers.

Our new home turned out to be a French barracks in Lille, and we drove along one of the roads used by the retreating BEF, where proof of how bitterly the German advance had been contested was visible. At almost every crossroads there were three or more crosses or rifles stuck in the ground, bearing British steel helmets or gas masks.

If Zuydcoote had had its drawbacks the French barracks were infinitely worse. We were allocated a barrack room up five flights of stone steps, covered with filthy straw bearing ample evidence of earlier human occupation. The latrines were blocked solid and we could locate no water for drinking or washing. We had to go down to a neighbouring building for the midday meal and by the time we got there the food was all gone. A French sergeant gruffly informed me that we would be lucky if we ever got any as orders were to feed French white troops, then the Goums and any coloured soldiers, next the British other ranks and last of all British officers. I went miserably to my favourite scavenging position at the main gate, outside of which there was a large crowd of French civilians. Word got around that I was a British officer and I soon had a good meal for Oswald and myself and promises of many more.

However, Oswald was not going to stand for this kind of treatment and in excellent German he ordered the sergeant of the guard to fetch a German officer. In due course the commanding officer arrived, accompanied by his adjutant, and meekly listened to a tirade from Oswald who had spent some time in Berlin when his uncle was British ambassador.

'Is this the way,' said Oswald coldly, 'that the German Army treats wounded British officers, especially those from the Brigade of Guards?' – pointing to me who lay apparently half conscious on the ground. 'As the nephew of a former British ambassador' he continued, 'I had the honour of meeting President Hindenburg, who I am certain would never have permitted the German Army to behave in such a dishonourable manner.'

Twenty minutes later we were driven away to a French convent near Roubaix, a temporary prison hospital for the

French naval officers from Dunkirk. The nuns burst into tears at the sight of us and after showing us to comfortable bedrooms insisted on washing my feet. I have seldom felt more out of place than having my filthy feet washed by a young nun streaming with tears. It seemed very wrong.

The tragedy of Mers el Kebir, when half the French fleet was sunk or put out of action by the Royal Navy at the cost of 1300 French dead, had just taken place and the welcome extended by the naval officers was understandably not cordial. In fact both Oswald and I feared that one or two of the younger officers might resort to violence, since their attitude was thoroughly menacing. However, the senior officer courteously introduced himself, and after ascertaining our names and regiments requested our presence at a meeting he called of all the officers. His address was short and to the point. 'England is fighting on and we are not. You will accord these two British officers the utmost courtesy regardless of your feelings. I shall make it my personal responsibility to see that this order is carried out and I can assure you you will regret any failure to implement it to the full.' We had no further trouble.

After the most pleasant week I was to spend in captivity the Germans turned up and we were all packed in a lorry and driven to the Faculté Catholique of Lille University, which was the collecting centre for all the British wounded until they were fit enough to be sent to Germany. The first person I saw was Airey Neave, later to be the first British officer to escape successfully from Colditz, and who was to work with me during the last three years of the war. I had met him before but nevertheless his opening words consisted of a short interrogation as to my education and military background!

'We have a small room upstairs where some of us play bridge and eat. We have steak for lunch. I hope you and Oswald will join us,' he concluded.

At that time there were some 300 wounded and about 70 RAMC personnel. The wounded other ranks were housed in the chapel and the officers two to a room upstairs. The bed, pillows and canvas sheets were French Army issue and decidedly uncomfortable and the French Army, under German supervision, were responsible for the general administration. The food was much the same as at Zuydcoote but slightly more plentiful and the Germans, in lieu of Red Cross parcels, allowed the French to send in gifts of food via their guardroom.

Every three weeks all the wounded were individually examined by German doctors to assess whether they were fit for despatch to POW camps in Germany. These periodical examinations were not without their lighter moments. The wounded naturally exaggerated to the utmost the suffering they were undergoing and their total unfitness for any kind of journey. Oswald Normanby, whose major wound in the ankle was as far healed as it was ever likely to be, complained that a flesh wound in his back was causing continuous and intense agony. The German doctors duly noted the fact and Oswald thought he had passed unfit to travel until one of them appeared to slip and, to save himself falling, put his hand and his whole weight on to Oswald's 'wound'. Busy gossiping with a colleague he took little notice until the doctor, roaring with laughter, said 'Ah, Lord Normanby, your wound is so painful you do not wish me to examine it and yet when I hit you there you take no notice! We will have to reconsider our decision.' We all laughed, including Oswald but he was allowed to stay.

A captain from the 51st Division was also caught out by German ingenuity. With a bullet through the right shoulder he maintained he had lost all power to lift his arm and should be repatriated as totally unfit for further service. Just as we were being dismissed the senior German doctor produced a block of chocolate and, throwing it in his general direction said, 'Anyone who can catch this with his right hand can keep it.' Though it was high above his head the captain brought off a magnificent catch. 'Germany,' said the doctor, 'and you may keep the chocolate!'

I was a border-line case until the examiner noticed the

splendid scar on my stomach, the aftermath of the bungled operation when I was three weeks old. He called over his colleagues who evinced intense interest.

'When,' enquired the senior, 'did that happen?'

'1916,' I replied.

He placed his arm on my shoulder. 'How very brave of you to fight again. However, for you the wars are really over. You will be sent to Switzerland as soon as it can be arranged.'

For once I had the sense to make no comment.

Half prison, half hospital, daily life was in no way unpleasant and was from time to time enlivened with amusing incidents. The sentries were reservists whose only ambitions were to return home as soon as possible and on only two occasions did they give us cause for concern.

One Sunday afternoon a sports meeting was organized in the courtyard and a number of Germans attended as spectators. All went well until the potato and spoon race, there being no eggs available. The Germans, who were all grouped round the winning post, had not observed the issue of potatoes and spoons. The first thing they saw was a line of men running towards them carrying, at arms length, a large potato in a soup spoon. Shouting 'grenades' some of them disappeared into buildings while those with rifles loaded them, pointed them at the runners, and cried, 'Halte! Halte!'

With commendable alacrity the order was obeyed and a few moments later the guard arrived, some 10 in number, armed with sub-machine guns with which they menaced friend and foe alike from the steps leading into the main building. It took considerable time to explain to the German officer the objects of a potato and spoon race and it was only after we had sliced up half a dozen potatoes – the Germans standing well clear of any danger – that calm prevailed. Even then the sports meeting was stopped.

The second incident was more serious. A number of French women, despite German orders and threats, persisted in their generous and courageous efforts to supplement our rations by throwing food parcels over the wall and barbed wire which separated the courtyard from the street outside. On one of these occasions I was having an animated discussion near the German guardroom with a senior German officer who spoke excellent English, when the German sentries lost their tempers and opened fire on the crowd. I waited around to find out what had happened and when the shooting and the hubbub had died down he returned and the following illuminating dialogue took place.

Self: 'What was that all about?'

The German officer: 'We have had to fire on a crowd of those senseless French women who, contrary to orders and frequent warnings, continue to throw parcels and God knows what else over the wall.'

Self: 'Are there many casualties?'

German officer: 'One or two dead and some wounded. I do not know the exact numbers.'

Self, very pompously: 'Not a very honourable act to fire on defenceless women and children.'

German officer: 'We are at war.'

Self: 'Not with the French – only us – and our army is not within 100 miles of here.'

German officer, with calm disdain: 'Will you stupid British never understand what war is? We are at war with anyone, anywhere, who at any time helps you, and will kill regardless of sex and age.'

Self (after a long pause and even more pompously): 'I hope you will forgive me if I go back to my room. I am not used to talking to people who hold such views.'

German officer, with genuine surprise: 'But you cannot let a trivial incident like this spoil our conversation.'

I walked away feeling that I was not as yet quite grown up.

Initially all the food parcels sent in were put in a common 'pool'; but as our numbers dwindled this system fell into abeyance. Most of the officers and the worst wounded other ranks, notably the blind, were 'adopted' by War Godmothers or Marraines de Guerre and received individual parcels. Oswald Normanby, as we all agreed befitted a member of the peerage was, every Sunday, the recipient of a magnificent

Ascot-type hamper full of luxury foods and often a bottle of champagne. However, for sheer persistency, continuity and life-saving, no Marraine de Guerre could compete with Madame Caron, who adopted me.

Nearer 50 than 40, she was married to a French gendarme, who regarded her enthusiasm for the British with a jaundiced eye, largely, I suspect, due to the effect it had on his meals. As a cleaner of the wards she had a '*laissez-passer*' from the Germans and every evening at six o'clock she would arrive with two plates – tied together with string – containing hot food, sometimes a steak and chips, occasionally a delicious stew, but never falling below a superb ham omelette. Attached to the plates was always a brown-paper parcel containing four slices of new bread thickly spread with fresh butter. On Sundays this repast was supplemented with half a bottle of wine and some chocolate. Even when the Germans, as a reprisal for some incident, forbade all food parcels and stopped all civilians entering the building, Madame Caron did not fail. My meals arrived daily, dead on time, delivered by a German sentry!

For several reasons relationships between the RAMC personnel and the wounded never reached the happy comradeship which had prevailed at Zuydcoote. There had been a number of stupid and trivial quarrels followed by two blazing rows. The first row occurred when the medical officers' mess ate some liver which we had managed to buy from the French and part of which we had given to the non-commissioned wounded. The second broke out when the senior RAMC officer forbade the singing of 'God Save the King' at an impromptu entertainment which was staged by the wounded, on the grounds that it would offend the German commandant and his officers who were invited to attend. Arrangements were made to 'muzzle' him and the Germans stood stiffly to attention for the National Anthem and the Marseillaise.

In passing it should be stated that the Germans endured, without comment, a character sketch of Hitler which in my opinion was in rather bad taste, but their enthusiasm for a similar one on Mussolini was such that they called for an encore. They were, however, completely mystified and ultimately somewhat shocked at the huge sign which was painted on the stage curtain:

JOIN THE GERMAN ARMY AND SEE
THE WORLD.
JOIN THE BRITISH ARMY AND SEE
THE NEXT.

Under the Geneva Convention – to which Germany was a signatory – captured medical personnel must be repatriated when there is no further aid they can render to those wounded they were tending when taken prisoner.

By the end of August there was little more that could be done for the wounded at the Faculté Catholique in Lille, and not unnaturally the anticipation of early repatriation was to the forefront of all the medical personnel's thinking. The German commandant was, however, no fool; he realized that escape must be in the minds of some of the combatant wounded and further that the buildings were totally unsuitable as a prison. He therefore informed the senior medical officer that, while repatriation was a matter to be arranged between the two governments concerned, he was not going to have any escaping and that he would shoot two RAMC officers every time anyone escaped. That he would carry out his threat was highly unlikely, though just possible, and this faint possibility was enough for all the wounded to be ordered by the senior medical officer to give their parole not to escape. Airey Neave alone refused and the following superb exchange of views took place between him and the senior medical officer.

The SMO: 'You refuse to obey my order and give your parole not to escape?'

A. N.: 'Yes, sir, You have no right to give the order.'

The SMO: 'I will have you court-martialled after the war for disobeying this order.'

Airey will, I am sure, forgive me when I state that he had already mastered the art of calculated arrogance; another officer present said it was part of the curriculum at Eton; however, be that as it may, Airey used it to the full.

A. N.: 'I shall not be court-martialled but you will be, and probably shot for cowardice in the face of the enemy.'

The SMO, white with temper: 'If you do not give me your parole I will have you locked in a room under guard.'

A. N.: 'Forcibly detaining an officer who wishes to escape will only make your case worse.'

The SMO: 'Go to your room. You will be confined there and only come out for meals.'

A. N., sauntering casually to his room: 'I do not want to come out for meals. I might get contaminated with defeatism by you or your colleagues.'

Reaching the door Airey turned round and delivered his parting shot.

'I will be sending you the names of two of your officers the shooting of whom would help us win the war.'

The breach was complete. The senior wounded officer gave orders that there was to be no further communication with the RAMC staff except on medical matters. A sentry, armed with a stick, was posted outside Airey's room and it was not long before he was sent off to Germany. It was to be nearly two years before we saw each other again, when he told me he was trying to draw the SMO's attention away from two more severely wounded officers who were planning to escape. Alas, they too were sent to Germany before their plans were completed.

How the German commandant must have laughed, but the last laugh was with the British as ultimately three officers got home from the Faculté Catholique.

5

Home James . . .

If in forcing us – apart from Airey – to give our parole the senior medical officer had stipulated that withdrawal could only be accepted by himself personally, the situation would indeed have been difficult. But this he did not do and it was a simple matter to find an RAMC officer who, ashamed of the behaviour of the commanding officer, was prepared to accept withdrawal on his behalf. Further, giving one's parole not to escape was no bar to making all the preparations so to do at the earliest opportunity. The problem was to decide where to make for when free and to discover what were the difficulties to be overcome. Other than that Western Europe was controlled by the Germans from Norway to the Pyrenees, (Sweden, Switzerland and Portugal excepted) little was known of the conditions outside, though a map cut from a newspaper showed that France was divided into the 'Zone Occupé' and 'Zone Non-Occupé' known, until the Germans in 1942 took over all France, as the 'ZO' and 'ZNO' respectively. It was also rumoured that the area of the ZO north of the River Somme was a forbidden area, known as the 'Zone Interdite' though what this implied was a matter for conjecture.

The nearest British soil which could be reached without crossing the sea was Gibraltar, over a 1000 miles south and of which some 500 would be through Spain, theoretically neutral but with strong pro-German leanings. Numerous though the imponderables were two things were clear, first that the nearer one got to Germany the more difficult it would be to get out and secondly that the only feasible objective was Gibraltar.

Initially I had hoped that Madame Caron, my Marraine de Guerre, would hide me until the anticipated hue and cry, which would follow my absence, had died down. However, she indicated that her husband would not co-operate but promised to find another safe house.

While I was waiting for the arrangements to be completed an event occurred which I cannot resist the temptation of calling 'the curious incident' since it so closely resembles the famous passage from Conan Doyle's short story 'Silver Blaze' which I hope I will be forgiven if I quote in part.

> 'Is there any other point to which you would wish to draw my attention?'
>
> 'To the curious incident of the dog in the night time.'
>
> 'The dog did nothing in the night time.'
>
> 'That was the curious incident,' remarked Sherlock Homes.

Amongst the wounded officers was an individual whose appearance, character and behaviour gave rise, not to suspicion – we were all still very naïve regarding the possible use of 'stool pigeons' by the Germans – but to doubts as to whether he really was an officer. Claiming to be a captain in the Royal Army Service Corps, he kept himself very much to himself and took little part in the day-to-day activities. Bearing in mind that the subsequent suspicions he did arouse in my mind may be ill-founded I will call him Paul Pepper, though that was not his real name.

Beyond passing the time of day I hardly talked to him though he did once say, 'Parole or no parole I am going to escape,' and we discussed possible methods. Then one day he just disappeared and, beyond the fact that he was last seen wearing full service dress including Sam Brown and cap complete with badge, no one knew how, when or where he had got out. More surprising was that the Germans like 'the dog in the night' did nothing. After 24 hours of wild surmising the affair was forgotten and I supposed would probably have remained so had I not, when walking through Lille some weeks later, seen several posters, complete with photograph in uniform, offering a reward for his recapture.

When the opportunity arose I enquired from the War Office whether he had arrived back safely and was informed that there was no officer in the RASC of his name who had been with the British Expeditionary Force and further that no such name had ever appeared on the German lists of British POWs. Was he a stool pigeon or agent provocateur? My views tend towards this solution of the mystery and that the Germans were much more escape conscious than we reckoned.

I now decided that 'he travels the fastest who travels alone' and therefore only discussed my plans for getting away with the senior wounded officer, Major de Salis of the Scots Guards and his room-mate, Major Carter of the Welsh Guards, both far too badly wounded to consider escaping. I was unaware that two other officers had similar plans.

At this point I must make it absolutely clear that my unauthorized departure from the Faculté Catholique does not merit the use of the word 'Escape' and if it is ever so described the only useful purpose would be to give the true escapers from Colditz and other POW camps in Germany and Italy a hearty laugh. Getting out unobserved was just about as difficult as leaving early a party to which your wife has forced you to go, without hurting her feelings or those of your host and hostess. To take the comparison a stage further – the Germans were my hosts and my wife was the individual to whom I had given an undertaking to remain until the proper time.

On 30 September the rumour went round that we would all shortly be moving to Enghien in Belgium en route for Germany. That evening the other two who planned to abscond, Captain Robertson of the Argyll and Sutherland Highlanders and Captain Griffiths of the South Wales Borderers went absent, and Madame Caron produced a safe address about a mile from the Faculté Catholique together with a password and a plan of Lille. I decided that I must go next evening and spent the day memorizing my route, arranging my place of exit, and to whom I would surrender my parole.

In the usual chaos that precedes any move the departure of Robertson and Griffiths had passed unnoticed and I felt it would be safe to use the same exit point, a small porter's lodge. During the day this was used as a guard-house but by some extraordinary oversight it was left unoccupied at night and I knew that a French-speaking RAMC corporal used the window to slip out for an occasional drink in the town. He promised to help me climb up to the window which was set high in the wall near the ceiling.

There were no feverish last-minute preparations as all the things I had to take with me I anyhow carried by day in the pockets of my half Belgian half French battledress. These consisted of my silver pocket flask and cigarette case, my wallet containing about £30 in French francs, two very grubby handkerchiefs and a box of matches. However, I did add two small rolls of crêpe bandages as the stump of my arm was still suppurating and Major de Salis kindly gave me a small pocket torch and a packet of 20 cigarettes.

I had decided to pose, if caught, as one of the French medical orderlies who were allowed to come and go as they wished, so I put a stretcher bearer's insignia, a white arm-band with a red cross, round my left sleeve.

The staff were having a farewell cocktail party to finish their supplies of liquor and I had no difficulty in finding an RAMC officer who promised to hold the withdrawal of my parole for two hours and to look after my diary, which incidentally he duly returned to me after the war.

The corporal, who was in the porter's lodge, told me that there was no time to spare as a German sergeant had just left after testing the locks on the gates and informing him that there would be sentries inside that night. From the window, in the half light I could see the sentry at the end of his beat on the corner of the street talking to someone, which gave me added confidence. It was common practice for them to gossip with French girls though unusual after dark. I would have been less happy had I known what I learnt after the war, namely that the other individual was an SS soldier, a company of which infamous units were taking over guard duties.

In sublime ignorance, aided by a good deal of pushing by

the corporal, I got through the window and, after hanging on to the sill for a few moments, dropped into the street, a fall of some 12 feet made easier by a small ledge in the wall half way down. Scuttling across the street I paused but there was no sound of pursuit and I set off at a brisk walk, hoping that I could find the house in the dark of the blackout.

From my plan of Lille I had calculated the distance to my destination as well as memorizing the turns I had to take. Luckily the route was not complicated and after I had completed the required number of steps – there were several hundred – I cautiously examined, by the light of my small torch, the door of a house. Incredible though it seemed it was the number I wanted and so I knocked as I had been instructed; three knocks and a 10-second pause. I had to count these out as I had no watch, and then give two more knocks.

The door was opened and a voice said quietly in French, 'Give me your hand and make no noise, there are some Boches about.' The passage, which was pitch dark and smelt faintly of antiseptics, led to a living room in which a short elderly man, his wife and a girl were seated and I now saw my guide was also a girl. After welcoming me and giving me a glass of wine, they introduced themselves as the family Carpentier, laughingly saying they were all practising dentists; hence the smell of antiseptics. Much as I hate visits to the dentist I found myself wishing that the two girls would have time to make a routine inspection of my teeth as they were extremely pretty.

As I ate a delicious omelette and chips the father addressed me in a voice totally without emotion though nonetheless kindly. 'Last night we had the honour of receiving two of your colleagues'; so this is where Robertson and Griffiths went to, I thought. 'Tonight we have the added honour of receiving you. However, the day has not been as calm as usual and twice German patrols have come along the road examining houses. Although they have not called here, I think it would be safer for all concerned if you did not sleep in this house.' He must have seen my face fall. 'No, do not worry, there will be no long journey. The house next door has been damaged by bombs but we have made up a bed upstairs and I have placed ladders on both sides of the wall that divides the gardens. One of my daughters will lead you there and collect you at dawn.'

It was a far more nerve-racking journey than leaving the Faculté Catholique as it had to be made without a light. However, in the end I lay down on a comfortable bed and was nearly asleep when pandemonium broke out in the street below. For some time I could not make out what was happening but in the end a German patrol arrived and I could hear a Frenchman explaining that a German soldier had been trying to assault a French girl against the door of the house I was in. The patrol leader was all for calling it a day and leaving with the soldier but the Frenchman, supported by others, wished him to search the house as who was to know how many French girls were suffering in silence upstairs! My host was protesting that it was all a waste of time as he knew the stairs were so badly damaged that it was unlikely that anyone could climb them in the dark. In the end his view prevailed but I spent a miserable night until rescued by one of the daughters at dawn.

My host was most anxious that I should be away before the patients started to arrive and hardly had I finished an excellent morale-restoring breakfast than a young and pretty woman – alas not as pretty as the daughters – arrived carrying a parcel of clothes which had seen better days. As I had not had a proper bath for four months and my bandages were saturated with puss – 'looks like cheese, smells like cheese and probably tastes like cheese,' as one of the doctors had said – the seedy black suit was well in keeping with my general appearance.

My guide told me she would take me across Lille to the village of Ascq not far from where we had been billeted in the Spring. We took a tram and after she had paid the fares she moved forward, leaving me alone. I thought at the time it was probably a security precaution but in retrospect I suspect she could not stand the smell. Apart from the fact that one of the sentries whom I had known by sight boarded the tram, but failed to recognize me, the journey was without incident.

I was again left on my own in the main square in Lille while we waited for another tram and had the pleasure of watching two French children sawing through the back tyres of a huge German lorry only some five yards from the sentry.

From the tram terminus to Ascq we walked some four miles, separated by about 100 yards which nearly caused a disaster. A German staff car going towards Lille stopped and as I realized the intention I tried to hide in the ditch which was only about two feet deep. Since it would have given no cover I abandoned the idea and obeyed the summons to come over to the car. The occupants were from the SS and I was half paralysed with fear. They all spoke at once and I could not make out what they wanted with the result that after a minute or two they drove on, convinced I suppose that they had encountered the local village idiot.

The safe house in Ascq was the presbytery, my host the village priest, and his motives for hiding me entirely those of charity. His main worry when I arrived was the text for his next sermon which his parishioners had requested should indicate how they should treat the Germans. The problem was complicated by the fact that the Luftwaffe band from the local aerodrome at Lesquin was billeted in the village and some of its members were devout Roman Catholics who regularly attended Mass. We used to walk in the walled-in garden in the dusk discussing possible solutions until one evening he said quietly, 'God has answered my prayers and given me guidance. He has sent me my text. "Render unto Caesar the things that are Caesar's and unto God the things that are God's." He never fails one.'

His housekeeper, a more worldly soul who was horrified at our evening walks and would not let me out of my room during the day, fearing that I might be seen by the neighbours, supplied my material needs in good measure. She was terrified of trying to dress my wounds but she did her best to clean me up and washed my shirt and handkerchiefs, with the result that when, after ten days, my guide came to collect me I felt fully prepared to face the problems ahead.

Back to Lille, this time to a small house in the back streets of the industrial suburb of Fives, to await arrangements to go by train to Paris.

Madame Veuve (the widow) Samiez owned the house through which a score of British evaders had already passed. Short in stature but vast in girth with a great bellowing laugh and a voice that could be heard the length of the street, her only passion in life was hatred of 'les Sales Boches' which she constantly declaimed in private and public. Whenever she went out to buy or scrounge food, waddling rather than walking, she never carried less than four German stick grenades suspended under her skirt from some portion of her underwear, and two British Mills grenades in her shopping bag. These, when the opportunity occurred, she would drop from the bridge over the railway leading to Lille, or roll them under a parked German vehicle. I do not think they ever went off as she did not know how they worked but this habit must have alarmed the Germans as much as it did me. Not surprisingly, she did not survive the war though no one seemed to know what happened to her. My guess is that she was blown up by one of her grenades, possibly with a number of other people.

Her first task was to provide me with a false French identity card which necessitated a photograph. It took a whole day to get this as our walk to Lille, grenades and all was not swift and there was a long queue of German soldiers in the store. However, all went well and it was duly affixed to a signed blank card stolen from the Maire at Lille. My father, when in due course he viewed the photograph, commented, 'If I were asked what you had been doing I would reply, "Seven years hard labour after a particularly sordid and unpleasant sex crime!" '

The difficulty of stamping it was overcome by gently rolling a shelled, cold, hard-boiled egg over the ink stamp on the photograph in her card and then rolling the imprint on the egg over mine. The results were not impressive but better than nothing and I now became Jean Dupont, a native of Dunkirk, where all the records had been destroyed, resident in the rue Esquemoise, Lille, a street consisting largely of houses and cafés of ill fame where the population was of a floating nature.

I cannot say I much enjoyed my stay 'chez' Madame Samiez. Apart from my fear that one day the Germans would raid the house and the conviction that sooner or later one of the grenades would go off, the other occupant, a stocky little private in a famous Scottish regiment, was, to put it mildly, bloody minded. His consuming passion was hatred of the officer class, which he gave vent to with monotonous regularity. While I could understand and, in some way, sympathize with his views, as the sole topic of conversation it became boring. In addition, he believed in the first come first served principle and occupied the only bed, while I slept on the floor covered by a dirty blanket and old newspapers.

I was not sorry when he moved on and a day or two later a middle-aged Frenchman came to collect me to put me on the train for Paris. He duly introduced my travelling companions, two huge Scotsmen, like my earlier acquaintance stragglers from the BEF, and a young Frenchman called Georges, who was to be our guide. There was some time to wait before the train left and as the station was full of Germans he told us to wander round for half an hour outside. Not unnaturally I gravitated towards the Carlton Hotel where I had spent many happy evenings during the phoney war.

My choice of route near as no matter cost me my freedom. Turning a corner I saw approaching me two German officers arm in arm with a girl I recognized only too well as a habitué of the hotel bar and with whom I had passed many amusing hours gossiping over drinks. No more! She had a regular 'boy friend' senior to me in both rank and age. To turn back would arouse suspicion and there was nothing to do but go on and hope for the best. She did not see me until we were about to pass when her whole face lit up with pleased recognition and they all stopped and turned round to look at me. Foolishly perhaps I looked back over my shoulder and, seeing her expression change knew instinctively she had realized who I was. She said something to the Germans and laughing they all walked away. The price on the heads of escaping British officers was several hundred pounds and I owe much to her loyalty and her quick wit.

Civilians were not allowed to enter the train until all the Germans were seated but long before that it was standing room only. A fat German corporal kindly invited me to hang on to his belt and as we rattled and swayed through the Zone Interdite I could not help thinking, 'Ah, my lad, little do you know that several thousand francs are hanging on to your belt.'

At Amiens most of the Germans got out; we all found seats and passed out of the ZI without having our papers examined. So great was the relief from the tension that the two Scotsmen started to talk loudly and I lit a Gold Flake cigarette, the smell of which is instantly recognizable to anyone used to the smell from black tobacco, as smoked by the French. We were in a Pullman car and were very lucky. Several people looked up but there were no longer any Germans nearby and nothing happened.

Arriving at the Gare du Nord in Paris we had three-quarters of an hour for Georges to take us by the Metro to a 'safe' hotel on the left bank of the river Seine.

Safe indeed it was, for when I wrote 'Dunkirk' on the registration form as my place of birth Madame laughed, tore the form in half and suggested I remembered I was French. Shamefacedly I re-wrote 'Dunkerque' and made sure I got the other details right.

Our instructions were to make contact with the local 'Old Comrades Association of the 1914–18 War', which organization would arrange for us to be flown, clandestinely by night, to England from a small disused airfield at Villacoublay. The plane, we were told, organized by the 'British Intelligence Service' left twice weekly and it says much for our faith in this great service that we believed every word!

In the morning Georges and I located the offices of the

Association only to find, as a huge notice nailed on the door announced in French, that it was closed 'by orders of the Geheime Staatspolizie' – better known as the Gestapo. This was a bad setback but worse was to follow as we pursued our emergency instructions to contact the commandant of the gendarmerie in the postal area where the 'safe' hotel was located. After a long wait we were duly conducted to his office and requested to explain our business. As Georges did so I watched the officer's face and it soon became abundantly clear that he was not going to co-operate. Holding up his hand for silence he turned to me saying, 'Do you mean to tell me you are a British officer in plain clothes?' I replied in the affirmative, 'And you have the nerve and audacity,' he continued, 'to come and ask me, a commandant of the gendarmerie, for help?' I nodded. He then stood up and shouted 'Monsieur, I am married and have five children. If you are not out of this office in one minute I will have you both arrested and handed over to the Germans.' We left.

To add to my personal depression the Germans chose that day to plaster the walls of the Metro with an announcement that all escaping British officers had five days grace in which to give themselves up, when they would be treated as POWs. After that period they would be shot out of hand. It also added that any Frenchman or woman who gave assistance to an escaping British officer would be shot without trial. I am not altruistic by nature but I was relieved to note that this threat was confined to officers. It would please my stocky little Scotsman, but I wondered just how Georges would react. I need not have worried, he merely shrugged his shoulders and said, 'It is war.'

After much discussion it was decided to send a postcard to Madame Samiez discreetly stating that all her friends were away on holiday and enquiring if she had any others we could call on. We chose a postcard as letters were subject to long delays for censorship and, the German posters apart, time was not on our side since our money was limited and the two Scotsmen had none at all. We only met after dark to plan the next day's operations and to arrange where and how we were going to eat. Meals always presented problems as most foods, other than luxuries such as oysters and fish, were rationed and also beyond our means. Further, speaking no French, the two Scotsmen could not go alone to a restaurant for any unrationed food such as vegetable soup, watery meatless stews, and the like. Usually we would give the Scotsmen any food Georges and I had been able to scrounge or buy, to eat in their bedroom, while we would lunch and dine in restaurants which were patronized by the Germans. This may sound strange but they had a generous issue of food coupons and the patron would frequently cut out enough tickets to cover their needs and ours.

As anyone who has been on the run is only too well aware 'getting nowhere' and 'hanging around' is not only morale-destroying but dangerous. Most people will dismiss anything they see the first time that is out of the ordinary but any repetition will make them think and talk. The two Scotsmen were tall and in no way French-looking and it was highly desirable that they did not become the subject of speculation and that we all had something to do.

Georges went off to Epernay to contact a rich uncle who might help with money, food and, I devoutly hoped, a bottle of champagne. The Scotsmen, who were both Roman Catholics, were instructed to make the rounds of the local churches with the object, during confession, of requesting the priest for help.

Their accents were so broad that often I could not understand what they said and I doubted if any French priest would so do. I therefore made them learn by heart some French sentences which ran roughly as follows: 'My father, in asking forgiveness for my sins I would also ask your help. I am an English private soldier trying to get back to England and require assistance, food and money.'

I decided to visit my pre-war friends in Paris, a hotel where I have stayed before the war, and the American Embassy. Alas, our foraging expeditions met with little success. The rich uncle proved a broken reed who refused to do anything which might prolong the war, beyond giving his nephew the price of his fare home and two tins of meat. The priests in the main gave some bread but I suspect they were mostly too poor to have any money to spare. My friends were sympathetic and lent me some money, while the daughter of the house, who was a trained nurse, expertly dressed my stump – and did it need it – also providing me with some fresh bandages. Despite their kindnesses, their attitude was very much 'we don't want to lose you but we think you ought to and relief when I did. The American Embassy was closed, having moved to Vichy, and I was smartly kicked out of the hotel; we were not the only people who had read the German posters. However, we were not betrayed, which was something.

When at last the reply to our postcard arrived we had the fright of our lives. In bold letters written in purple ink also on a postcard was the following: 'AWAIT THE PASSWORD. HELP WILL COME. LONG LIVE THE ALLIES.' Utterly unable to believe that this had not been picked up by the censors and that our arrest must inevitably follow in a matter of hours, we panicked. Collecting the Scotsmen with no more than a few minutes delay, we moved out to a hotel the other side of the city.

We were now in a real quandary. To leave our new address at the old hotel would mean we could be traced by the police; not to so do would mean that anyone who did come to our aid would not be able to find us. In the end we decided to try and cross the demarcation line, dividing the Zone Occupé from the Zone Non-Occupé, on our own and if this failed to return to Paris and discreetly re-contact our old hotel. Madame Samiez had given me the address of a friend at Romorantin, a town close to the demarcation line, who, she said, if still there *might* be able to help us. Next morning, cold, hungry and depressed, we took the first train to that town and after changing at Orléans reached our destination without being questioned.

Romorantin, which is divided in two by the river Sauldre, was teeming with Germans from a nearby Luftwaffe airfield and our first task was to find somewhere to park our Scotsmen where they would be inconspicuous and least likely to rouse comment. Crossing the bridge, which was guarded at either end by sentries, we came to the Municipal Gardens which were comparatively deserted, and so Georges and I left them on a secluded bench after providing them with a loaf of bread, some cold sausages and a bottle of beer. After partaking of an excellent, if early, lunch in a café – rationing seemed to be non-existent – we commenced our search for Madame Samiez's friend.

No one seemed to have heard of the address and so in desperation we decided to approach the local curé, whose house was the other side of the river. We always walked one behind the other some ten yards apart and this time by chance I was in front when we came to the bridge. I had not gone five yards across it before there was a roar of 'Halte! Halte!' from behind and an angry German soldier came running up carrying a rifle with a fixed bayonet. Convinced that I was about to be shot as a suspect saboteur I raised my hand and endeavoured to explain in the few German words I knew that I was a 'fliege offizier Englander'. Too angry to listen he drove me to the other side of the bridge and across at the point of his bayonet. I had omitted to read the large notice announcing that pedestrians must cross only by the right hand footpath; failure to conform led to risks of being shot at by the sentries.

The curé's house was a large stone building with a long paved corridor leading to his study but his replies to our enquiries were not encouraging. Yes, he knew the woman we were looking for but she lived some way away and he was very doubtful if she would help. However, he would go on his bicycle and find out. No, it would be better if we waited in his study. There had been a lot of alarms and rumours of British parachutists and the Germans frequently cordoned off areas and inspected all identity cards. We had chosen a very dangerous area in which to try and cross the demarcation line.

Off he went and the next 20 minutes were by far the worst I

experienced in the whole journey. The study had two windows set high up in the walls and from where I was sitting I could see the sky and some trees through both of them. Suddenly without warning or any sound a German helmet appeared at one and the top half of a German soldier at the other. Both had their backs to the windows and the second a Tommy gun slung over his shoulder. Georges sitting facing me had not seen them and as I put my finger to my lips and pointed, we heard the crash of German field boots coming down the corridor. The study door opened and the housekeeper ushered in a German officer. The curé obviously had not told her he was going out and she raised her hands in surprise at his absence but said nothing.

'Where is Monsieur le Curé?' demanded the officer in guttural French. We all remained silent. As far as I was concerned my lunch had started to come up and I was trying to repress it. Georges was simply paralysed with fear and the housekeeper not much better. The officer repeated his question. The housekeeper shrugged her shoulders, Georges's mouth opened and closed but no sound came out of it and some of my lunch spattered on to the floor.

'When will he be back?' the officer enquired of us. Georges's mouth continued to open and close but all he did was suck in air. More of my lunch arrived up but this time I succeeded in returning it to the proper place. The German realized he was not getting anywhere and said slowly and clearly 'Please apologize to Monsieur le Curé for any inconvenience we may have caused him. We are holding a training exercise designed to capture British parachutists. His house was selected as one of those to be surrounded. Please be sure he receives my apologies.' A crash of boots and he was gone – a few shouts and the others disappeared. I had just time to clean up the mess on the floor with my handkerchief before the curé returned. 'Madame is away,' he said. 'My housekeeper has told me what has just happened. The sooner you get away from here the better. Good luck!'

Georges went off to the station to buy our return tickets and I went to collect the Scotsmen, this time crossing the bridge on the right side. Tired and dispirited, we just got back to the hotel before curfew.

Next day the two Scotsmen decided to return to Lille and Georges said he would contact a school friend somewhere out in the country who might be able to help. We selected another hotel into which I moved and we agreed to meet there in four days time. I had privately made up my mind to apply for an official permit to cross the demarcation line, using the dying mother story as an excuse. However, four days one way or

the other would not make any difference so I passed the time by joining an English language course at the Sorbonne and the rest of the day meandering round Paris or in the cinema.

The only untoward incident that occurred was on the Metro when I was returning one evening to the hotel. The train was packed like the rush hour in the London Tube when a mischievous young girl took out her lipstick and started to write 'Sale Boche' on the back of the German soldier standing in front of her. Many of the passengers who could see what was happening started to laugh and the German realized something was going on but could not make out what. I was not amused as I knew that there was a risk she might be spotted when we would all have been arrested and interrogated, so I got out at the next station.

On the afternoon of the fourth day Georges returned with some money and food. Much to my surprise he was accompanied by the two Scotsmen who had been refused admittance to the Zone Interdite. How they had managed to avoid arrest is still beyond my comprehension. Georges went off to our first hotel but was back within the hour saying that Madame had gone on holiday and her replacement knew nothing about any message for us. We agreed to spend one more night in the hotel and then divide our resources and go our own ways.

I have always loved the Champs Elysées and decided to pay it a final visit before nerving myself to go to the German Kommandatur and try to obtain an official pass to cross the demarcation line. It was a lovely October evening and I sat down on a bench to admire the beauty of the chestnut trees and watch the passers-by. A man was already sitting there reading the evening paper which, after a while, he put down and turned to look at me.

'Where,' he said 'in the name of God have you been?' For three days I have been searching Paris for you, and in an hour I would have taken the night train to Lille.' He was the guide who had conducted me from Madame Samiez's house to the station in Lille – and some people say there is no such thing as luck!

I told him what we had been up to and he was rightly annoyed that we had been so stupid as not to leave our address at the first hotel. 'Madame,' he said, 'is completely loyal. Do you suppose she would have risked her life by housing you all unless this was so? Sometimes I wonder if you British ever think at all. However, as you are apparently incapable of realizing that you may have lost the war I have no doubt you will win it! Now to business. I will not see you again unless things go wrong. I shall require tomorrow to make the necessary arrangements. The day after you will all go to the Gare d'Austerlitz arriving at a quarter to seven in the morning. Standing by the newspaper shop or walking up and down the entrance to the station you will see a man wearing a black suit, black Homburg hat, with a red handkerchief in his top coat pocket, carrying a paper in his hand. You will not speak to him but pass close by saying clearly and loudly "MOZART" when he will drop his paper. You will follow him out of the station when he will give you the tickets and tell you the time of the train, the platform and where you are all to get out. You will give their tickets to the others and they will board the train one by one in the same coach – he will tell you the number – but not the same compartment. You will follow him on to the train and stand as close as you can to him but do not talk unless he first speaks to you. You understand?'

I repeated his instructions and gave him the address of our hotel with a heartfelt 'thank you'. It took me considerable time to persuade Georges and the Scotsmen that I had not gone off my head and started imagining things.

It was a cold miserable morning with driving rain and half the German Army seemed to be on the station, while there were only a handful of civilians which made the Scotsmen very conspicuous. Our guide was there but he did not even wait for the password, waving me to follow him.

'Excellent, excellent,' he murmured as he gave me the tickets and instructions, 'No one will worry about us on a morning like this.' He was right, there were no controls and we all boarded the train for Bourges without difficulty though I managed to get thoroughly cursed by an irate German sergeant-major for wandering into part of the platform forbidden to civilians. Going into the wrong place seemed to have a sort of magnetic attraction to me.

We all got seats spaced, as instructed, in one coach and after the ticket inspection, during which our guide and his female companion casually stood in the corridor opposite the Scotsmen in case any misunderstandings should arise, he beckoned me there to join him. 'I don't think there will be any difficulties at Vierzon, where we have to change, or Bourges, but if they are examining papers I will go behind one Scotsman. Tell Georges to follow with the second, while you will bring up the rear with my friend.' I asked him if they were part of an escape organization. He smiled and replied, 'We are the Institut Mozart and we are all music lovers. Let us leave it at that.'

Despite the optimism of our guides, at Vierzon the train was immediately surrounded by German soldiers who took up positions at all the doors, and we saw a group of uniformed men enter the first coach, presumably to examine and interrogate. It had long been agreed that, in an emergency, it was to be every man for himself and this I felt was one. At the opposite platform I could see our train for Bourges and I therefore slipped out of our compartment and made my way to the back of the train hoping to drop on the track unobserved and cross to the other platform. However, when I opened the back door of the last coach I was welcomed by a German soldier with a fixed bayonet. There was nothing to do but go back and hope for the best.

As I returned along the corridors I noted that the train was emptying fast and on arrival at our compartment nobody was there, while all the Germans seemed to have disappeared. Much perplexed I got out and was walking towards the Bourges train when a fat official came hurrying forward. 'Hurry up, my little Englishman,' he shouted in French, 'we cannot wait all day for our friends.' I broke into a trot and as I entered the carriage where I could see three of the others I heard the official shout to the engine driver, who was leaning out of his cab, 'All is well, our little Englishman is safe. Off you go.'

The explanation of all the fuss was ludicrously simple. Not knowing the exact time of arrival of the train from Paris, it was routine to put it under guard until the French and German frontier officials arrived, when a loudspeaker announced that anyone not going on into Unoccupied France could leave the train. But I would have been happier, if the railway official had curbed his enthusiasm in following our guide's request to help find me.

There were no controls at the station but, like Romorantin, Bourges was full of Germans and for the first time our guide seemed worried. As we walked into the town he said, 'We have got to pass most of the day here. There is no alternative. Tell the Scotsmen to wait in the park there and you and Georges come with us.' We followed them into the town and near the cathedral he pointed out a small 'Olde Worlde', run-down-looking, tourist café. 'We will all meet there at four o'clock this afternoon when you will again follow us. Good luck during the day.'

Georges and I returned to the park, showed the Scotsmen the location of the café and after telling them to be outside at a quarter to four, left them to their own devices. This may sound callous and even a cowardly act but was, I am sure, justified. Georges, if caught with them, would either have been shot or sent to a concentration camp for the rest of the war, where he would have been lucky to survive. I estimated that my return to England would be of greater value than that of two Scots privates. Where we made an error was not to think of the cathedral as a sanctuary for them for the day. Although we did go in for a short visit its potential entirely escaped us.

Despite our misgivings the Scotsmen turned up at a quarter to four and we told them to lounge around in the street, keeping the café under observation, and to follow some 10 yards behind the guides when they came out. Georges was to go next to help them in case of trouble and I allotted myself the position of 'tail-end Charlie'.

Georges and I had an unpleasant shock on entering the café. 'Olde Worlde' and run down it might look from the outside, but inside it was bright and gay and very much 'à la mode', and was obviously much used by German officers, a number of whom were already sitting around drinking beer. As there was no going back, Georges and I walked to a table, sat down and ordered beer. Conversation ceased and we were the cynosure of every eye, making me feel like the chief character in a Bateman cartoon. In our dirty crumpled suits, which in my case did not fit, grimy open-necked shirts and general unkempt appearance we made a poor showing compared to the immaculately turned-out German officers.

In fact we were just about as inconspicuous as a brace of nudists in the Royal Enclosure at Ascot. Our guides, when they came in a few minutes later and took their seats at a table by the window, were equally conspicuous and we were all very much a topic of speculation.

From where I sat I could see one of the Scotsmen the other side of the street standing near to a door through which German soldiers were coming and going, one of whom came out and went up to the Scotsman and started to talk to him. The guides also saw this and immediately got up to go, throwing some money on the table. Georges and I followed and were just in time to see the Scotsman run down the street towards his companion. The German re-entered the building and as I left the café I could see him, through the window, on the telephone. By now the guides had reached the two bewildered Scotsmen and they all turned down a side street followed by Georges and my terrified self.

It was astonishing how quickly the alarm spread; within a matter of a minute or so there were German motor-cyclists roaring through the streets and excited Germans armed with Tommy guns running hither and thither. A general alert had clearly been ordered but the reason for it appeared not to have reached the participants since no one tried to stop us. The side street led into a large square which was normally a market place but where some German troops were drilling. In the general hubbub I failed to see which way Georges had turned on reaching the square and, making a wild guess, I cut diagonally across it only to run into part of the German drill parade. Looking back I suppose it was the best move I could have made as I was harried across the square, in the right direction, by a furious German NCO whose lung power would have compared favourably with a regimental sergeant-major in the Brigade of Guards. No one would ever have looked for a POW on the run in a German drill parade.

At the other side of the square I found myself in front of Georges, and the Scotsmen and only just behind the guides. After 10 minutes fast walking, twisting and turning through side streets, we came to a house in front of which was an ancient farm lorry, partially loaded with chickens in crates. With a very brief farewell to our guides, who appeared immensely relieved, we were all four bundled into the lorry. Georges and the Scotsmen were put under and behind the chickens, while I sat in front, half hidden by sacks of vegetables piled on my knees.

Our new guide driving the lorry was entirely unperturbed when a German standing by his motor cycle held up his hand for us to stop. He merely waved a cheery greeting, shouted something incomprehensible and, receiving a reply in the same vein, drove on. Our destination was an inn some 500 yards short of the frontier posts and when we arrived there Phillipe, as our guide had introduced himself, ushered us into a large room full of Germans.

I shot out backwards, perspiring freely, but he only laughed and said, 'Well, if you are nervous, we will go to another room but I assure you there is no cause for worry.' I was worried, but three glasses of extremely potent local wine soothed my tattered nerves and we all joined the party in the first room.

It was quite a party too, being made up of half a dozen Germans under an NCO, waiting their turn to go out to patrol the frontier, and an assorted collection of individuals, some eight in number, waiting until it was dark to cross the demarcation line. The Germans were far from sober, the wireless blared out the BBC programme for Occupied France and all the drink was on the house, or rather Phillipe, which I have no doubt he could well afford, as the fee for crossing was 1000 francs or about £12 a head. As the daylight began to fade I went out for a breath of fresh air and watched a German car drive by with two officers in the back. I wondered whether they would call at the inn so I withdrew to the shelter of a hay stack. This proved an unnecessary precaution as after a brief visit to the frontier post itself they returned without stopping, though the sound of revelry was clearly audible.

At dusk the incoming patrol arrived and we all straggled out of the inn laughing and singing, to be marshalled into a somewhat motley flock and led across some fields, 100 yards or so behind the new patrol. After about a quarter of a mile we were told to crawl under a thick hedge down into a deep ditch, up the other side, and through a barbed wire fence into a meadow.

'France – Free France,' exclaimed Philippe, followed by, 'Damn, I have forgotten the mail. Wait here while I go and get it.' He did not take long to return. Carrying a huge sack of letters he led us across a couple of fields to a road on which, behind us now, we could see the lights of the frontier post.

'I leave you here,' he said. 'About twelve miles along the road you will come to a village called Dun sur Auron. I have reserved your rooms in the first hotel you will see. Good luck!'

Most of our companions who had brought bicycles with them disappeared into the night, leaving us and two noticeably pregnant women whom we helped along as best we could.

It was an uneventful walk except when, after about an hour, the upstair lights of a house suddenly went on and a voice shouted in German, 'Who are you?' We gave no reply and nothing happened though I wondered whether by error we had walked back into the ZO. My fears were unjustified and we located the hotel without difficulty and had a delicious hot supper and went to bed happy with the thought that we were half way home with the worst half behind us.

We were all in splendid form next morning as we set off by train for Lyons where, after a night in the usual back-street hotel, I called on the American Consul as the representative of our protecting power.

Diplomats representing a neutral country in a country that is also neutral must, like Agag, tread delicately in their dealings with individuals whose country is at war, no matter what may be their personal feelings. When the individuals are POWs on the run, and whose presence is not known to the local officials, the situation is indeed difficult and frequently the diplomat concerned will have nothing to do with them.

George Whittinghill, the United States Consul in Lyons

in November 1940 was, however, made of sterner stuff and gave me an enthusiastic reception in his office.

'After all,' he said, over the excellent lunch that followed, 'I cannot see that I am endangering my diplomatic status by giving you a good meal and official information about your position here. That Burgundy was so good I think we might try a second bottle. Don't you?' I agreed with alacrity and listened to what he had to say.

'International law regarding escaped POWs seems to be a little muddled here. As I always understood it, a non-belligerent allows escapers to return to their own country but the French have so far not agreed to this, largely I suspect due to German pressure, and they are rounding you all up and putting you in the Fort St Jean at Marseilles. However, I have a business friend working in Switzerland who, by chance, will be calling on me tomorrow. He is an expert on such matters and I propose you come to my office tomorrow morning to learn his views. Meanwhile, have you all enough money for your needs?' I replied that we were all right and accepted an invitation to dinner.

Raoul Beaumaine, the friend from Switzerland, was a man of many parts and after we had been introduced he said, 'I knew your father well in Berne in 1918. I hope he is in good health. It will be a pleasure to help his son.' I could not resist asking how he knew that father had been in Berne in 1918.

'My dear boy,' he replied, 'Your name has appeared on the Red Cross list of officers wounded and missing from the BEF and we were asked to find out from the Germans if you were alive. Your father has asked some friends of mine to send you parcels and only the other day the Germans reported that you had escaped. Hardly a difficult problem to solve! However, your future does present some difficulties. As George has told you, the French will put you in Fort St Jean where I do not know what will happen though I expect you will ultimately be repatriated. The alternatives are to come to Switzerland – I can arrange this – or try and get into Spain undetected.' Here George interupted, 'I have another young friend outside and I think he ought to have an equal chance.'

'Fair enough,' replied Raoul, 'call him in.'

He was introduced as Frank Clayton and told of the position.

'I propose we toss for it,' he said. We did, I lost and Clayton chose Switzerland.

Raoul shrugged his shoulders and turned to me. 'I am sorry I can only take one person but all in all I think it is for the best. On your wounds alone you will be repatriated. However, before either of you do any more I suggest you go and have a rest with friends of mine in Vichy who are constantly badgering me about how they can help Britain. As regards your companions, tell them to go to Marseilles and report to the Seamen's Mission which may be able to help them.'

Though the food was excellent, Madame, the soul of kindness and tireless in her efforts to make us feel at home, the 10 days in Vichy were not a success. I was violently ill for three days – overeating I expect – and when I recovered both Frank and I resented the fact that we were not allowed out after dark.

Twice we behaved like young undergraduates, grossly abusing the hospitality we were receiving, by breaking out and arriving back much the worse for wear. We were lucky not to be arrested and the second time not to be hurt when the ladder we were using broke. On the brighter side I had the first hot bath since escaping and was able to send a full report of my activities back to England via a neutral diplomatic bag. I also learnt the value of Vichy Water to assuage a hangover.

I have never quite understood why we were sent to Vichy, nor could I make out what our host did for a living. However, at the time this did not worry us and after a fortnight we parted on the best of terms, Frank for Lyons and I for Marseilles.

6

Mission in Marseilles

Marseilles, as the only large mercantile port in unoccupied France with ships serving the French colonies in Africa and the Near east, was, in the winter of 1940–41, the obvious base for escape to Spain, Portugal, Gibraltar and the free world. To it gravitated the men and women from the Occupied Countries who wished to go to England to continue the fight against Hitler or whose political activities made them liable to arrest by the Germans.

Marius, patron saint of all liars is also the patron saint of this city, which had a reputation for criminal activities second only to Chicago, and like Chicago it was controlled by gangsters. Add to all this a police force whose loyalty to Marshal Petain and the Government of Free France was doubtful, representatives of the German and Italian Armistice Commissions and a battalion of the Bersaglieri which Mussolini sent to show the flag, and you will have the background of the city which was to be the first operational centre of allied escape and evasion from France.

George Whittinghill had told me that entry into Fort St Jean, the temporary prison for all British service personnel 'on the run', was either voluntary by reporting to the guard at the main gate, or a matter of waiting until one was arrested and escorted there by the police. Remembering Raoul Beaumaine's remarks concerning the Seamen's Mission, I decided to go there first, to find out what the chances were of carrying on over the Pyrenees into Spain.

The Reverend Donald Caskie, who ran the Seamen's Mission, has fully described his activities in his book *The Tartan Pimpernel* and it is not for me to comment on the splendid work he did. Initially, as the name implies, it was a club run for British seamen calling at Marseilles but when, after the fall of France, no more of these came, it was kept open to help British refugees and later British 'escapers' and 'evaders' when, as might be expected, the social amenities and activities which the club offered were a cover for organizing escapes to Spain.

An hour in the club was enough to make me aware of the dangers of discussing any schemes for escape with the inmates. Moreover I was able to guess, accurately as it was to be proved, that the French police must be fully aware of most of the plots hatched within its precincts. In fact it was only allowed to remain open because it was such an excellent source of information about clandestine British activities. At this time I doubt if the French had any paid informer who was a permanent habitué, but later they certainly did. The result was that as British escape activities increased in Marseilles, to the irritation of the Germans, the French were always able to answer the latter's complaints by saying that they had the Seamen's Mission well covered.

Situated at the entrance to the Vieux Port, the Fort St Jean had achieved international fame as the collecting depot for all recruits en route for the Foreign Legion in French North Africa. The cold unfriendliness of all fortresses was further stressed by Marshal Lyautey's famous welcome to the legionaires, carved into the stone wall over the main entrance – 'LEGIONAIRES, YOU ASK FOR DEATH. I WILL GIVE IT TO YOU.'

On my arrival it housed some 15 British officers who were free to come and go as they wished, provided they were present at the weekly roll call on Monday mornings, and about 50 other ranks who were confined to barracks. Like Colditz reputedly escape proof, it took the British just four days to find a satisfactory exit. The latrines, like their military counterparts all over the world, were simple in the extreme. They consisted of a recess cut into the outer wall, the outlet being much like a chimney of a large open fire place with the waste matter of the users falling vertically down it into the sea below. Sewage disposal was left to the tide, while an iron bar across the recess provided the seat. By means of a rope tied to this bar the escaper would descend to sewage level and then duck under some two feet of the outer wall which, like an apron, divided the sewage from the sea but permitted the free flow of water. Clothes and shoes were carried in a waterproof bag and the swim to the nearest jetty was reputed

to wash off most of the sewage. An accomplice would retrieve the rope and the operation was always carried out after dark so as to permit dressing unobserved on the jetty.

The members of the officers mess were continually changing as parties or individuals went off by train to the Spanish Frontier, where they either crossed successfully, or were arrested and sent back under police escort to try again with the minimum of delay. One individual actually travelled back to the frontier in the same carriage as the police escort who had a few hours previously delivered him to Fort St Jean. New faces from the north arrived at frequent intervals but rarely stayed for more than a few days to recuperate and reorganize.

I stayed a week in the fort and then took a room in a small secluded hotel, which was in fact a 'Maison de Rendezvous', called the 'Hôtel Cécile'. This move was greatly facilitated by the French commandant in the fort offering all the officers their weekly rations in bulk at the Monday morning roll call. These could be sold in the city black market for exorbitant prices providing ample funds for my modest needs in the hotel.

It was not long before I realized that to try and cross the Pyrenees in winter would be foolhardy. I therefore settled myself down to await repatriation, promised weekly by the French authorities, as a '*Mutilé de Guerre*.' However, before this could take place it would be necessary to be passed by a medical commission and declared unfit for further military service. Meanwhile I joined whole-heartedly in the favourite local pastime of investigating alternative methods of returning to England.

Initially all escape plans were by individuals or pairs and no thought was given to a possible escape organization. However, as time marched on and the difficulties of escaping mounted, largely due to the shortage of money and the tightening of French security measures under increasing German pressure, it became obvious that efforts must be co-ordinated and controlled if any successes were to be achieved. Luckily the right man was in the right place when one of our number, Captain Ian Garrow,* volunteered to take on the task. His was a bold and courageous decision which was to influence the whole future of escape and evasion from France, though none of us sitting round that café table overlooking the Vieux Port appreciated its immense significance.

Ian Garrow, a Seaforth Highlander, had evaded when the 51st Division was overwhelmed at St Valéry-en-Caux

* Now Lieutenant-Colonel Ian Garrow, DSO.

in June 1940 and had led a party of men through to Unoccupied France. Tall, every inch a Scotsman, and speaking little French, he did not seem likely to survive very long. However, his quiet determination to do what he believed was his duty left no room for argument and, perhaps more important, the only other possible candidates had all been prisoners, albeit for a short time, but were nevertheless known to the Germans. That my assessments of Ian Garrow's chances of survival and potential to achieve success were entirely wrong was due to failure to appreciate what he had to offer and complete ignorance of the attitudes to our activities of the Vichy Government police force and security services.

Cool, calm and collected, slow of speech and never indulging in histrionics, Ian Garrow portrayed a British characteristic which the more volatile and voluble French have always admired. In addition, he had a certain mystique which fascinated and inspired his helpers in Marseilles and, as the months went by and he was not arrested, gave them a a feeling of security.

It was the head of the department in the French security services for Marseilles who, when he came to England in 1942 to join the Free French, filled in the gaps in the puzzle. He told me that they were fascinated by Ian Garrow whose every movement they knew but they simply could not believe that the British Intelligence Service could ever employ anyone whose physical appearance alone made him an impossible choice for an agent. 'The Germans,' he coughed in some embarrassment, 'with whom we had, of course, to liaise, agreed and asked us to find out who was really organizing the escapes to Spain.'

The onset of winter increased the dangers of crossing the Pyrenees and most of December 1940 and January 1941 were spent in planning and organizing for the spring. Ian Garrow concentrated on looking for individuals who were prepared to travel to the north of France to recruit local helpers with 'safe' houses. Here the evaders could be hidden while they were being provided with forged identity and ration cards (usually 'acquired' from the printers) and civilian clothes for their journey to Marseilles with one of these men or women as a guide. He also set about finding safe houses in Marseilles itself. Like me he considered that except in an emergency the Seamen's Mission was too risky to shelter evaders while arrangements were made for guides to take them to the Spanish frontier and over the Pyrenees into Spain.

Evaders frequently offered to stay on in France and help but they rarely had the necessary qualifications, the most important of which was to speak fluent French. An exception was a certain Paul Cole who had arrived in Marseilles in November 1940 and stated that he was a sergeant in REME. He claimed to know the whereabouts of a number of evaders in the area of Lille and even though his French was vile, Ian Garrow accepted his offer to return to the north, a decision with which I concurred. During the following twelve months he made a number of successful trips and came to be regarded as an excellent guide. On the two occasions we met, and talked, I found him a rather colourless character with a faintly subservient manner which I disliked. Physically tough, he had a weak face with close-set eyes and was in no way my idea of a man capable of ruthless action, ingenuity and cunning. My judgement could not have been more wrong.

Meanwhile, during the winter of 1940–41, Richard Illingworth, an Army officer who had been captured in Belgium but had escaped during the march to Germany, Mike Maloney, an RAF fighter pilot also an escapee who shared a room with me in the Hôtel Cécile, and I devoted our energies to looking into the possibilities of sea escapes and liaising with French, Belgian and Polish officers and men who were trying to get to England.

Mike, who was over six feet tall with a mop of fair curly hair and a wide open face, did not merge into the background of Marseilles as all good evaders should. He made matters worse by wearing a long black overcoat with an astrakan collar that had not only seen better days but had been made for someone even taller than Mike and of considerably larger girth. Perhaps Richard Illingworth did not set a very good example with his canary-coloured polo-neck sweater, black coat, pin-striped trousers, black beret – two sizes too small – gloves and umbrella. 'But,' as he remarked, 'I am at least "official" and therefore it is my duty to dress like an officer and gentleman though I must admit the shortage of clothing makes this somewhat of a problem.' By 'official' he meant that he, like myself, had reported to the French authorities and was more-or-less on permanent parole from Fort St Jean.

Mike had not bothered to report himself on the grounds that his stay would be brief and he did not wish to trouble the French authorities. However, he was finding it more difficult to leave France than he had anticipated, largely because he refused to try crossing the Pyrenees into Spain. 'I have done enough walking already to last me for the rest of my life,' he complained, 'and anyhow I could not possibly climb mountains in this coat!' Knowing Mike's impressive escape record since being shot down over northern France in June 1940 we forbore to argue.

He had crash-landed successfully and had then walked some 40 miles to the coast, hiding by day, travelling by night and living off what he was able to steal from gardens and fields. He had managed to find a rowing boat with oars which the Germans had as yet failed to seize and set off to row the Channel in the dark. Unfortunately wind and tide were adverse and dawn had found him barely two miles off shore. The Germans had opened up with machine guns but the range was too great and he had rowed clear. They then turned on the artillery but a rowing boat is a very small target and they had finally been forced to send out an air-sea rescue seaplane to capture him.

He was sent to Lille for interrogation but was so obstreperous and unhelpful that he was sentenced to a month's solitary confinement in the local gaol, theoretically as a punishment for having stolen the rowing boat. The Germans underestimated their prisoner and he escaped from the small exercise yard by the simple expedient of knocking out the guard and a German soldier who was strengthening the wire on the top of the wall of the yard, and using his ladder to climb the wall. Still in RAF battle dress and in broad daylight he managed to get clear of Lille without being re-arrested and had walked south to Lyons, receiving occasional assistance from farmers and small café owners.

He had crossed the demarcation line between Occupied and Unoccupied France in the dark without realizing he had done so; in itself no mean feat as the line was actively patrolled by the Germans. Near Lyons he had met a Frenchman, Georges Le Maire, who had invited him to stay at his house for a week's rest and recuperation. He had also provided Mike with civilian clothes, an excellent forged identity card and a considerable sum of money, enabling him to complete the journey to Marseilles by train.

We three had been working together for some weeks when we were joined by another out-of-the-ordinary character, June Sheffield, a pretty young American girl who originated from Fort Worth in Texas where shortly before the war she had won a local beauty competition, the prize for which included a month's stay in Paris.

June or 'Texas' as we always called her, had remained in Paris after the month was over and had joined the Franco-American Ambulance Corps in 1939, ending up in Marseilles after the Armistice in June 1940. She was now awaiting repatriation to the States and living on a very generous allowance granted her by the US Consul General in her capacity as a distressed American citizen. It was evident that she was extremely fond of Mike and prepared to go to very considerable lengths to help him, including hiding him, and sometimes myself, under her bed when the police raided the Hôtel Cécile where she was also staying.

From time to time we were helped by other evaders but in the main they came and went, frequently ending up in Fort St Jean, which was now much more closely guarded. Major 'Napoleon' Brinckman* of the Grenadier Guards, was a superb example of one who only went! His presence was reported to us and I made contact with him in a café but he was not interested in discussing any plans with me. He merely stated that he was on his way to Algeria. We had

* Now Colonel Sir Roderick Brinckman, Bt.

already dismissed this possible route as likely to be out of the frying pan into the fire as it had often proved to be, but he was cleverer or luckier than others and succeeded in reaching Gibraltar.

Our first and, very nearly successful, scheme was not of our own making. In December I was approached by a French contact who said that Paul Carbonne – the chief of the most powerful gang in Marseilles and the lover of the famous Manouche* (probably Europe's most famous gangster's moll) – desired to contact a British officer. A meeting was arranged in one of the many restaurants he owned and I was invited to dinner, not with the great man himself but with one of his assistants. The food was exquisite and the wine of similar quality. However, I was somewhat surprised when everyone stood up and bowed as the chief passed through to his private sanctum. His plan was simple and had it been carried out I have little doubt but that it would have succeeded. Briefly, he was prepared to provide an ocean-going tug with crew to take as many British as she could carry to Gibraltar. His estimate of the numbers would certainly meet our requirements, since there were some of our 'clients' who were self-confessed deserters whose best contribution to the war effort would be to continue as a burden on their captors. Further, he promised to provision the tug and to guarantee that there would be no interference by the French authorities. If we were worried he would also provide an escort to deal with any possible Italian naval reaction! His price? My word of honour that the tug and crew would be permitted to return to Marseillies and that the British Government would in no way interfere with his activities when the war was over.

Escapers are noted for their willingness to commit their government to honouring pledges about which it has not been consulted and I pointed out that I was not an accredited representative of His Majesty's Government. He shrugged his shoulders and gesticulated in the true French fashion. 'I am informed,' he said, 'that officers in the "Garde Royale" have very considerable influence in State affairs.'

* *Manouche*. Roger Peyrefitte. Hart Davis, 1973.

I do not think there was any 'leak' of information on our side as there was no need to reveal the scheme but merely to warn certain individuals that there might be a sudden summons to take part in an escape. Plans were well advanced even to 'D' day, when I received a summons from the great, man's adjutant. He informed me, with deep regret, that the scheme was off. I enquired why and after a long pause he paid me a great compliment. 'My chief has received a personal message from Marshal Pétain informing him that, provided he has no further contact with the British, he can rest assured that the Government of France will accord him all aid in the conduct of his business. He has asked me to express his personal regrets and requests you to accept his card as a small token of remembrance.' In three cafés in Marseilles I never paid for a drink or a meal again – an 'Access Card' in every possible sense!

There were any number of other schemes. Most I have forgotten but the memory of two remains. The first was to take over and sail to Gibraltar a small liner in which, for three days, all the undesirables had been confined during the visit of Marshal Pétain. We turned it down as it involved arming escapers with the consequent risk of being shot if the plan failed. I learnt of the second when I was approached by a Frenchman, who stated that he was working for the British Intelligence Service. He had devised a plan to hide a number of escapers in the deep freeze of a ship going to Algiers and then Lisbon. I only turned it down when he handed me an automatic pistol and a couple of clips of ammunition which act I felt might be an excuse to arrest me while carrying arms.

Life was not all business and we had our relaxations which by day consisted largely in 'taking the mickey' out of the German and Italian Armistice Commission members and Mussolini's Bersaglieri contingent. The Germans were difficult as one never knew quite how far one could go without serious repercussions; the Italians on the other hand were easy meat.

General Wavell was advancing in North Africa, and it

became a routine practice to chant out to the sentries in front of the Bersaglieri headquarters the names of towns captured and the number of prisoners taken as the campaign developed. The officer officiating always wore as a buttonhole a large stick of macaroni, decorated with an oversize black mourning ribbon, and at the termination of his act he offered 50 francs to anyone in the admiring crowd who could name an Italian victory since 1900. The results were always the same; the guard was turned out, the French police summoned, the British officer was arrested and marched out of sight, only to be released to continue the performance when next he had the energy. The game finished when the Italians withdrew the sentries and replaced them by a stout French gendarme.

A more serious and important demonstration of our sentiments was given at the public funeral of two French victims of a stray bomb, killed when the RAF attacked shipping outside the harbour. The Germans and Italians were determined that this dastardly act should not go unnoticed and sent uniformed representatives, carrying wreaths, to march in the funeral procession. The presence of two British officers in plain clothes, also carrying wreaths, each bearing a small Union Jack, immediately behind the relatives of the deceased and well in front of the Germans, was deeply appreciated by the crowds lining the streets, but not by the Germans and Italians.

Money for escaping was running short and Ian Garrow thought that we might be able to raise some from the British civilians still resident on the Côte d'Azur, the only difficulty being that we were not allowed to leave Marseilles. However, General Huntzinger, the local area military commander, granted me leave of absence together with a *laissez-passer*, and although my money-raising efforts met with little success I passed a very happy Christmas and New Year with a charming Swiss family who had a villa at Cap d'Ail.

Returning in January to Marseilles, I learnt that the medical board was, at long last, to become a reality. However, before the board was convened I got mixed up in a series of events which, apart from the knowledge I had gained on escape and evasion, were the only happenings the War Office took much interest in on my return to England.

Our relationship with the American Consulate was distant and formal but as our Protecting Power we maintained it, if only to draw our monthly Displaced Persons Allowance. One day I received a message, through a third party, that if I met a Mr X at a certain hour at a certain café I would learn, in that splendid legal phrase, 'something to my advantage'! Invitations to learn something to one's advantage were a daily occurrence and usually resulted in a glass of pernod and a request for help to escape, or a loan. However, I knew that Mr X was vaguely connected with the American Consulate though in what capacity I had no idea. A restaurant was as good a rendezvous as any since all their proprietors had long since realized that, after a good black market menu, the next most important draw was tables where plots and plans could be discussed without risk.

Mr X had a strange story to tell. A few days previously an anonymous telephone caller to the Consulate had stated that he had information of vital importance to America's future and that he would telephone next day for a date, time and place where he could meet a representative from the Consulate. Such messages are not uncommon in neutral countries in time of war, and they carry a high element of risk as they may well be a trap designed to involve diplomats in espionage. On the other hand, they may be genuine and the information of great importance. A meeting had duly been arranged and the anonymous caller said that his information was primarily for the British and what he really wanted was to meet a reliable British officer who was likely to get back to England in the near future; this was why Mr X had chosen me, since as he knew the medical board was due to meet in a few weeks' time. Would I be prepared to meet the individual concerned?

POWs who involve themselves in espionage sacrifice all rights under the Geneva Convention and, if caught, suffer a spy's usual fate. This might well be a trap to involve one British officer in espionage activities and, by implication, the rest of us. On the other hand it might be a genuine effort to pass valuable information. I asked Mr X for 24 hours' grace; he had two days before the caller would ring for an answer, as I wanted to consult Richard Illingworth and a French officer of whose loyalty I had no doubt. We all agreed that we could not dismiss the matter but, unless we had some proof that the information was likely to be of very high value, it would be an unjustified risk to meet the informant. I passed our view to Mr X who fully understood and said that he would arrange for a further meeting and would try to obtain more details.

The results as far as I was concerned were not encouraging. The individual said he had been working before the war for the French Government on the formula for a new gas of such high killing potential that, when perfected, the tiniest drop would kill instantly. Captured in 1940 he had now perfected the formula, and it was shortly going into full-scale production. He added that in 1936 he had been in touch with the British Government but had been told that even if the formula was developed production on a scale sufficient for use in a war would never be feasible.

When asked what he was doing in Marseilles he replied that now his work was virtually over he had been granted a month's leave in the south of France. He was staying in the same hotel as the German Armistice Commission and he was not allowed to take any papers out of the hotel but if a British officer would meet him there he saw no difficulty in passing him an envelope containing the perfected formula and plans for production.

The immediate outcome was something of an anticlimax. I agreed to meet him and duly sat myself at a small table in the hotel foyer, hoping that I looked like someone waiting for a friend to come down from his or her bedroom, but with rapidly draining courage as German officers passed to and fro. As he had not turned up after half an hour I left but I declined to repeat the performance when the inventor informed Mr X that there were too many German officers about for him to dare to approach me.

The sequel was not without interest. The scientist turned out to be well known to the back-room boys in England and had the reputation of eccentric brilliance which never achieved practical perfection. He had once succeeded in interesting Churchill in a machine for use in the field of higher mathematics; it had not worked.

By the end of January Ian Garrow's efforts to organize and co-ordinate evasion over the Pyrenees were beginning to meet with success and he had succeeded in establishing contact with the British Mission in Madrid, under Sir Samuel Hoare, and with the Consulate in Barcelona. In Marseilles itself he had a number of devoted helpers who would hide evaders awaiting departure to Spain and had even succeeded in recruiting guides to go to the Zone Interdite to collect evaders who were hiding in the area – largely in the Departments of Nord and Pas de Calais.

No one would claim that Marseilles was the birth-place of evasion or even organized evasion. The human race has been indulging in this pastime from the time when Cain tried to evade the wrath of God after killing Abel up to the twentieth century when Nurse Edith Cavell was shot by the Germans in 1915 as head of an organization passing British soldiers from occupied Belgium into neutral Holland. The importance of Marseilles was that it offered all the facilities necessary for men and women of courage, foresight and daring, to lay the foundations of a great evasion network from which many of the subsequent organizations in enemy-occupied France and Belgium could trace their origin. Even in the formative months many people were involved and it is perhaps invidious to name individuals but without Ian Garrow, Monsieur and Madame Louis Nouveau, and Nancy Fiocca as prime movers I doubt if much would have been achieved.

It was the Nouveaus who provided the first 'safe house' in their apartment on the Quai Rive Neuve overlooking the Vieux Port, and for more than two years this was an operational headquarters. A middle-aged French couple with one son and owning a small import/export agency, there was no sacrifice too great for the cause of de Gaulle and Britain.

Their success in recruiting 'helpers' of similar calibre was of immeasurable value, as were their contacts with the municipal authorities.

Nancy Fiocca, a slight dark vivacious Australian girl married to a Frenchman, also had a wide circle of acquaintances and friends who gave help but it was her irrepressible energy and refusal to admit failure that did much to carry the organization through the difficulties of the early days. With all the Australian contempt for British stuffiness she and I crossed swords with the first words we exchanged.

'A Guards officer I hear. One of those pampered young men who live a life of ease and luxury in London society on other people's money.'

'Where,' I enquired quietly, 'did your grandfather come from? Wormwood Scrubs or Pentonville?' We were never friends but nonetheless I have high praise for her work.

'We don't want to lose you, but we think you ought to go,' was becoming Ian Garrow's theme song whenever he met me and as I heartily agreed it was time to be off we were both delighted when I was called before the Mixed Medical Commission, as it was styled, early in February 1941.

7

The Last Lap

In a largely misspent life during which over indulgence in alcohol and under indulgence in sleep has been one of my many failings, I have suffered and observed the results of many a 'night out on the tiles'. However, nothing will ever equal the mass hangover that the 25 wounded candidates for the Mixed Medical Commission managed to achieve. We had been warned by the American Consul General that the examination would be extremely thorough and that only those genuinely unfit for further military service would be granted repatriation.

Those of us who considered themselves 'borderline' cases took him at his word. We got down to our homework which consisted of drinking continuously for two days and nights, not sleeping, where possible, opening our wounds and rubbing salt into them and, of course, not washing or shaving. As the senior officer I was the first to be interviewed and I can just remember the gasps of horror from the six doctors, two appointed by the Americans to represent the Germans, two by the Swiss to represent Britain, and two nominated by the Vichy Government. Beyond confirming my identity no questions were asked and there was no examination.

A week later we rejoiced in the news that we had all passed; however before this occurred I had to consult a French doctor if only to have my wounds cleaned up. As helping evaders was a punishable offence I felt it only fair to explain my position. But he merely grunted and performed an excellent if painful job. When thanking him and offering payment, which he refused, I remarked ruefully that he had hurt me. 'I meant to,' he replied, 'I loathe the British. You killed my great grandfather at Trafalgar and have stolen all our colonies.'

'Why,' I asked in surprise, 'do you risk possible punishment to help me?'

'Solely because I hate the Germans even more. It is my duty to France to give aid to anyone who is fighting them. When you have beaten them you will be weak and we shall then conquer you. Goodbye.'

While arrangements were being completed for our repatriation Ian Garrow asked me if I would go over to Cannes and see if I could raise some money from my friends and acquaintances there. This time, pledging the credit of the British Government, I had considerable success but unfortunately the evader whom Ian Garrow sent over to collect the cash had as a girl friend a member of the gang which had robbed The Blue Train before the war. She was kind enough to leave a small sum behind but it was a costly lesson!

Ian Garrow and I had talked over the possibility of trying to smuggle out a couple of genuine evaders with the repatriation party or of asking two of the more lightly wounded to stand down in place of two more highly trained evaders, such as pilots, who would have had to act the part. We dismissed these ideas largely because several of the wounded were obviously in need of care which the French would not or could not supply and we felt we were not justified in taking risks which might endanger their future well being.

Security precautions at both the station in Marseilles, where in late February 1941 we boarded the train for the Spanish frontier, and at the frontier itself were very strict and I was very glad we had tried no funny business as we would undoubtedly have been caught out. Although we had a splendid send off from a large number of friends who had come to the station to say goodbye, I was depressed and unhappy at leaving Ian Garrow and some of the others to face what I felt instinctively would be very unpleasant music. Although I knew that it was best for all concerned in the future of evasion that I returned to England to give a firsthand report of what was going on, I could not rid myself of the feeling that I was running away. The only consolation was that I might be able to arrange for Ian Garrow to receive some help from outside though I could not visualize the form it would take.

The train journey under escort, first by French then by Spanish police, to Gibraltar, via Madrid, was enlivened by an incident at the Franco-Spanish frontier when one of the party, a private soldier who had fought with the International Brigade in the Spanish Civil War, got drunk and started to abuse General Franco. With infinite tact and efficiency the Spanish authorities and the representative from our Consulate at Barcelona dealt with the difficulty and I thought it was the last we would hear of it. Alas, it got to the ears of Sir Samuel Hoare, British Minister without portfolio in Madrid who, on our arrival there, welcomed us with an icy speech about his personal difficulties, terminating by forbidding us to leave the hotel or consume any alcohol during the two days we rested there. We also appreciated a member of his entourage referring to us as 'the scum of the BEF.' However, the Rolls-Royce representative in Spain put everything right by giving us his views on Sir Samuel, two large barrels of white and red wine, and all the cigarettes we needed.

At Gibraltar, where we arrived late one evening towards the end of February our reception was not much better, but at least there was the excuse that we were unexpected, being overdue by two days following damage to the line by flooding. Nevertheless, I feel that the sergeant-major, who was hastily summoned by the driver of the lorry from the frontier to the barracks where we were to be billeted, might have chosen more friendly words to welcome us back on British soil than, 'Come on you lot of dozy idle bloody bastards, stand up and let's see who you are and what you all look like.' I just had enough energy left to tell him who we were and what he looked like.

Sir Samuel Hoare's frigid welcome in Madrid may well have been justified by a complaint from the Spanish Foreign Secretary about the incident on the frontier and sergeant-majors are notably short-tempered but even today I find the behaviour of the Port Embarkation Officer, to whom I applied for a passage to England, quite incomprehensible.

The RAF had been kind but firm in refusing to fly me back and the subsequent interview with the Port Embarkation Officer was a nightmare. While admitting that there was a convoy leaving next day he said there was no room for me and that I must wait for the next one which might be anything up to a month. Appreciating that space in an aircraft is limited, I could not believe that in a convoy of five merchant ships, one escort and a submarine there was no room for one emaciated evader. When I pointed this out he merely told me to mind my own damned business and get out of his office.

However, as the proverb goes, it is not what you know in life that matters but whom you know and before the war I had once met Admiral Sir James Somerville, the Commander-in-Chief of 'H' Force, which was based on Gibraltar. Dinner that night with Sir James on board his flagship HMS *Renown* was a memorable welcome home and his words to his secretary were music in my ears. 'Please present my compliments to the Port Embarkation Officer and request him to arrange a passage for Captain Langley with the convoy, preferably in the escort ship.' I hardly expected to be greeted as a friend by the Port Embarkation Officer when I went to collect my travel warrant but I could have done without his views as to the legitimacy of my birth.

HMS *Scarborough*, a pre-war survey ship, had had a very rough time as an escort to Atlantic convoys during the winter and the nervous tension of some of the officers and crew was only thinly veiled but this is no way affected the kindness and hospitality with which I was treated. However, I did not find it easy to adjust myself to an atmosphere which was very different from that which I had known when on leave in January 1940. I was intensely surprised at the cold bitter hatred of the Germans that the horrors of the Battle of the Atlantic had engendered in men who had never seen a live German in uniform. Busy with my own affairs I had never thought much about life in wartime England and was appalled to learn of the casualties and devastation caused by German bombing.

More personally, I found it exceedingly difficult to accept

the routine of three meals a day, as I had become accustomed to eating when I felt hungry, and to hoard food. It became almost a routine for the first lieutenant to say to me at the end of a meal, 'There is really no need to put that slab of butter, those lumps of sugar and that piece of meat in your pocket. We have plenty of food on board.'

Day to day life in HMS *Scarborough* was never dull but,

for me at least, it became intensely exciting when one dawn revealed two small vessels ahead of the convoy. Questioned by morse as to their identity they claimed to be Norwegian whalers from the Antarctic making their way to England. One immediately started to sink and while we were picking up the crew from the lifeboats the other made off. To everyone's surprise the survivors included a German naval officer and three ratings. After a long chase we caught up with the second vessel which then scuttled herself and we had another German officer and three more ratings – all prize-crews from the

'Scharnhorst' which had captured the whalers in the Antarctic and ordered them to make for Bordeaux.

Guarding the POWs presented problems and the captain asked me whether I would help as far as the officers were concerned, adding that I would no doubt much enjoy so doing. Frankly I hated the idea. Both were big men and in the small confines of the cabin I was sure that a concerted attack would succeed, though I might kill or wound one with the large .45 revolver with which I was armed. The only thing I felt I could do was make quite certain that if the eventuality arose I did at least get one. I therefore passed my four hours 'on watch' with the loaded and cocked revolver pointing at the stomach of the senior of the two who spoke good English. After two sessions he said he was frightened that the revolver might go off by accident and he asked whether I would accept their parole not to try and escape when I was on guard. I agreed. Life was much more comfortable and I fear I fraternized more than I should have done, even to the extent of drinking a glass of sherry with them in the evening. This last was a gesture of protest against a member of the crew who asked me if I would petition the captain for permission to throw all the Germans alive into the furnaces!

It was a bitterly cold morning in March 1941 when we docked at Liverpool and as I stood shivering on the quayside I momentarily envied the German POWs who were met by a fine reception committee. Everyone seemed to know what to do with them but no one had any idea what I should do. Despite the fact that the first lieutenant had given me an identity card the military police at the dock gates were loath to accept my story. It was only after endless delays and frustrating arguments that I was finally handed over to the RTO who decided to telephone the War Office for instructions.

After further delay the order came that I was to report to the officer in charge at the Great Central Hotel at Marylebone Station in London. The words 'under escort' were not mentioned but the RTO refused to let me take the next train, saying that he would arrange for someone to accompany me on the first train next morning to help me carry my luggage. I refrained from pointing out that this was hardly necessary as it consisted of one small brown paper parcel containing a pair of dirty pyjamas – a gift from the Swiss family in Cap d'Ail – washing and shaving kit and some ham sandwiches, kindly provided by the first lieutenant who had understood my fear of being without food.

Despite the kindness of the RTO who lent me a pound, I spent a miserable evening in the Adelphi Hotel which had been partially requisitioned. I was obviously and, I suppose, understandably, the object of the deepest suspicion. My efforts at conversation at the bar were not encouraged and even the barman refused to talk to me. Finally, after a poor dinner, I went to bed with the only consolation that I had managed to telephone my home and, though the line was appalling, arranged to meet my father in London the next afternoon.

My travelling companion, a sergeant in the Military Police, had clearly been ordered to make sure I talked to no one and not to talk to me. We travelled in a reserved carriage and it was with obvious relief that he handed me over to the NCO at the reception desk at the Great Central Hotel.

'We were expecting you,' said the latter, 'I will take you to the captain's office.'

What a relief to be expected and to find someone who seemed to know who I was.

A young captain rose from his chair to greet me.

'I am de Bruyne – usually known as Bruno,' he said, 'I cannot tell you how much I have been looking forward to meeting you. Take a pew and make yourself comfortable.'

I looked at his immaculate uniform and badges of the Intelligence Corps. He seemed all right but I was mystified by the letters BSAV on his shoulder.

He answered my unspoken question. 'British South American Volunteers. I live in Chile.'

Well, I thought, you have come a hell of a long way to fight a war!

'I am from the War Office, MI 9 to be exact,' he continued. 'We are responsible for helping POWs to escape and one of my jobs is to interrogate those who get back to England.'

'Will it take a long time?' I enquired.

'Today, no. I have read the report you sent from Vichy and the letters you wrote home from France.'

'You have met my parents then?'

He smiled. 'No, they were intercepted by the censor. All I want now is the names of the people who helped you and the latest news from Marseilles with special reference to Ian Garrow's activities.'

'You know all about him then?' I asked.

'Broadly, yes. The details, no. In his last message he indicated that an officer who had worked with him would be coming straight back to England. We guessed it would be one of the repatriation party which was originally routed through Lisbon. Your arrival at Gibraltar and immediate departure caught us by surprise.'

I laughed. 'You were not the only one who was surprised!'

He laughed in turn. 'We are slowly learning that escapers usually do the unexpected. I suppose that is why they escape! Did you meet Major Brinckman?'

Ah, I thought, so you know about him.

'Yes,' I replied. 'You are much better informed than I realized.'

'Thank you. We shall I hope be even better informed when you have told me all about Ian Garrow. Now, what is really happening?'

The interrogation left me ample time to report to Regimental Headquarters in Birdcage Walk and I set off in a much happier state of mind, being materially better equipped with money, a ration card, petrol and clothing coupons. However, I was not altogether sanguine as to my reception as I was still wearing my final evading attire, consisting of a somewhat loud and oversized brown and white check 'plus four' suit, a light blue shirt and matching tie, both very much the worse for wear, gigolo-type black and white leather shoes and a black beret. All this would be very much 'de rigueur' on the Riviera but hardly in accordance with the strict regimental regulations which required young officers in plain clothes in London to wear a dark suit and tie, a stiff white collar, black shoes, a bowler hat, and to carry brown gloves and a neatly rolled umbrella. However, the Brigade of Guards can 'take it' as well as dish it out and Colonel John Wynne-Finch, the Regimental Lieutenant-Colonel only winced very slightly as he rose to greet me with the words:

'Welcome back. You must have a good story to tell, I must hear it some time. However, I don't suppose you have anything much to add to the report you sent from Vichy?'

'No, sir.'

'Good. Now, what do you want to do?'

To be asked my wishes for the future seemed to indicate official approval of my recent activities, and I felt relieved.

'I have little doubt,' continued the colonel 'that a medical board will declare you unfit for further military service.'

I was appalled and my face must have shown it.

'However,' he added, 'unless you wish to terminate your career with the regiment I see no reason for you to go before any board.'

'I would like to rejoin the 2nd Battalion.'

The colonel smiled. 'There are others you know! Perhaps in due course, but I think at present you need some less active occupation. I have in mind ADC to the Governor General of New Zealand.'

I had not the faintest idea who he was or whether he governed from England or New Zealand. However, unless they have suicidal tendencies young officers do not argue with regimental lieutenant-colonels.

'Yes, sir.'

'Right, off you go for a month's leave. You will receive instructions about where to report for your next appointment. Goodbye, enjoy yourself.'

When not eating, sleeping or working, Father passed the time writing letters and he was thus occupied when I joined him in Brooks's Club. His greeting was the most affectionate I had ever received.

'It really is good to see you back. Get yourself a drink while I finish this letter, and telephone your mother to tell her you have at last arrived.' As he picked up his pen he added as an afterthought, 'You must have had a damned interesting time.'

My welcome home was all that the prodigal son would wish but I rapidly became bored and restless. Everyone seemed to have something to do while I had nothing to occupy the long day except to wander about without even a dog to keep me company. I suppose I was very mildly suffering from what, at the end of the war, was loosely referred to in medical circles as 'Gefanganitis', a mental and physical disturbance caused by the difficulties of readjustment after being a prisoner. The only bright spot was when Father persuaded the governor of the local open Borstal that it would raise the inmates' morale if I gave them a talk on what he insisted on calling 'my escape'. I felt it was a subject which was best left unaired as far as Borstal boys were concerned but once Father got an idea little would stop him activating it. I have never had a more attentive and enthusiastic audience, eight of whom were sufficiently stimulated to escape in the early hours of next morning. The governor was not amused!

Despite my restlessness it was with considerable surprise and apprehension that two days after my talk at Borstal I received instructions to report to Regimental Headquarters as early as was feasible next day. Beyond having reported my return while improperly dressed I had had no time to commit any misdemeanour and it never occurred to me that I could be summoned to RHQ for anything but a reprimand. Somewhere, somehow I had obviously erred and would now pay the penalty.

The Colonel's opening words were far from reassuring.

'You are well aware of the immense power of the Brigade of Guards in all matters concerning the employment of its officers?' I nodded. 'As a last resort we can always appeal to the Monarch.' God, I thought, what have I done now that merits possible appeal to His Majesty King George VI.

'However, in your case,' he continued, 'we can do nothing and I am further informed that the Monarch would be powerless to intervene.' Too numbed with shock I could think of no crime where the King could not use his royal prerogative of mercy; my situation could obviously not be worse.

'It goes without saying that I personally can do no more than give you the orders I received yesterday by telephone.'

'Yes, sir.'

'You will go at 12.30 this afternoon to the Savoy Hotel where in the foyer opposite the restaurant you will see a man dressed in a dark suit, wearing a red carnation, with a folded copy of *The Times* on the table at which he will be seated. You will make yourself known to him.'

There was a silence while I digested these facts. 'What do you think it all means, sir?' I enquired.

The colonel glanced nervously towards the door of his office, which was closed. 'I think,' he said in a whisper, 'it must be the Secret Intelligence Service.'

III. LIVES TO FIGHT

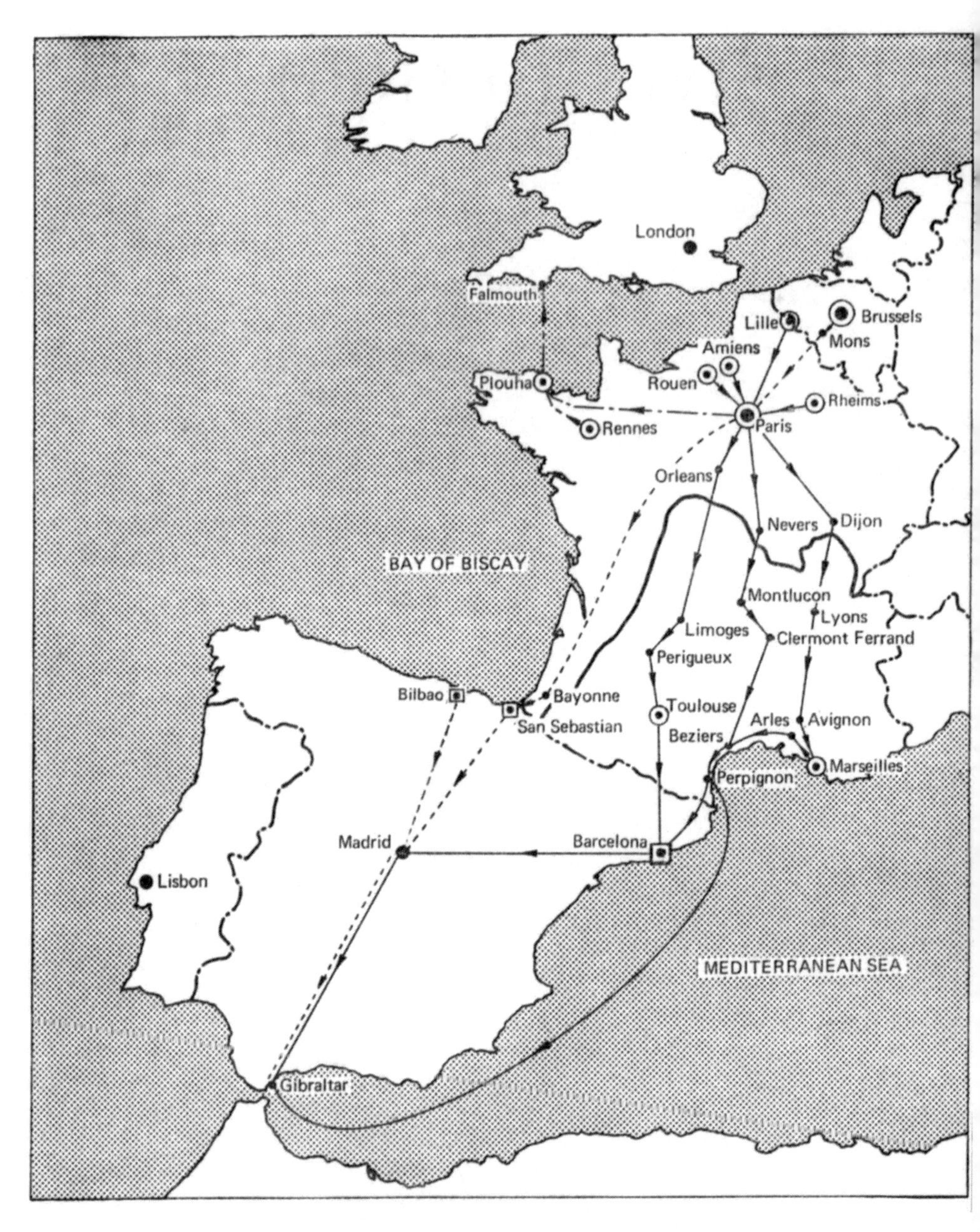

THE THREE EVASION ROUTES

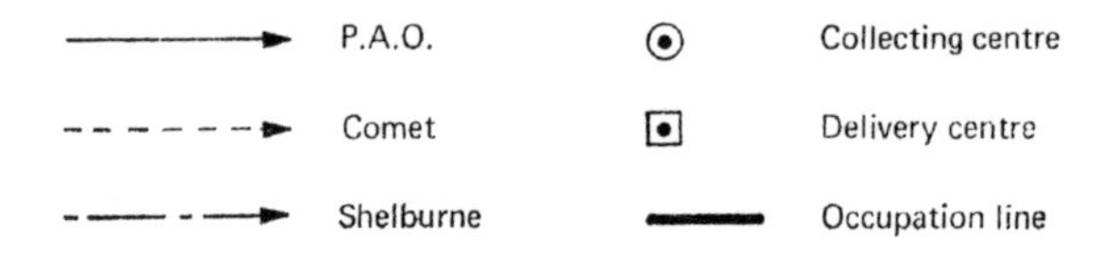

8

The Resurrection of IV Z

It was not my first visit to the Savoy Hotel. Father had given me a superb 21st birthday party there four years before and I had no difficulty in locating the man I was to meet who was dressed as described. He introduced himself as Colonel Claude Dansey, and my first impression was very much of a benign uncle, with his white hair, blue eyes and general air of benevolence; but this was quickly erased as he looked me sharply up and down and with a grunted 'Hm' said, 'F.O.L.'s son and wounded. What a bit of luck.'

I merely stared in amazement and he proffered me an explanation.

'Your father worked for me in Berne in 1917 and 1918. Some of my young men are finding it difficult to explain to their girl friends why they are not fighting. However, be that as it may, I am going to ask you the same question as I did your father when he joined my staff. What do you want?'

'I am sorry, sir, but I do not quite understand.'

'Surely I make myself plain. It is always much easier if you get what you want before you start working, then you don't spend half your time worrying about your possible award. Now an MC or an OBE? A DSO is more difficult and you are too young for a CBE. However, there are plenty of foreign decorations available. I am told that the Poles have the nicest ribbons – the Order of Stanislaus, or some such other outlandish name is very much sought after. I call it 'Pologna Prostituta' as it is immensely popular with the women. Take your choice but be quick about it.'

I replied that I did not want anything.

'Just like your father. Well, do not come complaining to me that you have not been properly looked after. Waiter!'

The response to his call was as swift as a guardsman responding to a shout from the regimental sergeant-major.

'Two large dry martinis and tell Henry pre-war gin and none of that ersatz martini he dishes out to the Americans. I presume you drink dry martinis?' he asked as an afterthought. I assented in the certainty that if he had said strychnine and cyanide on the rocks my reply would have been the same.

'What am I to do?' I enquired, gaining courage from the dry martini.

'I never talk business in public. You do not know who is listening. Waiter! These were excellent, two more, please, and ask Mr Manetta to show us the menu in the Grill.'

Manetta, the maître d'hotel of the Grill came over and whispered something in the colonel's ear.

'Excellent, you know how I like it.'

A further whisper. 'Yes, could not be better. How are your friends on the island?'

Manetta said they did not much like the food and were very homesick.

I was very much in the dark until the colonel condescended to explain. 'Most of the big boys in the restaurant world in London are Italians and when Italy declared war many of them were arrested and sent to the Isle of Man. I like them to think I was responsible and if I am not well looked after they will follow. Manetta says he has some excellent steak and a fresh Stilton, I hope they will be to your liking. Of course, I never would dream of taking any action however poor the food.'

No, I thought, I bet you wouldn't, but I should not like to be in their shoes after you had eaten a couple of bad oysters.

The colonel apparently preferred to eat in silence and our conversation was limited to queries by myself and short snapped answers which I felt would have been even more caustic had not the food and wine been excellent.

'When do I report to you?'

'Tomorrow, of course.' I ventured to point out that it would be Saturday and that I had only had five days' leave.

'All right, I suppose Monday will do, but don't forget we are at war.'

My next question as to where I was to be billeted was even less appreciated.

'Good God, man, you find your own accommodation. You will get a lodging allowance.'

'What uniform do I wear?' called for a further outburst.

'Plain clothes, of course. You are not in the army now. As far as I am concerned you can wear uniform to take out your girl friends but don't go telling them all about us or you will be in trouble.' I made a mental vow to imitate a Trappist monk.

'Well, off you go and report at 10 o'clock Monday morning at this address,' he said, scribbling on the back of a card. 'I have got some more work to do.'

I proffered my thanks and as I collected my hat I glanced at the card which was neatly inscribed 'Captain Charles Pomfret-Seymour, CBE, DSO, RN, The Naval and Military Club, Pall Mall'. On the back was written 'Admit, informing ACSS of arrival', followed by an address. I was later to learn that the colonel had a passion for aliases, the only difficulty being that he often forgot which one he had chosen for the day.

Broadway Buildings, opposite St James's Park Underground Station, where I duly reported was according to the brass plate at the entrance the head office of the Minimax Fire Extinguisher Company. A casual observer might well have wondered how on earth this company had managed to retain so large a staff in time of war and equally why there was a constant coming and going of uniformed despatch riders and military cars. The entrance hall was large enough to accommodate 15 or 20 people and it was frequently used by passersby to shelter from the rain. They were left undisturbed unless they tried to pass the reception desk, when they were politely asked their business by two middle-aged uniformed porters. However, these were the days before Ian Fleming and John le Carré had got down to the job of modernizing the intelligence services of the world.

Uncle Claude, as Colonel Dansey was widely called, wasted no time in getting down to business. 'Just listen to me and don't ask any damned silly questions,' he said. 'The likes of you in France and Belgium are causing me considerable trouble, which is being made worse by the apparent inability of the RAF to remain airborne over enemy-occupied territory. My job, and that of my agents, is to collect information about the Germans' intentions and activities, not to act as nursemaids to people who seem totally incapable of doing much to get back on their own.' He pressed the bell for his secretary.

'Miss Reade, who controls Hengist?' The pretty red-headed girl replied 'Captain Caines, sir.'

'Right, ask him to come to my office, please.'

Captain Edward Caines was obviously somewhat apprehensive of the reason for this sudden summons.

'Good morning, Teddy. If I read your messages right Hengist has picked up another pilot. From the way he rakes them in you might think he is a homosexual. Rare I know in France but always possible. Is he one by any chance?'

'He is not a he, sir, he is a she.'

Uncle Claude slammed the desk with his fist.

'How many times have I told you not to go recruiting women and above all not without my agreement. A fine fool I would have looked if I had recommended him for the DSO and he turned out to be a woman.'

'I did not recruit her, she recruited herself when Horsa was caught.'

'That is beside the point. I will not have any of your organization run by a woman. They simply are not trustworthy. Do you understand?'

'Yes, sir.'

'Right. Now what are you going to do about the pilot?'

'I don't know.'

'I thought so. Well, this is Captain Langley who has recently escaped from Lille and knows all about the escape lines in France. His job will be to take over all British Service personnel who come into the hands of our people and arrange for them to be sent back here. Tell Hengist to hide the pilot for a couple of weeks when Langley will take him over.'

Teddy Caines withdrew and Uncle Claude turned to me. 'You understand now what you have to do?'

'Yes, sir.'

'Good, then lets get one or two further points clear. Theoretically you will be on loan from MI 9, which is commanded by Colonel Crockatt. In practice you will be on my staff and under my orders in MI 6. Is this clear?'

'Yes, sir.'

'While you will liaise with Colonel Crockatt on routine matters you will not give him any detailed report of your activities without my agreement.'

'Yes, sir.'

'Now I suppose we must fit you in here.'

He picked up the telephone and dialled a number.

'Good morning, Colonel. Dansey here. Have you still got any vacancies in your department?'

Colonel Heydon-Home, as I was to know him later, might be serving his country from an office but he addressed the telephone as though commanding a battalion on a ceremonial parade and his voice was clearly audible.

'Yes, IV Z never reported on mobilization.'

'What was he supposed to do?'

'How the hell do I know if he never turned up.'

'Well, he has now. Captain Langley is his name and he will be seconded to me.'

The telephone backfired several times and Uncle Claude said soothingly, 'I don't suppose you do want him. Don't worry, he will be paid by us. All you have to do is inform the War Office that IV Z has now turned up and has been seconded for special duties.'

The telephone emitted a low rumbling assent and Uncle Claude turned back to me.

'Well, there we are – all settled. Miss Reade will help you with any letters or reports you may have to write and will find you a room. I have already agreed your appointment with Colonel Crockatt but you had better go and see him in the next day or two. Don't hesitate to come and see me if there are any difficulties and don't forget to arrange with Captain Caines to remove that pilot off Hengist. I can't have sex interfering with our work.'

Miss Reade was most helpful, even though the only room available was used for making tea. 'After all,' as she remarked, 'you will at least get yours hot!' Colonel Heydon-Home might not approve of my appointment but nevertheless he wasted no time and I had hardly acquired a table, chair and blotting pad before a large file arrived labelled 'IV Z'.

I was duly impressed, until I started to read the contents of the file. The opening minute was dated April 1919 and requested advice as to the desirability or otherwise of permitting the Germans to manufacture Luger pistols for export. From then on until 1924 it had meandered round the War Office with occasional visits to the Foreign Office, the Board of Trade and the Home Office, collecting some interesting signatures, not least of which was that of Major Bernard Montgomery. As it had not been closed I could only assume that IV Z had died in harness at his desk and some vigilant clerk had awaited the appointment of his successor.

Well, IV Z was back in business and his first act was not going to be to let down his predecessor, so I addressed the file back to the War Office with the covering minute 'Closed pending outcome of present hostilities'.

Dealing with Teddy Caines' and Hengist's pilot was not so easy and I had to confess that there was no ready-made solution. All I could propose was that Hengist arrange for the pilot to be conducted to Marseilles and contact made with Ian Garrow through a mutual friend whom I knew would help. Teddy, however, was not prepared to ask his agents to have direct dealings with an escape organization. We compromised by agreeing that Hengist would be requested to arrange for the pilot to be passed into the unoccupied zone and put on a train to Marseilles with instructions to go to the Seamen's Mission and ask for Ian

Garrow. Despite my apprehension all went well and in due course the pilot arrived safely in Spain and later in England.

All the talk of Hengist, Horsa, IV Z and the casual reference to MI 9 and Colonel Crockatt left me completely confused. Major de Bruyne had said MI 9 were responsible for helping POWs to escape and yet I was on loan from that organization to Uncle Claude who seemed to be taking a very direct interest in evasion, if only in France. I asked Teddy Caines what it was all about.

'Yes,' he said, 'I am not surprised you find everything a little confusing. I cannot myself quite understand why you have been sent here but, be that as it may, this is the background. We are MI 6, the Secret Intelligence Service of popular fiction, with the task of gathering information from all over the world about the intention, plans, etc., of any country which may be at war with Great Britain or may be a potential enemy. My job here is to collect information from France and as you know, Horsa was one of my agents there. We have similar organizations in all enemy-occupied territories and we are all responsible in the first instance to Uncle Claude.'

'And Germany?' I queried.

He laughed. 'I simply do not know. We keep ourselves very much to ourselves. The less you know the less you can give away.'

'MI 9 with its headquarters in Beaconsfield and commanded by Colonel Norman Crockatt is responsible for helping and encouraging British POWs to escape. MI 19, also at Beaconsfield, has the duty of interrogating and looking after German POWs.

'Then there is MI 5 which deals with enemy spies, agents, call them what you like, in this country.

'Finally,' he heaved a sigh, 'there is the Special Operations Executive – usually shortened to SOE and commonly referred to as "The Baker Street Boys" since their offices are in that street. Sabotaging the enemy's war effort is their trade, though if you get Uncle Claude on the subject you would think their main efforts to date have been sabotaging our own.

'There you are, that's the background, no doubt you can fill in the gaps as you go along.'

I was very grateful for this information, but still not quite clear as to why I had been lent to Uncle Claude. I felt I must find out as soon as possible.

I made a point of meeting Colonel Norman Crockatt, later Brigadier, commanding MI 9 a few days later. As a young officer, serving with the Royal Scots Fusiliers, he had been twice wounded in the First World War, during the retreat from Mons. Recalled to the army in 1939 to form MI 9, he had attracted the immediate loyalty and devotion of all who served under him. His cheerful greeting, words of congratulation on getting back home, and his enquiry as to how I had got on with the old buzzard in London, warmed my heart. 'However,' he continued, 'we will leave him for the moment as I expect you want to know what this is all about.' I nodded and the background he gave me made everything much clearer.

MI 9, which was formed in September 1939, had by May 1940 achieved considerable success in making fighting personnel 'escape minded' and in encouraging the relatively few POWs in Germany to try to escape. The fall of France, Belgium and Holland not only brought about a considerable increase in the number of prisoners but also presented an entirely new problem, that of 'escapers and evaders' in these three occupied countries.

Norman Crockatt had immediately appreciated the likely trend of future events and was considering what action to take when the first evaders crossed into Spain in June 1940. Here they were arrested and interned in a camp at Miranda del Ebro, some 120 miles north-east of Madrid.

At this stage Uncle Claude took a hand in the game, not from any real interest in the fate of the evaders, but to ensure that any clandestine work on their behalf was controlled by MI 6. He did not want yet another independent organization like SOE, which he had disliked since its inception, since it was not responsible to MI 6 and he considered its personnel to be rank amateurs in 'cloak and dagger' work. He conducted a personal vendetta against them which it must be admitted occasionally had its amusing side.

I was in his room when news of the destruction of the great French passenger liner, the *Normandie*, by fire when interned in New York harbour, was announced. He immediately picked up the telephone and as soon as he was through to a senior officer in SOE said cheerfully 'Good morning old boy, Dansey here. My heartiest congratulations on your latest battle honour. Keep up the good work!'

On another occasion I was accompanying him on one of his rare visits to the Baker Street offices when it was noticed he raised his hat every time he passed a junior officer in the corridor. Finally our conducting officer could no longer resist the temptation of enquiring the reason for this extraordinary gesture. 'Why, Colonel Dansey,' he asked 'do you raise your hat to every junior officer?' Quick as a flash Uncle Claude replied, 'My dear sir, anyone in your organization who remains a lieutenant for more than 24 hours deserves a congratulatory salutation from me!' In fairness it must be admitted that in the first flush of enthusiasm and inexperience SOE made some remarkable blunders, two of which elicited the epic comment from Uncle Claude, 'One the act of God, the other the act of a fool.'

Appreciating that there was a very real chance that MI 9 might try and go it alone on the lines of SOE he approached Norman Crockatt with an offer to help with the work of recruiting guides to conduct evaders over the Pyrenees and through Spain to either the consulate at Barcelona or the headquarters of the British Mission in Madrid, which was headed by Sir Samuel Hoare – later Lord Templewood.

As MI 9 were totally ill-equipped to undertake such work, Norman Crockatt had little alternative but to accept the offer, which included the suggestion that the task be delegated to Donald Darling, a young man who had been in Spain during the Civil War and had an intimate knowledge of the Franco-Spanish frontier from Andorra to Port Bou on the Mediterranean coast. This choice could not have been bettered, but the price was very high. Uncle Claude had achieved his object and for the next four years MI 6 were to control all MI 9's clandestine operations in Holland, Belgium, France, Spain and Portugal.

Donald Darling, code named 'Sunday', who bore a striking resemblance to the great film actor Herbert Marshall, worked unceasingly from July 1940 onwards to accomplish his mission and by the Spring of 1941 he had built up a courier service between Ian Garrow and Barcelona which convoyed a number of evaders through to the British Consulate, from which they were passed on to Gibraltar. Unfortunately, in March 1941, his activities became known to the Spanish Government which, under pressure from the Germans, forced him to leave Spain for Lisbon where his drive and energy were much less effective.

Such was the position in April 1941 as outlined by Norman Crockatt who then proceeded to put a brake on my impetuosity.

'Your first task is to settle down with Uncle Claude. Do not go rushing around like a bull in a china shop,' he warned. 'It is going to be a long war and mistakes made now will not be easy to rectify. However much you and I may think it is wrong, the fact remains that evaders and escapers in the occupied countries are as yet very small beer. If you get across the intelligence and sabotage boys in London you will do more harm than good. Take it quietly and remember we are playing very much a lone hand and although we have got some cards up our sleeve we have got to be damned sure we use them at the right moment.'

Settling down in wartime London under Uncle Claude presented some problems, a number of which had nothing to do with my new appointment. For the first few weeks I lived in the old Berkeley Hotel but was firmly though kindly requested to leave when one morning I foolishly left in my wash basin two unexploded German incendiary bombs which I had picked up in Green Park during an air raid. A colleague in the office, Christopher Rhodes, who occupied a flat in No 5, St James's Street, which was rented by MI 6 suggested I slept on the sofa in the living room until I could find alternative accommodation. I stayed two and a half years until Uncle Claude discovered what was happening

and ejected me on the grounds that the lease permitted only one occupant.

I rarely saw any of my pre-war friends who were almost all in the Forces and when I did the atmosphere was strange and unreal. I took very seriously the warning not to discuss my activities in France and refused to talk about them. They were not very interested in the Dunkirk campaign and about the only thing left to discuss was the whereabouts of mutual acquaintances, some of whom had already been killed, thus adding to the general gloom.

Meetings with old girl friends were equally unfruitful, largely I think because they had written me off for the duration of the war and found it difficult to accept the fact that I was once again in circulation. However, I had a year's back pay to my credit; Milly, the famous proprietress of the Bag of Nails night club made me a free member for life; Rosa Lewis offered me continuous hospitality in the old Cavendish Hotel and my barber insisted on trimming my moustache at no cost, in recognition of services rendered! It was not very long before I abandoned any hope of rejoining the regiment and settled down to the task of tackling the problems of escape and evasion from France, Belgium and Holland as presented by the Germans and Uncle Claude.

Two weeks in Broadway Buildings were sufficient for me to form a picture of the setup and to appreciate the truth of Norman Crockatt's warning that 'escapers and evaders were very small beer'. Everyone went out of their way to make me welcome but they also made it abundantly clear that nothing must ever be allowed to interfere with their work of collecting from all possible sources, by every feasible means, the world over, information about enemy intentions on land, sea and in the air. I found myself in sympathy with them over the difficulties and dangers which evaders caused to their organizations in enemy occupied territories but in disagreement with the general view that the fate of evaders was of little importance so long as they did not disrupt any intelligence sources.

In May 1941, as Donald Darling had been ejected from Spain, Uncle Claude decided to send me there and to Portugal, to find out what was happening.

9

Bricks Without Straw

Uncle Claude arranged that I should travel as Mr Lewis, an architect touring various consulates and embassies, to assess the repairs and maintenance required and the cost. When I pointed out that I new nothing about architecture or the profession he merely grunted and said, 'Don't be a bloody fool. Nor do the Portuguese or Spanish immigration authorities. If you are worried buy a book on the subject.' Armed with the appropriate Penguin, a large notebook and a generous supply of pencils, I duly flew to Lisbon where I was met by Donald Darling. He was full of plans and bubbling with energy but it was painfully obvious that beyond making contacts with high-ranking neutrals who could obtain visas to visit Vichy or Unoccupied France and might carry messages for Ian Garrow, there was little he could do.

In Madrid the situation was even worse as Sir Samuel Hoare, British Minister without Portfolio, had officially put the kiss of death on any escaping activities other than negotiation with the Spaniards for the release of the British interned at Miranda del Ebro. His excuse was that his personal position was far too delicate to take the risk of involving his mission in underground work. In so far as at least two of its members were already involved in subversive activities this hardly rang true. The fact was that he did not care a damn about escaping and was not going to make any effort to help unless officially ordered so to do. Those of his staff with whom I was supposed to work naturally adopted the same attitude and it was obviously a waste of time and energy to attempt to stir them to take action.

Things were a little better in Barcelona where Darling's replacement, who went by the code name of 'Horse', was doing his best but even with local support the creeping paralysis that emanated from Madrid stultified much of his effort. Nevertheless there was a keenness to achieve something and with a little luck I felt Sir Samuel Hoare might drop dead, be assassinated or replaced, I could see no other solution.

It would have been a dull and depressing visit had it not been for the unexpected arrival from Unoccupied France of an individual who had been of some help to me when I had gone to the Riviera during the winter of 1940. Bobby Stuart was a well-known character who spent much of his time ridiculing those who took themselves too seriously. Not long before I met him he had had a notable success in Cannes where he was living in a hotel.

Due to the difficulties of getting money from England he had run up a debt of some £800 in the casino. The 'Doyen' of the British colony who always wore a stiff collar and an Old Etonian tie, it was rumoured that he slept with them on, had organized a 'whip round', in his words 'to save the honour of England'. After receiving a long, pompous lecture on the evils of gambling, Bobby was despatched to the casino to settle his debts.

An hour later his benefactor saw him at the hotel bar. 'I hope, my dear sir, that this has been a lesson to you,' he said.

'Yes,' replied Bobby. 'I lost the whole lot in 20 minutes and £200 more. I now owe them £1000.'

The French had finally granted Bobby Stuart an exit visa and he was on his way back to England when we met unexpectedly in the lounge of the best hotel in Barcelona. Knowing well of his inability to treat life seriously, I was perhaps foolish to tell him I was travelling under an assumed name but I did not want him to introduce me to his travelling companions by my right name. My worst fears were instantly realized. 'Just the man I wanted to meet,' he practically shouted, 'you see that fat overfed Hun in the chair over there?' I glanced the way he pointed and mentally congratulated him on a very apt description of the individual concerned. 'Well, the hotel manager told me this morning that he is the local Gestapo chief. I think you ought to know.'

Maybe he was right but the fat overfed Hun took umbrage at the public announcement of his identity and called the hotel manager. Calm was only restored by the hotel manager undertaking to see that Bobby left on the first available plane. I think he would have done so in any event as only a few minutes later, in order to demonstrate how shoddy the hotel fittings were, he hooked his umbrella on to a vast chandelier and gave it a tug. Not only did the chandelier come down but a considerable portion of the ceiling as well!

I left by the first Iberian Airways plane next morning and Bobby followed in the Lufthansa plane, having been personally escorted to the airport by the hotel manager.

I spent a few more days in Madrid doing the rounds of certain neutral consulates which Darling had informed me might be willing to sell a few blank passports for use by high priority escapers in France. In all cases I was most cordially received, given refreshment and politely informed that while my proposition was of considerable interest it would have to be referred to their respective governments. The price I offered was clearly not high enough.

As if to make amends for his behaviour on my previous visit Sir Samuel invited me to lunch at his house to celebrate the engagement of a very distinguished Spaniard who had arranged for a supply of food parcels to supplement the somewhat inadequate prison food on which the British were expected to live in Miranda del Ebro. Unfortunately the invitation went not to the Spaniard's fiancée but to his mistress who, as a middle-aged woman with a considerable sense of humour, could not resist the temptation to accept. The error was noted by another guest who knew both parties and was soon common knowledge to everyone present except our host and hostess. Even then all might have been well had not Sir Samuel made a congratulatory speech after the meal and Lady Hoare proposed a special toast to the 'fiancée' reminding us that on occasions like this the woman is so often forgotten. This was too much and the laughter that followed demanded explanation. Lady Hoare, like Queen Victoria, 'was not amused'.

It was only next day that I ran into trouble which put an end to my stay in Madrid. At a private dinner given by a senior member of the Mission a lively argument developed as to the advisability or otherwise of demanding the unconditional surrender of Germany. I expressed my views that peace should be sought with any German political party other than the Nazis. Despite the promise of our host that anything said would be 'off the record' I was summoned by Sir Samuel and given 24 hours to leave Madrid for having expressed views contrary to the policy of His Majesty's Government.

Bobby Stuart was delighted as he was already in trouble with Sir Samuel first for complaining, both verbally and by letter, that there was no visitors' book available for signing at the Embassy, and secondly for an incident over his passport which he had left behind in the hotel in Barcelona. When he had realized his loss he had asked the girl in the Lufthansa office to arrange for it to be collected and flown over in the next plane and the porter at the Embassy to call for it. The manager of Lufthansa wrote a stiff note to Sir Samuel on the undesirability of British subjects flying in German civilian aircraft and of porters in uniform calling at the company's office.

On my last evening Bobby gave a dinner party to celebrate our joint misfortunes and when I ultimately got to bed I did not seem to have been asleep for more than about 10 minutes when the telephone rang and Bobby asked what time the bus to the airport left. I replied, 'At half past eight,' and he said, 'You had better get a move on. It is 20 past now.' I glanced at my watch which showed a quarter past seven and presumed I had forgotten to wind it up. Tie-less, unshaven, with much of my clothing sticking out of my suitcase and in a complete panic I shot down the main staircase, dropping pieces of gear en route to the accompaniment of the cheers and applause of the hotel staff whom Bobby had summoned with the words, 'Come to the main hall where you will witness an event of considerable interest.' The manager was also there in his pyjamas in response to Bobby's message that one of his guests was about to leave without paying. The clock showed 7.30!

In Lisbon Donald was amused. He too had already crossed swords with Sir Samuel on several occasions, though we could neither of us see a way round all the difficulties.

On my return to England Norman Crockatt was philosophical about Sir Samuel's reactions. 'From what I know of the old devil I would rather deal with Laval,' was his comment, a reference to the famous or in many people's view, the infamous Hoare–Laval Pact, and Uncle Claude was simply delighted. 'You were beginning to cost me money as I had a bet you would not last five days. However, it was to be null and void if you were finally chucked out. You have done what I wanted and shown that bastard we mean business.'

I was very depressed as I had achieved nothing which would help Ian Garrow and I did not know what to do next. I could not foresee that waiting in the wings for their cue to come on the stage were two of the greatest stars of Escape and Evasion 1940–45, namely Lieutenant-Commander Patrick Albert O'Leary and Mademoiselle Dédée de Jongh. However, just before they made their debut life assumed a rosier hue when Squadron Leader Mike Maloney, my companion in many a Marseilles adventure, arrived in England in June 1941 after an epic 'do it yourself' escape from Unoccupied France.

Not long after my departure from Marseilles Mike had at last hit upon a simple and, as it turned out, fool-proof method of returning to England, which involved little physical effort. It was a brilliant concept which I think was the brainchild of Texas. She and Mike travelled to Vichy in the rôle of a very sick man going to take the waters with his attendant nurse. They relied on his false identity card and her papers from the Franco-American Ambulance Corps, but actually were never questioned by the police. They were much helped by the fact that Mike looked the part as he had been very ill in December with an attack of jaundice and, in my opinion, probably owed his life to the devoted nursing of Texas. Once in Vichy Mike approached the Eire Embassy and requested an Irish passport. The consul responsible for issuing passports was in a dilemma. He knew perfectly well that Mike was not

registered as an Irish citizen resident in France and Mike had perforce to come clean. On the other hand, the consul was duty bound to replace the lost passport of any genuine Irish national. So he compromised by agreeing, provided Mike's claim to citizenship was substantiated by Dublin.

Confirmation by letter through the diplomatic bag would have taken a long time and it was therefore decided to risk cabling, the cost of which Texas paid. There was no reaction from the French censorship and a week later Mike was the proud possessor of a genuine Irish passport.

No more back street hotels, no more eating in dirty little restaurants off unrationed food, no more queasy feelings every time one passed a policeman or a member of the German–Italian Armistice Commission. Mike was an Irishman and he did not care who knew it.

Once Mike's credentials were confirmed the consul became fully co-operative. He permitted him to draw all his arrears, back to June 1940, of the distressed citizens' allowance, issued him with ration cards and gave him an advance sufficient for Texas and himself to travel in luxury from Vichy to Lisbon once the necessary travel permits were issued. This the French, Spanish and Portuguese authorities were only too delighted to do for citizens of two great benevolent neutral countries, the USA and Eire.

Their journey out of France and across Spain and Portugal was a veritable triumph. Mike had bought an 'Anthony Eden' hat, had had the overcoat altered and borrowed Richard Illingworth's umbrella and gloves on the promise to return them in England. Texas purchased a new travel outfit and it was not surprising that they were accorded the attention and service usually reserved for diplomats and oil kings; after all Texas had once been a beauty queen!

Their parting in Lisbon, where Texas took a boat for America and Mike the plane for Shannon, must have been distressing for both of them. Their personal feelings for one another apart, they had achieved together something of a saga in the annals of escaping.

It would be pleasant to record that Mike, Texas and I all met again after the war but as the years go by the chances become dim and the mystery that surrounds Mike's ultimate fate is less and less likely to be solved.

On returning to England he was posted as a squadron-leader to a wing stationed in Suffolk not far from my home. He was very late for our reunion party and my parents who regarded failure to arrive on time – even in wartime – as unpardonable rudeness, gave him a somewhat cold reception. However, all was forgiven when he apologized and excused himself by saying he had shot down a Heinkel bomber during the late afternoon and had been unable to resist the temptation of going by car to view the wreckage.

In the following months we met whenever duty permitted and although he was often his old gay self I noticed that he would have sudden fits of depression and I wondered what was on his mind. He would rarely talk of his escape and the days in Marseilles and never referred to Texas; the whole subject was obviously distasteful to him. Modesty? Battle fatigue? Disillusionment? I could not ever guess.

Then he went missing – nothing spectacular, he just did not return from a routine patrol over the North Sea. I did not even see anything in the press but heard of his loss from a mutual friend in the squadron. Beyond the fact that he had a brother in the Irish Army I knew nothing about his private life. He had never talked of his parents, his youth or his home. Flying had seemed the be all and end all of his life.

Time marched on and with the liberation of France the task of tracing, awarding and thanking the brave men and women who had risked all to help evaders and escapers was put in hand. In due course Georges Le Maire who had helped Mike in his escape in 1940, was contacted and came to Paris to the office of the Awards Committee. His first question was naturally how could he get in touch with Mike. He was told of Mike's return to England and of his ultimate disappearance. Then came pure drama.

'But that is impossible,' said Le Maire. 'He called on me again in 1942. He only stayed for dinner and the night, saying he was in the hands of an organization and did not require help this time. I asked no questions – what you do not know you cannot tell. I am sure you understand. He was collected next morning by a man whom I did not recognize and that was the last I saw of him.' Nothing could shake Le Maire's story and it seemed impossible that he could have imagined the whole affair. Discreet enquiries were made as to his background but nothing of any value in solving the mystery was revealed. He was an ordinary middle-class Frenchman who had risked his freedom and life to help Allied evaders. He was a widower and the old woman who looked after him was unaware of the true identity of his guests. Dead end!

The Air Ministry gave details of Mike's last flight. Three Spitfires had taken off, Mike in the lead with the other two in échelon behind. They had passed over Orfordness, flying east, and that was the last that was ever heard or seen of the three aircraft and the pilots. It was presumed that an order for the formation to wheel right or left had been misunderstood and that there had been a triple collision with no survivors. No wreckage and no bodies were ever recovered. Dead end again.

I have many theories but no solution. However, one strange incident that occurred in Marseilles, remains clear in my memory, though if it has any significance the mystery only deepens. We were enjoying a bottle of champagne one evening in Texas's room, 'by kind courtesy of the American tax payer,' as Mike put it when Texas suddenly said something in German. I do not speak the language so did not understand what she had said or Mike's reply also in German, which was given in anger. Before she could say any more he knocked her off the bed on which she was sitting, picked her up from the floor, threw her on the bed upside down, seized her hairbrush, pulled back her skirt and gave her six of the best with the words, 'The bitch said she did not speak German. That should teach her not to.' After a couple of hearty howls Texas in her best American informed us as to her views on British men in general with special reference to Mike's ancestry. We then finished the bottle of champagne and the incident was never referred to again.

'Mike Maloney' may still be alive so I have given him a

'nom de guerre' and, with the passage of time, I have forgotten 'Georges Le Maire's' true name. I do not think the mystery will ever be solved but I am convinced that 'Georges Le Maire' was telling the truth.

10

Patrick Albert O'Leary

Mike Maloney had little news of interest to tell us as the courier service set up by Donald Darling was functioning well and we received regular, if of necessity brief, reports from Ian Garrow. It was in one of these which arrived in June, 1941, that he requested us to obtain security clearance for, and permission to enrol, a man calling himself Patrick Albert O'Leary. The first task was mine but only Uncle Claude could grant permission for him to join the organization.

O'Leary's story was that he was an officer from the armed merchant cruiser HMS *Fidelity* who had accidentally been left behind during a night landing of agents near Collioure on the French Mediterranean coast. Arrested, the French had accepted his cover story, that he was a Canadian RAF evader trying to steal a boat to sail to Gibraltar, and had sent him to join the other British prisoners at St Hippolyte du Fort, near Nîmes, where they had been transferred from Fort St Jean, shortly after I had left Marseilles.

Verifying his service with HMS *Fidelity* was simple. Originally SS *Rhin*, a French 'Q' ship, she had been recommissioned in the Royal Navy as HMS *Fidelity* after the fall of France. Her officers and men had been enrolled in the Royal Navy and had been granted the equivalent rank. The commanding officer, Commandant Peri, had changed his name, becoming Captain Langlais, and his girl friend was commissioned in the WRNS where she achieved the unique distinction of being the first Wren to go to sea on active service.

O'Leary had indeed been First Officer at the time of the night landing operation, but what worried Uncle Claude was that there was no record of his previous activities other than his statement that his real name was Albert Marie Guérisse who, as a Belgian army officer, had come over to England at the time of Dunkirk. Norman Crockatt and I proposed approaching the Belgian authorities in London for further information, but Uncle Claude, who had the lowest possible opinion of the security of the various refugee governments, refused to permit this, saying we might as well hand him straight over to the Gestapo.

'Once the Belgians know we are interested in Guérisse they will guess he is working for us and it is merely a matter of time before the news gets back to Belgium and the Germans.' Norman Crockatt and I looked glum. We had not thought as far ahead as that!

Uncle Claude smiled and said helpfully, 'I don't think he is a German agent as he already knows enough of value to go straight to them rather than into prison; I advise we agree. Garrow has met him and I think we are justified in relying on his judgement. Further, from what I hear of Captain Langlais I much doubt if anyone with pro-German sympathies would survive many hours in his company.'

The message of acceptance 'Adolphe doit rester' as requested by Garrow went out over the French BBC news service. One of the greatest escape organizers of the war had joined us.

Uncle Claude called me to his office next day. 'I have told Colonel Crockatt that any future reference to anyone, and by anyone, I mean anyone, of Guérisse's real name and nationality is as good as signing his death warrant. You understand?'

'You will give him a code name for the field and a different one over here,' he continued, 'and for God's sake watch out for the Belgians. They will get to hear that you have one of their people working on escape and do their utmost to find out who he is. I've warned you what will happen if they succeed.'

This was the first time I became fully aware of the necessity of security in England as well as in the field. I therefore arranged that in future all communications sent to us from sources in England, other than from official intelligence departments, should be addressed to Room 900 at the War Office. Messages from the organizations abroad were to be addressed to Room 055A, also at the War Office. All agents and the most important helpers in the field had code names which were changed if it was felt that they might have become known to the enemy.

Although we now felt these security arrangements were desirable they occasionally caused confusion, notably when an evader carrying a message for Room 055A found that the department responsible for his evasion was located in Room 900, the name by which we became generally known.

Though the guide and courier service was functioning very efficiently it was obvious that there was a limit to the number of evaders who could be brought out by this route and my thoughts turned to the sea. If agents could be landed in France from Gibraltar surely evaders could come back on the return journey.

On the purely naval side there is very little increase in the risks involved in picking up one or 20 men though in the latter case the ship may have to be stationary in the danger area, that is to say close to the hostile coast, for a slightly longer period, depending on the numbers of men to be embarked and the 'ferrying' boats available. From the land side the risks are greatly increased with every additional individual to be embarked especially when they do not speak the language of the country and are utterly dependent on their guides. An agent or two can hang about in the rendezvous area for several days without arousing suspicion but not 20 men who have to be fed and hidden, and who are likely to become fractious and difficult to handle if there is any long delay. Radio communication with the organization is an absolute essential and the operator must not only be trained in the art of transmitting and receiving from enemy-occupied territory but also in the maintenance of his radio and the way of encoding and decoding messages.

There was an enormous demand for men and women either of French nationality or who were sufficiently conversant with the French way of life to be able to work and move around in France without arousing suspicion but the supply of individuals with the necessary courage to risk their lives in this dangerous work very limited.

As a late arriver 'escape and evasion' was very much at the tail end of the queue and it was not for another six months that the situation changed.

The reasons for this dilatoriness were not difficult to find. The Air Ministry still regarded a bomber or fighter which failed to return to base as lost, crew and all, and were only slowly beginning to appreciate the high potential of evasion by those who got clear of the aircraft uninjured. Equally Uncle Claude was not going to waste, as he felt, valuable potential agents on what he regarded as a thoroughly unproductive clandestine pastime. Norman Crockatt and I were therefore very much lone voices crying in the wilderness for something which we knew was highly desirable, but we had no facts with which to prove our case.

However, on the home front considerable progress was achieved, notably in making the operational personnel of the RAF thoroughly evasion conscious. Interrogation of returning evaders had clearly shown that many were being captured during the first few hours after successfully landing by parachute or getting out uninjured from their crashed aircraft, solely due to making no effort to leave the area and hide up before the Germans could organize search parties.

Briefing combat personnel on escape and evasion techniques was therefore put in hand and weekly courses were held in London for the intelligence officers from the fighter and bomber stations; I lectured on the Do's and Don'ts when evading in enemy-occupied territories, for repetition to pilots, navigators and crews.

All flying personnel were now equipped with a small compass, a knife for cutting away the parachute harness should the 'landing' be in a tree, silk maps of the countries over which they were operating, as well as money and a small emergency pack which contained food in highly concentrated form, pills for purifying water, matches, a razor and shaving soap, a needle, cotton, a water bottle and fishing line. I never heard of any evader catching a fish but many said it helped to pass the day when hiding near a river or stream and that it was useful for keeping up the trousers if one's braces broke! They were also advised to carry a small passport-size personal photograph for use on forged identity cards.

Much thought had been given to the desirability of giving addresses of 'safe houses' but it was felt the security risk was too great and this was only done for key personnel in highly specialized operations such as the Commando raid on the German radar station at Bruneval in France – and then the men were required to memorize the details. The wisdom of this decision was confirmed in a tragic manner when one returning pilot, contrary to the strict routine orders given during his interrogation, gave the name and address of the family which had hidden him to a friend. The latter was killed over northern France and the Germans found the address in his wallet. The whole family were arrested and the father and mother shot for collaborating with the enemy.

The logical sequences of the perfect evasion were now firmly established. To get clear of the point of landing or crashing was of the utmost importance, hiding up if necessary to avoid pursuit. When the danger of immediate capture had passed the next step was to approach, at dusk, a small isolated farm and ask for help. If this was not forthcoming the evader should continue to walk south towards Unoccupied France, repeating the process until a promise of help was forthcoming. The instructions of any helper should be carried out without question. The helper was unlikely to have direct contact with an organization but would have friends, or friends of friends, who had. On their side the organization would first check an evader's bona fides by radio to London, and then, after equipping him with civilian clothes, shoes and false papers, would arrange his return to England either overland via Spain and Gibraltar, or by sea if this were possible.

Blank forged identity cards and passes, official rubber stamps, ration cards and even French cigarettes made in

England, could be smuggled in over the Spanish frontier. However, radio contact was absolutely essential if any of these supplies were to be sent in by parachute and if any evasion was to take place by sea or air.

Even though the perfect evasion was as yet a pipe dream 'Operation Sugar Beet' as I somewhat facetiously named it was the first clear indication of what could be achieved with even our antiquated methods of communication, and a foretaste of the potentials of organized evasion.

Early one morning in July 1941 a Gibbs – 'Defend those Ivory Castles' – toothpaste tin was handed to the porter at the British Embassy in Madrid by an individual who refused to give his name or nationality, merely saying it was for the British Ambassador. Tins such as this had false bottoms which could be made into a hiding place for messages or paper money and I had used one for this latter purpose during my journey through France. Initially there was considerable speculation as to why anyone should want to give Sir Samuel Hoare a half-consumed tin of toothpaste and the concensus of opinion was that it was a member of his staff who wished to poison him. However, someone made the right guess and the following message was extracted:

'To the War Office. Brigade Major and self hiding in farm where six of us had Christmas Dinner in 1939. Former badly wounded in knee but now able to walk. Please send guide to rescue and acknowledge receipt of message over French BBC Broadcast, incorporating words "Sugar Beet", which we are tired of breeding.' The signature was only partially legible followed by the words 'Officer Commanding Infantry Brigade' and a date some weeks previous.

The writer had obviously been deliberately vague in order to provide the Germans with the minimum information should the message fall into their hands. No difficulty was experienced in identifying the two officers and a close female relative, sworn to secrecy, confirmed both signature and hand writing, also giving us considerable pleasure by commenting, 'What? Old George weeding sugar beet and mucking out the cow sheds – that will do him good – best thing that has come out of the war so far!' To many junior officers it was also a pleasant thought to visualize a rather fat and bad-tempered brigadier with his austere disciplinarian brigade major working as farm hands. However, senior officers were in very short supply and the suggestion that their continued

agricultural activities might do much to help the Entente Cordiale (since farm labour was reported to be in short supply in France), had to be turned down.

Had the message been written under German pressure? This was possible but very unlikely as at this early stage German reaction to evasion had been negligible and limited to threats to shoot any 'helper'. Such threats had almost always been carried out although, as far as is known, no evader from the BEF had ever been executed, though one escaper from a prison hospital in Lille had disappeared. In any case when the farm had been located, Ian Garrow, who would arrange the rescuing, could be warned of a possible German trap.

Who had been at the Christmas Dinner and would any of them remember the name and location of the farm? Records showed that the brigade had suffered considerable casualties in May 1940 and only one of the 'possibles' had returned to England; he was now in New Zealand. A cable was despatched reading: 'Did you have Christmas Dinner with your Brigadier and Brigade Major 1939? If so can you name farm and indicate location as information received reports they are hiding there?' The reply was helpful but by no means the solution – 'Yes but cannot recollect name of neighbouring village or farm but believe could identify from large-scale map of area.'

Where was the brigade on Christmas Day? War Office records were limited to 'Brigade H.Q. closed down in Le Mans area 13.00 hrs. 24.12. and moved by road to Jerusalem. Route Joppa Jedda Johannesburg Jericho Jedburgh. Re-opened 06.50 hrs. 26.12.' To confuse German Intelligence routes and code names for French towns between Le Mans and the BEF staging area around Lille had been frequently changed and no one could identify with any degree of certainty the list of towns. For a period it looked as though the brigadier and his brigade major would continue their farming activities for the duration if their rescue depended on the efforts of Room 900. Nevertheless, it was decided to acknowledge receipt of their message and the following went out for five days over the BBC French 'Messages Personnels' programme. 'Sugar Beet, Sugar Beet, William Orange will gather in harvest as soon as he can. Continue ploughing fields and scattering good seed on the land,' It was hoped this would mean nothing to the Germans and that the reluctant farm hands would correctly place 'William Orange' as the War Office and carry out the instructions to stay put.

It was now decided that a risk must be taken and officers were sent to contact relatives of the brigade HQ staff with a request to view any letters and diaries covering the move north. That it was a risk was shown by an event a year or two later when a letter from a very senior retired officer to a relative in Dublin (where the Germans had an embassy) was retained by the censors as it contained an absolutely accurate description of the cold-blooded murder of an escaping British officer in Italy as conveyed by MI 9 to the next-of-kin, under oath of secrecy.

However, the risk appeared justified when one letter from a junior officer to his fiancée, with a splendid disregard for security, contained the following paragraph: 'Despite the fact we were on the move to our battle line in the north we had a very jolly Christmas evening. Of course, most of the drink and good things were packed in the lorries but we made up for it by a high old evening in 'Lion D'or' at . . .' obliterated by the censor – but he had failed to cut out the name fully, and very careful work built up the name FLEURY. To this achievement was added the information in a letter from New Zealand to the effect that 'The Brigade had passed most of Christmas night a few miles south-east of ROUEN'.

At this point consideration was given to the possibility of the RAF doing some low flying over the area by day in the hope that the two tillers of the soil might be out in the fields and wave a handkerchief. Reluctantly it was abandoned as being likely to arouse German suspicion and possibly result in a combing of the area by German troops.

Examination of further letters and diaries and interrogation of officers from other brigades which had gone north by the same route elicited the fact that all night stops had been a few miles north-east of Fleury and that brigade HQ was usually situated around three or four small farms near a major crossroads. Study of French large-scale maps limited the possibilities to about four. The relevant maps were flown to New Zealand and the officer was requested to cable the name and map reference of the farm, and return the maps with the farm ringed in blue should it not have a name.

The reply was 'All joy. Absolutely certain farm is one of

two' – here followed map reference – 'will never forget the noise the owls made throughout the night from the wood to the north. Dinner was in the most southerly farm where Brigadier and Brigade Major slept. Owners were rather more than normally pro-British.'

The relevant information was sent by courier from Barcelona to Ian Garrow, together with two photographs cut out of their passports, for use on forged French identity cards, and instructions to rescue them as soon as feasible. He was further instructed that whoever collected them should introduce himself as 'Guillaume d'Orange' and ask for Monsieur la Bettrave Sucrée, only using the brigadier's real name as final confirmation of his bona fides. A further message was sent out over the BBC French broadcasts saying 'Mr Sugar Beet. A reaper calling himself William of Orange will contact you soon. Follow his instructions.' A guide was sent from Marseilles to the farm and the two officers were safely conducted through to Spain. In the light of events to come it was perhaps a clumsy and amateurish operation which had greater success than it probably deserved.

In September 1941 we heard that Ian Garrow had received reports that Paul Cole, the English sergeant who was helping escort evaders down from the north of Franch to Marseilles, was using evasion funds to support a mistress and indulge in high living. Then, in October, Garrow was arrested by the Vichy police and sentenced to imprisonment in Fort Meauzac in the Dordogne. He gave away nothing under interrogation and Pat O'Leary immediately took over command; but it was our first setback.

In November Paul Cole was confronted with proof of the accusations that had been made against him; unfortunately he gave his accusers the slip and fled to Lille. Early in December he was arrested there by the Abwehr (the German military counter-espionage service) and within a week a number of our staunchest helpers in the north were also arrested; some were tortured and shot.

It was a disaster of the first magnitude and it took all Pat O'Leary's courage and driving energy to rebuild what was now officially designated the 'PAO' organization (after the initials of Pat's nom de guerre). All that we could do from London was to continue sending in money by guides who conveyed parties of evaders back into Spain and pass on the information that we were training a radio operator.

Jean Ferière, as this radio operator was named on his false French identity card, was very much my ewe lamb and I nursed him with all the devotion of a mother with her first born. It was an exhausting and frustrating association for both parties and at times I almost despaired. Where the average agent became proficient in coding and decoding in a matter of days Ferière took weeks and was for ever forgetting the key phrase of his personal code. The head of the section responsible for radio training informed me that his speed of transmission was such that he would be picked up by the enemy radio detection vans as soon as he came on the air and almost certainly located and arrested the second time.

The results of his 'field training' were equally unsatisfactory. Sent out to the suburbs of London to find a lodging house from which to transmit messages he invariably aroused the suspicions of the land-ladies within a matter of minutes and was usually arrested before he even got his radio working. Whenever he did succeed in transmitting he was so slow that he was used by trainees in radio detection for practice purposes and was always located. On an exercise in avoiding pursuit he once managed to board a crowded bus only to fall off some minutes later and was lucky not to be run over by the bus behind with his pursuers aboard. Socially he was equally uninspiring, his only topic of conversation being silk stockings for which he had been a salesman before the war.

However he was my only hope, and in March 1942 I planned to fly to Gibraltar with him. There I would introduce him to Pat O'Leary, whom I had not yet met, and who was to be smuggled out of France for the conference. Donald Darling would also be present as he had just been transferred to Gibraltar from Lisbon.

Just before we left England I received a horrifying report from the Special Branch at Scotland Yard. A middle-aged English woman, who had been living for many years on the French Riviera, had recently been granted an exit visa by the Vichy Government. On her return to England she told the authorities that a few days before her departure an Englishman had been arrested by the French police and charged with stealing. Although she knew him by sight she did not know his name, but was confident she would recognize him from a photograph.

Anxious to learn if he was one of the 'wanted' men believed to have fled to France before the war, Scotland Yard showed her a number of photographs, amongst which was one of Paul Cole. Picking this up she said, 'No, that's not him, but this charming man called on me in 1941 to borrow money to help our men escape from France.' Scotland Yard were extremely interested in her information as Cole was 'wanted' on a possible manslaughter charge and they approached MI 9 in the hope of finding out more about his activities in connection with evasion in Unoccupied France.

MI 9 were handed a copy of Cole's criminal record, which included a term of imprisonment for larceny, and a description of his methods of operating as a 'con' man, usually claiming to be an army officer. Scotland Yard were unaware that he had joined the army, their information being that he had got out of England posing, in stolen battle dress, as a sergeant returning to the BEF from leave. In MI 9 we now did what we should perhaps have done earlier, which was to call for his army record. When Ian Garrow and I had first met him in Marseilles we had accepted the army pay book he produced as sufficient proof of his identity and honesty. But from his record sheet we learnt that in April 1940 he had absconded from his unit taking with him the funds of the sergeants' mess. This new information began to throw a very sinister light on the arrests which had been made in France during the previous few months.

When we arrived in Gibraltar my first impression of Pat O'Leary was of a man with immense drive and energy who would never admit defeat and, as I got to know him better, I learnt that the supply of these most desirable qualities was almost inexhaustible. His modesty, shyness and delightful sense of humour effectively masked a first-class calculating brain and the indomitable courage he was to show in the future. However, what appealed to me most during our long hours planning was his complete understanding of our difficulties and no word of recrimination at our lamentable efforts to support his activities in the field, particularly when I had to confess our serious sin of omission in failing to check Paul Cole's bona fides.

We all agreed, in the light of the revelations in London, that Paul Cole had probably not 'broken' under threats of torture but had been working with the Abwehr for some time. Pat undertook to instruct all members of his organization to kill Cole without any further questioning if they came across him again.

During our talks we covered a great many subjects and Pat told us the story of his life. He was a doctor by profession and had served in that capacity with the Belgian First Lancers. With considerable diffidence he requested that his work with us should not be made known to the Belgian Government in London and I could not but wonder whether he held the same views as Uncle Claude regarding their security.

I could see Pat thought little of Ferière as a man, but the possession of a radio transmitter and a set of codes was ample compensation. Pat's proposals for evasion operations ranged from air-lifting evaders in bombers from a disused French aerodrome, or by flying boats from lakes, to sea-borne evacuations from the Mediterranean coast. I knew that the latter were the only ones that would receive consideration in London and detailed discussions were confined to such possibilities.

As I said goodbye to Pat and Ferière, before they set out on their long journey through France, for most of which they would be concealed in the boots of cars, I realized that we had in Pat a born leader and a very great man, just how great time was to show.

I flew back to London with a feeling of intense elation, so different from my return from Spain and Portugal in the previous year. At long last we were on the road to success.

11

A Comet from Brussels

The task of supporting and expanding Ian Garrow's pioneer work in Marseilles had taken up most of my time so far and I had given little thought to the potentials of evasion across the other end of the Pyrenees. Theoretically a line running through Lille–Paris–Bordeaux–Bayonne by train, and then over the Pyrenees on foot into Spain, could be organized. But the entire journey to the Franco–Spanish frontier would be through German-occupied territory, a fact which I thought would deter even the most courageous helpers. The frontier post at Irun was manned by German guards which would necessitate evaders crossing the River Bidassoa, a mountain torrent which runs along the border between the two countries. This I considered to be a further deterrent.

It was true that a few evaders from Belgium had successfully crossed into Spain in that area and further that they had received help to reach the frontier zone but their information about their helpers was vague and never contained any names or proposals that we might make contact. It had therefore been a considerable surprise when the British consul at Bilbao reported in August 1941 that a few days previously a young Belgian girl had come to the consulate with a British evader and two young Belgians whom she had 'escorted' from Brussels. Further, she stated that she and her father had been helping the British since August 1940 and were confident that they could organize an escape line from Brussels via Paris to San Sebastian. All she required was money for train fares, food, and payments to the frontier guides.

The consul, whom I had met in Spain and knew to be extremely sensible and level headed – he had had the task of escorting the Duke and Duchess of Windsor into Spain on the fall of France – accepted her story and proposition but added a word of warning that it might be a German trap. This caution was quite unnecessary as far as Uncle Claude was concerned since he instantly envisaged the build up for another 'Venlo'* incident. Norman Crockatt, however, saw the affair in a different light and tactfully said he was sure Uncle Claude was clever enough to play along with the Germans and deal with any plot that might subsequently

develop, meanwhile receiving a dividend of evaders every time the former made contact with the consulate.

Uncle Claude merely grunted and said that the consul was a damned fool to have paid out for the first party. He added that in any case the Foreign Office must be consulted as their man was involved and that he would ascertain their views. This was not, of course, strictly true but Uncle Claude was not going to have any bloody amateurs, especially soldiers,

* In the winter of 1939 two British intelligence officers, Captain Best and Colonel Stevens, had been kidnapped by the German Abwehr when attending a meeting with the latter's agents in a café on the Dutch side of the frontier post at Venlo in Holland. This incident had not reflected much credit on the British SIS!

taking any decision where he was involved. Crockatt said he understood and that he would have all interrogation reports checked to see if there was any mention of a young Belgian girl as a helper.

The interrogation reports were helpful; a young girl whose description tallied with that from the consul was reported as a helper but it was some Red Cross letters from Belgium that clinched the matter. Between September and December 1940 three letters had been received by anxious parents in England from a certain Mlle Andrée de Jongh, saying that she had been able to visit their wounded sons in the German hospital in Brussels and had given them food. The name was that of the young girl and even cynical Uncle Claude had to admit it was highly improbable that her charity was instigated by the Germans or motivated by pro-German sentiments.

The consul was given the go-ahead to provide the money she had requested for her next visit, scheduled in October, and arrangements were put in hand to transport her 'parcels' as she called her party of evaders from San Sebastian to Gibraltar. The work needed a co-ordinator and organizer in Madrid and all I could do was to say who I felt should not be allotted the task! Uncle Claude's choice could not have been better – a young diplomat Michael Cresswell* whose courage, ingenuity and tact was just the support Andrée de Jongh (later to become famous as 'Dédée') needed. He was given the code name of 'Monday' and Dédée 'Postman', commanding the Postman Line, though this was later changed to 'Comet' under which it achieved international fame.

In January 1942 we had received some splendid news about Airey Neave whom I had last seen in September 1940 as he left the prison hospital in Lille on the first stage of the journey to a POW camp in Germany. He had escaped from Colditz and reached Switzerland, the first British officer to make a successful escape from what we knew was the punishment camp for inveterate escapers. After much heart searching, it was decided to entrust Pat with the task of arranging for his onward journey through Unoccupied

* Now Sir Michael Creswell, KCMG.

France to Barcelona. It was not an easy decision to reach as had he been arrested en route there was a very real chance that the Germans might persuade the French, and possibly even the Spaniards, to hand him back to face a court martial for some trumped up criminal charge. The verdict of guilty would have been inevitable and if he had not been shot he would certainly have been sent to a concentration camp for the duration of the war.

All went well during his journey and in Marseilles he met some of Pat's chief colleagues, notably Louis Nouveau, in whose flat he stayed, though not Pat who was at the planning conference in Gibraltar. Our reunion in London was made even more pleasurable for me as I knew Norman Crockatt was going to ask him to join Room 900. He accepted the offer and in May 1942 I put him in charge of Comet and escape and evasion from Belgium and Holland, with the code name 'Saturday'.

Comet was unlike any other escape line that came under our jurisdiction – control is too strong a word. The last decision always rested with the men and women in the field, as from the outset Dédée had made it clear that she would brook no interference from outside. The line was Belgian, would be run by Belgians and any help would be gratefully received; but payment of money was simply reimbursement of expenses and in no way gave us the right to issue orders.

This was an attitude that Uncle Claude deplored though he quickly realized there was very little he could do about it; however, it did not make our task any easier, especially when things went wrong, as they inevitably did with every underground organization, and his comments were caustic in the extreme. Unlike 'Monday' and Airey I never really got the measure of Comet which was more a club of patriots who, devoted to the cause of Britain and her allies, were prepared to suffer torture and death at the hands of the Germans which, alas, many of them did, rather than a tough ruthless underground organization with a hatred for all and everything German. My admiration for their bravery and unconquerable spirit in the face of disaster never wavered but at times their intransigence and failure to make use of some of the help we offered them, notably in the field of security, nearly drove me frantic.

The constant refusal of members of Comet to accept a radio and operator in Brussels, on the excuse that it would give us control, was always a very sore point. We never had the faintest intention of issuing orders since we knew only too well that it would be a waste of time and energy as we had no means of ensuring they were carried out. On the other hand, it would have permitted us to pass on rapidly all information we received on the work and identity of traitors, German agents and agent provocateurs whose task it was to destroy the evasion organizations. Further, and perhaps more important, it would have enabled them to obtain a quick check as to the bona fides of RAF and other allied personnel whose behaviour excited their suspicions. Finally, they would have been able to alert us when things went wrong, and saved us making plans based on situations that had ceased to exist.

Comet never undertook any sea evacuations as the Belgian coast line was too short and well guarded for such operations. The evaders, the occasional escapee from Germany, and their conducting 'helpers' always travelled by train from Brussels to Paris and thence to the Bayonne – St Jean de Luz area where Dédée had arranged a number of safe houses where they stayed in hiding until the guides led them across the river Bidassoa or over the Pyrenees to San Sebastian or Bilbao. The guides then returned to France, taking with them money and any messages we had for Dédée or her successors.

The evaders were then smuggled down through Spain, via Madrid, to Gibraltar, in a splendid 'Taxi Service' organized by Monday in Madrid. As I have implied, apart from money there was little tangible help we could give Comet but the enthusiasm and tireless work of Monday and Sunday in Gibraltar gave great encouragement.

Both Dédée and Pat were requested to send out only British, and later American, fighting personnel or helpers whose activities were known to the Germans and whose usefulness, at least temporarily, was finished. Pat kept very much to the spirit of this request but Dédée occasionally threw in an odd Belgian whose claims as a helper were thin but whom she felt would help the war effort. Her choice was always excellent but it never ceased to arouse the fury of Uncle Claude when he read the radio message from Sunday listing the latest arrivals in Gibraltar. Norman Crockatt was also not best pleased at what he regarded as misuse of MI 9 funds and Airey and I would receive rebukes from both quarters with orders to tell Dédée to stop sending out foreigners on pain of a cut in the money supply. Needless to say we never passed on these instructions.

After all the bitter disappointments and frustrations of 1941 the prospects for evasion in the second half of 1942 were much brighter. On the home front Airey quickly settled in with me, and brought about a near miracle by injecting into me some courage when facing up to Uncle Claude. Previously he had always reduced me to a petrified jelly which had great difficulty in even saying the required 'Yes' or 'No'.

Meanwhile in the field Dédée on one occasion sent back the entire crew of a bomber shot down over Holland, while Pat was sending back fighter pilots shot down during daylight sweeps over northern France.

As a result of these two successes someone in the Air Ministry tumbled to the fact that an aircraft lost over enemy-occupied territory did not necessarily mean that the crew must also be written off. The low rumblings of appreciation reached Norman Crockatt and strengthened his hand when dealing with Uncle Claude. Not that the latter softened much. That one might as well have tried to dissolve iron in boiling water as melt Uncle Claude was illustrated by a conversation between two septuagenarians I could not help overhearing in Brooks's Club about this time.

'I wonder,' shouted one, into the deaf aid of the other, 'what has happened to that fellow we shared a tent with just before the relief of Mafeking?'

'You mean,' bellowed the other, 'the fellow who used to fill stockings with sand and go out at night and slug Boer sentries?'

'Yes. But I cannot remember his name. Claude something.'

'Dansey,' replied the other. 'If he is still alive I will bet he is mixed up in some dirty work.'

In fact, even Uncle Claude was impressed by Dédée's courage, tenacity, and powers of physical endurance, which inspired all who worked with her. He also grudgingly admitted that Pat had done splendid work to make good after the disasters that followed the treachery of Cole and Ian Garrow's arrest. He was prepared to allow us to give Comet and PAO full support but refused to sanction any plans which envisaged setting up completely new organizations either as an insurance against German counter-evasion activities or to cover areas, notably Brittany, where nothing existed. It was a policy for which we were to pay dearly in the future.

12

The Navy Joins In

I never expected that Jean Ferière would make a name for himself as an intrepid radio operator. If he had had any real potential he would have been snapped up by MI 6 or SOE long before I got hold of him, but it was a disappointment that his nerve broke after only one transmission. Pat packed him off to his wife and family as to be reunited with them was apparently the real reason for volunteering to return to France, and he obtained the services of a French operator.

Uncle Claude did not like wireless sets being worked by someone about whom we knew nothing and he therefore acquiesced without comment when I proposed as a replacement Alex Nitelet, a young Belgian fighter pilot who had been flying with the RAF. Shot down over the north of France with the loss of an eye, he had evaded through the PAO organization and now, since his wound barred him from active flying, volunteered to rejoin Pat as his radio operator.

Training presented no problem as he was already proficient in the art of transmitting the Morse code but getting him to Pat was altogether a different matter. Smuggling through Spain was becoming more difficult and there was the added danger that he was known to the Spanish authorities as he had passed through Miranda del Ebro. If caught and identified the Spanish might well stop permitting the repatriation of evaders caught and imprisoned there on the grounds that we were using them as spies. Pat had no knowledge of the technique of arranging a reception committee for a night landing by a Lysander or a parachute operation. In any case Alex's disability added to the risks of parachuting either to a reception committee or 'jumping blind' as it was called when an agent parachuted by night from a converted Halifax bomber, with no one to meet him.

However, I discovered that SOE had a Lysander scheduled for the May 'moon period' to pick up an agent on the run in Unoccupied France. The officer responsible for 'laying on' the operation said that Alex could go over as there were no passengers for the outward journey, provided Uncle Claude gave his agreement. After giving me a long lecture on the dangers of mixing up evasion with sabotage, he assented prophesying that this would be the end of my second radio operator. He was damn nearly right!

The Lysander got bogged down on the landing field and the pilot, Flight Lieutenant Mott, RAF, was arrested by the Vichy police and sent to the prison camp at Fort de la Revère on the Riviera which had replaced St Hippolyte du Fort at Nîmes. Alex escaped and succeeded in reaching Louis Nouveau's flat in Marseilles but he was a very shaken man and his first message was largely indecipherable. All that the experts at the decoding centre could make out of the jumble of letters was the sentence 'Cui Cui a stoper', though who or what 'Cui Cui' was I never made out! However, from then on he was a superb operator and we were now all set to put into action plans discussed at Gibraltar for a large sea evacuation of evaders from the Perpignan area.

Donald Darling was not only an individualist and opportunist of high order but he was also 1500 miles from Uncle Claude and therefore, provided he was not caught out, able, within limits, to go it on his own. He had twice succeeded in arranging for evaders to be picked up either by one of the two feluccas, manned by Polish naval personnel, or by the armed British trawler *Tarana* serving with the Royal Navy. All three of these ships were based on Gibraltar and had from time to time picked up or landed agents and supplies on the French coast in the Gulf of Lyons. This, of course, had necessitated the help of other intelligence or sabotage organizations but as all had gone well no questions had been asked.

The plans Pat, Donald Darling and I had discussed at our meeting in Gibraltar were much more ambitious and envisaged up to 50 evaders, the maximum which *Tarana* could accommodate; embarkation was to be at Canet Plage, a prewar pleasure resort near Perpignan with an hotel and empty bungalows which could be used as 'safe houses'. It was not easy to convince the Naval Operations Officer in Broadway Buildings that Pat was capable of carrying out the immense task of having this number of people, most of them without any knowledge of French, at a prearranged place on the beach at midnight. However, he had heard much about Pat from Captain Langlais, of HMS *Fidelity*, and agreed that the risks were justified.

We christened the first full-scale evasion plan 'Bluebottle'. Arranging recognition signals, passwords, day, hour and exact point of contact required the utmost accuracy and the minimum chance of any misunderstanding. In the timing alone there was plenty of scope for error with British Summer Time, British Double Summer Time, Greenwich Mean Time and Mid European time to be sorted out. Once out of sight of land *Tarana* would be disguised as a small coaster and would fly a neutral flag, usually Moroccan or Spanish, but while she could receive messages she could only break wireless silence in an extreme emergency.

Although I was fully confident of Pat's ability, I went through hours of worry that some vital figure might have been wrongly encoded or decoded, that there was some important factor we had overlooked or that some untoward incident, such as an accident on the railway between Marseilles and Perpignan, might wreck the whole scheme. I knew only too well that if anything went wrong on our side it would be a very long time before we would be allowed to try again. Failure of *Tarana* to arrive at the rendezvous would be less serious as there was a fair chance that many of the evaders would be able to cross the Pyrenees. Nonetheless, it would be a very severe blow to the morale of Pat and his devoted band of helpers.

However, all went well and early in July 1942 *Tarana*

arrived in Gibraltar with 34 evaders, largely RAF personnel, including Squadron-Leader Whitney Straight and two gallant helpers, Leoni Savinos and his wife, who were so deeply compromised with the Germans and the Vichy authorities that Pat had deemed it essential to get them out of France.

The return of Whitney Straight was a relief in more ways than one. He already had a very high reputation in the RAF and the fact that he was a prisoner in Fort St Hyppolyte was

known to the Air Ministry which was for ever asking what we were doing to get him out. The trouble was that, as a born evader and escaper, he was doing most of the 'doing' himself, leaving us little time to help. He nearly succeeded in being repatriated as unfit for further military service, but the party to which he belonged was stopped, it was said on the direct orders of Hitler, just short of the Spanish frontier, as a reprisal for the bombing of the Citroen works at Boulogne-Billancourt. Furious at the failure of this scheme, Straight had sent a highly inflammatory personal cable to Churchill. It was passed to me with the acid comment that if only I would do something positive difficult incidents like this would not occur.

The success of 'Bluebottle' showed that large-scale sea evacuations were feasible and in the autumn we attempted a second evacuation. On two successive nights the ship failed to make contact with the shore party. Pat returned to Marseilles, where he had left the wireless set, not wishing to take the risk of it being captured should the police close in on Canet Plage, and sent a furious message which contained the sentence 'Pas plus de bateau que de beurre au cul', which can be roughly translated as 'No more a boat than butter on your behind'. *Tarana* meanwhile sailed some 100 miles towards Gibraltar before breaking wireless silence to inform us that there had not been a bloody Pongo or Blue Job on the beach.

There was no time for recriminations as Pat had 50 evaders hidden around Canet Plage, whose capture became increasingly probable as the hours passed, while fuel in *Tarana* was running low. Every instruction to Pat and *Tarana* was checked and rechecked and as far as could be seen there were no errors. Someone had blundered but all that mattered was that there should not be a recurrence if a third attempt was made. The Navy agreed to try again and Pat, who had perforce to wait in Marseilles for our decision, telephoned the news through to the Hôtel du Tennis, the operational headquarters and main hiding place. *Tarana*'s shore boat landed 400 yards north of the agreed contact point and was only just seen by the left-hand man of Pat's outpost.

More than 40 evaders and several helpers were embarked and *Tarana* returned without incident to Gibraltar. Everyone involved was furious over the delays but all unanimous that those 'chairborne' clots in London were responsible. As Airey and I were far the most junior all recriminations were, by common consent, channelled on to us.

One thing was certain when working with Pat, there was never a moment of relaxation. The row over Bluebottle II was still going strong when he asked for food, clothing, money and cigarettes to be parachuted to him. The RAF agreed the selected dropping point, a football ground outside Nîmes, but unfortunately the pilot had difficulty in identifying the town and did three low runs over it before spotting the reception committee's recognition signals. The roar of the Halifax's four engines woke up everyone, including the chief of the police who, although he was destined to be a recipient of a case of whisky as a gift, had to take some action and Alex Nitelet and two other members of the reception committee were arrested.

Pat was once again without a radio operator and so final arrangements for a third sea rescue, Bluebottle III, had to be made through another organization's radio operator. Pat had none of Uncle Claude's inhibitions about using other networks in an emergency. Fortunately the operation was a complete success and Uncle Claude's comments were limited to muttering about our good luck.

The three sea operations had rescued over 100 RAF personnel, four Commandos who had evaded after Dieppe and a number of helpers, two of whom were to go back and perform fine work as members of SOE.

It was with immense pride and pleasure that in November 1942 I sent the following message to Pat: 'Le Roi t'a accordé le DSO je dis le DSO, mille félicitations' (The King has awarded you the DSO repeat the DSO. A thousand congratulations).

One of the helpers evacuated by Bluebottle II was Paula Spriewald, an attractive young German girl whose hatred for Hitler had caused her to leave Germany before the war. Shortly after her arrival in England she was the centre of an incident which might have had serious consequences.

Pat had asked Paula to get in touch with Captain Langlais, his old commanding officer, and pass him all the news. Somehow she found out that he was on leave staying in the Ritz Hotel and without further ado called on him there early one morning. The first I heard of the matter was when Langlais came through on the telephone. He was so excited that I could hardly understand what he was saying but I gathered that he had caught a German spy and unless somebody came quickly he intended to shoot her.

I had only met Langlais twice and could not for the life of me make out how he knew my telephone number or why he should appeal to me for help. It later transpired that he wanted a namesake of mine who worked with one of the French sections and with whom he had had considerable contact. However, there was obviously no time to be lost, so I hurried round to the Ritz and raced up to his suite.

Paula, streaming with tears, was cowering on her knees in a corner of the room with Langlais standing over her, waving a loaded and cocked revolver, and shouting 'Sale Boche – Sale Boche'. It was some minutes before he calmed down sufficiently to listen to my explanation of Paula's reason for calling. When he grasped the fact he immediately called for the room service and ordered three dozen oysters and a magnum of champagne. We were still trying to comfort Paula, who was having mild hysterics, when a waiter arrived and said that the chef had told him it was too early to have oysters and champagne.

Picking up his revolver Langlais rushed out of the room and a few moments later an under-manager came on the phone imploring me to come down to the kitchens as Langlais was threatening to shoot his chef. Luckily I was in uniform, otherwise I think we would have all been handed over to the police; as it was it cost Langlais a five pound note, two magnums of champagne and innumerable oysters before all the injured parties could be persuaded to overlook the affair.

Throughout that summer Comet sent through a steady stream of evaders and later in the autumn we were able to send Pat a new radio operator called Tom Groome, a young Australian, who had lived in France and spoke excellent French.

However, there were ominous signs of trouble ahead, the first of which was the arrival, by Bluebottle I, of Christine Wolf Derwent. An extremely attractive and intelligent woman in her late twenties, with more than her fair share of sex appeal. When interrogated at Gibraltar she said she had been living in France before the war and had escaped from the internment camp at Bescanon, where the Germans had sent all the British women they had rounded up in the Occupied Zone. She further frankly admitted that her husband was serving a prison sentence for robbery with violence, adding that she did not wish to see him.

Pat had stated in a radio message that he was sending her out as she was insistent she had information of importance to pass to the British Government, the nature of which she had refused to divulge. In a private despatch to me which accompanied her he added that she knew Ian Garrow and other members of the organization but that he found her social activities very disrupting. All this information I passed to Uncle Claude, who merely grunted and said, 'When you meet her I will send Brown with you to hear what she has got to say.'

I knew little about Brown except that at some time or other he had been with Scotland Yard, his appearance suggesting that he was probably a rising young policeman at the Sidney Street Siege and that he did odd jobs for Uncle Claude. As we waited for Christine's train to arrive at Charing Cross Station he said, 'I always call myself Robinson when on business. How do I refer to you?' I replied that as Christine had been instructed to contact me by name it would be better if I did not assume an alias.

'A mistake, a great mistake,' he muttered, half to himself.

'Captain Langley, I assume,' said Christine as she arrived at the ticket barrier looking quite ravishing, 'and?' she queried: 'Mr Robinson,' I said formally. 'We have booked you a room at the Waldorf Hotel in the Aldwych. I propose we go along there now as you must be tired after your long journey.'

'But why two of you?' she asked as we sat in the taxi. One up to you I thought as Robinson replied, 'I often accompany the captain when he meets people to help carry the luggage. Porters are difficult these days you know.'

She laughed but I could see she did not believe him. As she

was filling in the registration card at the reception desk Brown idly picked up her passport and put on his glasses, leaving the case open on the counter. Inside the lid I saw neatly inscribed 'Property of Mr H. Brown' together with an address.

Christine turned to him and said sweetly, 'Next time you call yourself Mr Robinson I suggest you do not carry Mr Brown's glasses. I further propose you go back to Mrs Brown as I have things to say to Captain Langley which are not for your ears, that is unless you are actually Colonel Claude Dansey.'

My God, I thought, as we sat down to dinner, Uncle Claude is not going to be best pleased when he learns that this woman knows his name.

During the meal I asked her about Pat, whom she obviously disliked, unlike Ian Garrow for whom she had a high admiration. However, the whole subject obviously bored her and I waited with interest for her to come out with what she really wanted to talk about.

Suddenly she said, 'Let's get down to business. I suppose you work with or know of Colonel Claude Dansey?'

'Yes,' I replied cautiously.

'Good. You can get in touch with him tomorrow?'

I nodded.

'Right. Please tell him I want to see him as soon as possible. Now, I am tired and am going to bed. If the Colonel is not interested, please add that I know all about "Zee Loewe" and "Zee Adler", "Sea Lion" and "Sea Eagle" in case you do not speak German. Goodnight.'

Uncle Claude's face remained utterly impassive as I recounted our conversation and only when I had finished did he comment. 'I gather she caught Brown out; he is getting too old. Do you know what those two names mean?'

'No.'

'Well, Sea Lion is the German code name for the invasion of England and Sea Eagle that for the occupation of Spain and attack on Gibraltar. She must have been in contact with some highly placed Germans. Anyhow, I am not going to see the woman until I know more about what she wants. It is your job to find out. No tough interrogation – kindness and sympathy. I will get in touch with MI 5, which can handle that side. Do you understand?'

'Yes,' I replied and rose to leave.

'You will have to cut down on your visits to the Bag of Nails and the Cavendish Hotel for the next week or two,' he commented as I left.

'Damn the old bastard,' I thought, as I went to my office to ring up Christine, 'is there nothing he does not know?'

She was a most pleasant dinner companion and took Uncle Claude's refusal to meet her with equanimity, though she was very outspoken in the comments on her interrogation by MI 5.

I used to meet her interrogator most mornings and we both had to admit failure, as she adamantly refused to pass her information to anyone except Uncle Claude. However, one evening she suddenly said, 'Well, this does not seem to be getting anyone anywhere I suppose I had better tell you at least part of my story.'

I smiled hopefully.

'After we had been in the prison camp for about three months some of us were called for reinterrogation,' she began. 'At least that was the excuse given, but in actual fact it was to find out if we would work for the Germans. By that time I was nearly crazy at living with all those squawking women and their bloody children.'

'And not a man for miles,' I interrupted. She gave me a dazzling smile. 'Well, there were the German sentries but I like my friends to be officers – preferably British. Anyhow, I said I did not wish to be a spy and asked what the work was. "Nursing British wounded airmen" I was told, and listening to what they had to say. I could not see much harm in that so I agreed. My escape was faked, all very simple, I merely reported sick, the doctor diagnosed measles and I was put into an isolation room from which a young German Officer collected me in the evening. He took me to a hotel near St Jean de Luz and I was allowed to go where I liked provided I reported back before dark. Nothing much happened for a week when a German officer took me out to dinner.'

'What was he like?' I queried.

'Very good looking; tall and blond, and speaking perfect English.'

'Rank,' I enquired.

'He said he was a colonel in the German Intelligence Service, and that far from wanting me to work for Germany he proposed I work for England.'

I refilled our wine glasses and said, 'Go on.'

'He told me that there were many Germans who hated Hitler and would like to do away with him but must have British help and an undertaking to make a fair peace. He proposed that I returned to England and saw Colonel Dansey, whom he said was in a position to help and obtain the required undertaking about a peace treaty. If he agrees I am to go back, when the colonel will arrange to be parachuted into England to discuss plans for dealing with Hitler.'

'How did your Colonel propose you went to England?' I asked.

'He said there was a very fine escape organization working in Marseilles, and that if I went there I would have no difficulty in getting in touch with it.'

'Did he give you any names?'

She hesitated. 'No, but he did say it was run by a British officer and that if I went to the Seamen's Mission someone there would tell me how to find him.'

'How long did you stay in Marseilles?'

'About nine months I suppose.'

'Why this long delay when you had such important information?'

'Ian Garrow said if he sent me to Spain I would probably be caught and put in a Spanish prison. He advised me to wait until he could arrange a boat.'

I pulled myself together, remembering Uncle Claude's warning about interrogation.

'Well, I must be off to bed. I'll tell the colonel what you

have told me and no doubt he will see you. Meanwhile I will meet you for dinner tomorrow night.'

Uncle Claude remained silent for some minutes after I had made my report, then said 'It would be of interest to know the colonel's name. Try and find it out. But much more important is it to ascertain how many other Germans she met, where and for how long.'

To my query as to the German's name, she replied, 'I will tell you if you give me your word of honour as a British officer that you will never reveal it to anyone else.' I hesitated for a fraction of a second and she laughed, 'I can see in your eyes that you are making up your mind to lie. Nothing doing.' She was absolutely adamant that her only contact had been the colonel, always after dark, over drinks and dinner.

It was only a day or two later that a parcel arrived from Gibraltar, sent by Pat through some other organization, with a laconic covering note: 'I have been through Christine's flat and enclose her private papers which I think you may find interesting.' Uncle Claude smiled grimly as we studied a large photograph of Christine who was undoubtedly looking her best. However, it was not her glamour that caused the smile on the face of the tiger but the general composition of the picture. The background was the bonnet and radiator of a large Mercedes, with the German Army number plate easily readable, a bottle of champagne standing on one mudguard, and the débris of a picnic in the foreground. Grouped round Christine were four German officers in uniform with their glasses raised, as if toasting her beauty.

I never saw Christine again; she was detained in prison under the Defence of the Realm Act. But I still feel the postcard I received from her when the war was over, with the message, written in green ink, 'I will get you yet, you bastard!' was unjustified – as was Uncle Claude's comment on my expense account: 'This is really a case, Jimmy, where you should pay the War Office.'

It was a logical assumption that the Germans had kept Christine under observation while she was in Marseilles and that they were probably well aware of the method of her departure. Adding this to the information that Paul Cole must have supplied when he turned traitor, we estimated that the Gestapo must have a very full picture of the PAO oraganization, including a description of Pat. What we did not know was that Goering, becoming very disturbed at the number of RAF pilots and crews who were evading capture, had given orders that all evasions were to be ruthlessly crushed and the Luftwaffe secret police used to reinforce the Gestapo and the Abwehr.

Airey and I assumed, wrongly as it turned out, that the first strike would be at the PAO organization. I therefore suggested to Pat that he should hand over to Tom Groome and come to England for a rest period and to plan for the future. I knew, at the bottom of my heart, that he would never leave, even though things appeared to be quiet and Tom Groome would be fully capable of keeping the organization going. His reply was that he should try and engineer the escape of Ian Garrow, whom he had learnt was shortly to be sent to Germany, from the prison at Meauzac.

Uncle Claude and I, for once in agreement, felt that the risks were not justified to save one man but Norman Crockatt and Airey disagreed, pointing out that Ian's magnificent work and self-sacrifice should be recognized by some effort to save him from almost certain death in a concentration camp, and in January 1943 Pat was given the OK to go ahead. The plan was for Ian to walk out disguised as one of the sentries when the latter were relieved; speed was vital as it was known that his departure was imminent. Help from inside was essential and one of the French internal security guards was persuaded to smuggle in the uniform. In obtaining his services Pat showed how great a planner he was by matching up the reward offered to the risks involved, namely three years' salary, cash down, and a further half year's as a bonus for success.

Pierre Ulmann, a devoted helper in Toulouse and a tailor by trade, helped by his wife made the required uniform in 48 hours and all was ready when without warning the sentries from the French Army were replaced by gendarmes from the

Vichy police. This setback might well have wrecked the whole plan but the Ulmanns, working through the night, produced the new uniform, cap, badges and insignia all in 48 hours, an incredible achievement. This, together with a revolver and faked papers, were smuggled in and Ian, weak though he was after almost a year in prison, successfully walked out with a group of gendarmes going off duty. Pat accompanied him on the dangerous journey through France and over the Spanish frontier and his last words to Ian, as he turned to go back, were, 'Can this go on much longer?' – a phrase which was to haunt us in London for months to come.

In my radio message to Pat informing him of Ian's safe arrival in London I went as near as I dared to ordering him to come out via Spain or by Lysander. His reply was a request for another parachute drop of supplies. I knew that Pat would never come out now and that it was only a matter of time before he paid the price of the magnificent work he had done during the past year which had resulted in some 300 evaders returning to England.

13

Blows and Counter-Blows

In October 1941 the Gestapo had questioned Dédée's father about the whereabouts and activities of his daughter but they took no further action at the time. Then, in the spring of 1942, just after the Abwehr had struck at the PAO organization, they arrested several important members of Comet in Brussels. Dédée and her father quickly moved to Paris.

We never discovered how the Germans got their information. There was no sign of treachery nor were 'agent provocateurs' used. Possibly they had kept an evader under observation from the moment he was first hidden in a farm and followed him through his journey to Brussels, noting the addresses where he was hidden.

For a few days during early May 1942 it looked as though the Brussels end of the organization had been crippled beyond recovery but Dédée, from her new headquarters in Paris accepted the offer of Baron Jean Greindl, or 'Nemo' as he became known, to undertake the work of reconstructing it.

At the age of 36 he had already made a name for himself in the Congo administering the family coffee plantations. Lightly dismissing Dédée's warning that he would be lucky if he survived six months, he put all his superb organizing ability at Comet's disposal. So swiftly did he act and with such drive and determination that in June, barely six weeks after the disasters, he sent back the survivors from a bomber that had been shot down early in May.

All through the summer of 1942 a steady stream of evaders came through from Belgium en route for Spain, but in November of that year the Gestapo renewed their offensive. First they again penetrated the Brussels group, using Germans posing as Americans flying with the RAF, and being helped by Belgian traitors, notably a man called Prosper

Desitter. Jean Greindl escaped arrest, but he was forced to send out a number of key men and women, including Peggy van Lier, whom I was later to marry. The activities of all of them were obviously known to the Gestapo but even then it was with difficulty that Jean Greindl persuaded them to leave.

Finally, in the spring of 1943 the Germans struck the whole length of the line. Jean Greindl, Dédée and her father were all arrested. This time it was the work of Belgian and French traitors, backed by information given by evaders who, when arrested, broke under the threat of execution as spies.

It seemed incredible that Comet could survive, but survive it did, due largely to the matchless courage and unconquerable spirit of the few who remained and inspired others to take up the challenge.

During the same period 'PAO' was equally hard hit. Tom Groome was arrested in January 1943 while actually sending out a radio message about an air drop. He gave away nothing under interrogation and it was the work of traitors that led to the arrest of Louis Nouveau and then of Pat himself. The prime traitor was a trusted guide, Roger le Neveu, known as Roger le Legionnaire, who personally arrested Pat in a café in Toulouse at the point of a pistol. At the time we thought that Roger had agreed to work for the Germans, following arrest and threat of torture. Later we learnt that he was already in German pay when he volunteered to work for PAO and there is little doubt that he used information supplied by Cole to make the first contact.

At first there was little we could do in Room 900 except give the widest possible circulation to the description of the traitors and reiterate warnings as to the danger of 'agent provocateurs'. However, as the numbers of evaders returning to England dropped away the Air Ministry began to ask questions which triggered off widespread recriminations in London, some of them directed at Airey and myself. Where were the trained reserves to replace the losses in PAO and Comet? Why had we not built up embryo organizations to step in and take over? In other words, what the hell had we been doing all the time?

The Air Ministry went as far as to propose that Norman Crockatt be replaced by a senior RAF officer and that all evasion should come under their jurisdiction. It was rumoured, with what truth I do not know, that the whole matter was discussed by the War Cabinet and that Churchill had decreed 'No change'. Be that as it may, we were ordered to redouble our efforts and at last promised all the moral and material support we so badly needed.

Our objectives, apart from helping in the reconstruction of Comet (PAO was virtually a write-off) were to found an organization in Holland, new ones in France and to achieve my ambition of sea evacuation from Brittany.

There was virtually nothing in Holland and Airey had to start from scratch. In Belgium Comet slowly recovered under the leadership of Baron Jean-François Nothomb, a young Belgian who took over from Jean Greindl. In France there was a small nucleus of PAO helpers in Paris who had escaped arrest but lacked a leader. In Toulouse Pat's chief organizer, Françoise Dissart, a French woman aged 60, gallantly continued to send small parties over the Pyrenees but we decided that her association with Pat had been too close to risk sending her a radio operator.

During the 18 months I had been working four people had been trained and sent into France. Three of these were the radio operators for PAO, Jean Ferière, Alex Nitelet and Tom Groome, all of whom had been arrested. The only survivor was Mary Lindell, Countess de Milleville, who had been sent in during October 1942 to found an organization in the Limoges area.

Her exploits have been fully chronicled in two books* both of which make no secret of the fact that we did not get on together, and still do not, as is borne out by our exchange of courtesies (*sic*) when we met again some 25 years later at

* *Saturday at MI 9*. Airey Neave. Hodder and Stoughton, 1969. *No Drums, No Trumpets*. Barry Wynne. Arthur Barker, 1961.

an evasion reunion in Holland. Our brief conversation ran roughly on the following lines:

'Good afternoon, Mary. I do not suppose you remember me?'

'Only too damned well I am sorry to say.'

'I think you were a little unkind to me in the book *No Drums, No Trumpets.*'

'Nothing to what I would be if it was revised.'

'A pity as I think you got things wrong.'

'That may be your view but it is not mine.'

Time, it would seem, is not always a healer! The truth of the matter is that Mary is a woman who brooks no opposition but prefers to use a battle-axe rather than the more usual feminine charm when dealing with difficult males. However, it was her handling of Uncle Claude at the one and only interview she had with him that will always be a happy memory.

Before arriving in England from France Mary had already served a nine months' prison sentence in the Occupied Zone for her part in helping Major Jim Windsor-Lewis* of the Welsh Guards to evade in 1940. Despite this she was determined to go back and made it abundantly clear that she would raise hell if any obstacles were put in her way. If Airey and I were dubious as to the wisdom of sending her back Uncle Claude had no such doubts and agreed to inform her that he would not sanction her mission. He never got round to that as Mary took control of the interview and informed him of all his shortcomings as far as helping evaders were concerned. When he pointed out that he was only trying to save her life she replied that it was not her life he was interested in but his reputation.

For once Uncle Claude had met his match and after she had left said to me, 'Spare no effort to get her to France as soon as it is humanly possible.' He was not the only member of the 'Establishment' in London that held this view, with the result that she went without a radio operator.

Her mission was not as fruitful as Airey and I had hoped

* The late Brigadier James Windsor-Lewis, DSO, MC.

but her rescue, in December 1942, of two of the survivors from the famous Bordeaux raid by the Royal Marine Commandos* bore witness to her indomitable courage and tenacity of purpose. The immediate result of the lack of direct communication with Mary was that she received no help from us and the Commandos were naturally vociferous in their complaints when they arrived back in England, via Spain, and they had ears in high places.

There was another major row but by now Norman Crockatt was a past master at protecting his ewe lambs and we were not the only subjects of a witch hunt in intelligence circles. The outcome was the appointment by the three services of 'watch-dogs' in Broadway to look after their interests. The Navy was represented by a Royal Marine of distinction and renown, the Royal Air Force by an eminent airman and the Army by General 'Moses' Beddington, a distinguished cavalry officer of the First World War vintage, one of whose tasks was the supervision of Airey's and my activities.

General Beddington's nickname 'Moses' was due to a tactical error by his family, who were stockbrokers, in changing their name which caused a wit to post a notice in the Stock Exchange reading 'God said unto Moses, thou shalt be Beddington.' Highly intelligent, he instantly appreciated that plans which Airey and I had formulated during the 'infighting' were so far advanced as to make any interference of doubtful value, and he therefore gave us full support.

The steady increase in evaders from the USAF and the formation of an American counterpart to MI 9 – MISX – were factors we had to take into account and which might well have given rise to difficulties, but with great wisdom MISX curbed their very natural desire to 'get cracking' on their own and agreed to accept and profit from our experiences and to supply us with any material help we required. At this time the favourite weapon of my agents, a ·32 Colt automatic pistol, was virtually unobtainable in England and I asked our American liaison officer if he could help.

* *Cockleshell Heroes*. G. E. Lucas Phillip. Heinemann, 1956.

'Sure, captain,' he replied 'no problem.' A month later he proudly gave me 20 with the necessary ammunition. As it was not a regulation service weapon I could not resist asking how he had got them.

'Plumb easy,' he said. 'I cabled the War Department, asking them to request the Mayor of Chicago to put out an appeal to the gangsters. I have 300 more when you want them.'

Their enthusiasm for evasion was a real tonic though I was occasionally embarrased by this, notably at their reaction to my advice concerning the use of civilian clothes when evading. The Germans, as far as we could ascertain, accepted the practice of evaders changing into civilian clothes as soon as they could obtain them, and permission had been granted for pilots to take with them a pair of their own grey flannel trousers for use when they successfully crash-landed. I passed this information to a very senior Air Force general who turned to his staff colonel with the words, 'Bert, get on to Washington and arrange for every flyer to be issued with a pair of grey flannel trousers.' My God, I thought, this is going to be a different war.

In the field it was not so easy. To enable our organizations to check the bona fides of an evader, every four months we issued them with a questionnaire and a set of correct answers. An evader had to give the correct reply to seven out of 10 questions. The questions were such that anyone familiar with life in war-time England could answer. 'Who is Jane?' was almost a regular – she was the famous heroine of the Daily Mirror strip cartoon. 'What is the weekly coffee ration?' another; it was never rationed. The Americans could not be expected to know the answers and we had to compile new questionnaires. The fact that many of the Americans bore German names was a potential source of danger and their insatiable desire for chewing gum and coffee necessitated a change in any supplies we were able to parachute in. However, these were comparatively minor problems compared to the main business of keeping organized evasion working effectively.

Choosing and training agents was no easy task as Jean

Ferière had already taught me. Courage and patriotism simply are not enough when facing a superbly organized and utterly ruthless enemy, though these two qualities are major requirements. To achieve success the individual must be quick-witted, capable of making decisions at a moment's notice, cunning, ruthless when required and with the capacity to recruit men and women with similar qualities. Physical strength is a help, provided it is not so conspicuous as to call for comment, but the power to endure long periods of intense strain, both mentally and bodily, is essential. A sense of humour is a help but less important than the ability to lead and inspire others.

My relationship with the Free French Intelligence Service, the BCRA,* through Colonel Passy, had always been excellent. It was less satisfactory with the Belgian equivalent,† largely due to my fear that I would inadvertently give away Pat's identity. And although it was non-existent with the Dutch, Airey soon remedied this and we were supplied with some first-class potential agents. Training these in all the techniques required, e.g. radio communication, codes, night landing by Lysander, parachute operation and recognition signals for sea operations, went superbly during the early months of 1943, and despite some initial set-backs I was able to inform Norman Crockatt that the outlook for the autumn and winter of 1943 was most promising.

That 'cracking' Brittany would be a tough job I was already aware, as two earlier attempts made in conjunction with the BCRA had failed. In each case the agents whom we had put in were French naval officers; the first had been denounced by a colleague and the second shot by a German officer in a brawl over a woman. However, I decided to have a third try, led by one of the few agents we had in training at the time of the Comet and PAO dêbacles, a White Russian brought up in Paris called Vladimir Bouryschkine. He had been one of Pat's helpers sent back in Operation Bluebottle II, when his activities had attracted the attention of the Vichy police

* Bureau Central de Renseignements et d'Action.

† Sûreté Belge.

or, to use the current phrase, he had been 'blown'. I gave him the code name of Valentine Williams, after the author of the famous Club Foot spy novels, always shortened to Val.

Training Val was exhausting work as he was for ever making enemies by pointing out the deficiencies in our methods, usually justifiably but nonetheless irritatingly, to those responsible. Parachuting him into France with his wireless operator, one of the Canadian commandos who had escaped via PAO after the Dieppe raid, became a legend with 161 Squadron at Tempsford. During three consecutive 'moon periods' they set out and returned nine times, due to the inability of the pilot to locate the chosen dropping area. Keeping Val happy during the day drove me nearly mad. The 'secret house' at Godmanchester, where agents spent the hours before leaving and slept if the parachute operation was unsuccessful, rapidly bored him and he insisted on making a tour of the local pubs. His vociferous complaints of the inefficiency of the RAF, to all and sundry at the bars, soon attracted the attention of the local security authorities and, through them, Uncle Claude, who vented his wrath on me and threatened to send Val to Wormwood Scrubs for the rest of the war.

When Val and his radio operator did at last reach France they were dogged by bad luck in their efforts to organize sea evacuations from Brittany. Their radio was captured and although they re-established communication through another organization's wireless Val was arrested before the replacement radio, which we had perforce to send overland via Comet, arrived. However, they both did good work in resuscitating part of PAO in Paris, and in arranging for a number of evaders hiding in Brittany to be escorted to Spain.

Val was imprisoned in Rennes and his radio operator was ordered to return to England via Spain. Val's subsequent escape and return to England excited the suspicions of Uncle Claude who refused to accept his story and had him sent to Wormwood Scrubs as a suspect double agent. He was ultimately cleared and released but the fact that this shameful treatment, and the meagre award of the BEM, did not embitter him gained the admiration of all his friends who knew the true story.

It was the reversal of one of the worst errors of judgement that I made during my time with Uncle Claude that finally set us on the road to success in Brittany. Some months before, in October 1942, I had reluctantly refused the offer made by Sergeant-Major Lucien Dumais of the famous Canadian regiment, the Fusiliers Mont-Royal, to work an evasion in France. Dumais was another survivor from the Dieppe raid who had returned to England via the PAO organization's Operation Bluebottle II. Tough, wiry and a born leader, he was obviously just what we required. As a French-Canadian he spoke fluent French but the crux was his accent, which my contacts with the Free French assured me would swiftly lead to his arrest. I was not so sure, but felt I was not justified in turning down this warning and so Dumais went to North Africa as a Canadian Army observer in 'Operation Torch', the invasion of Algeria. I never knew what his terms of reference were, but Dumais interpreted them as being an observer of enemy activities and organized his own private army behind the German lines, which work received high praise from the Army Commander.

Returning to England when the campaign was over he approached me again and this time I had no hesitation in accepting his offer and he started training in the summer of 1943. In October he landed in France by Lysander with his wireless operator, Ray Labrosse, who had been Val Williams's radio operator and was now going into France for the third time, to set up Organization Shelburne.

Airey Neave's task of resuscitating Comet was greatly helped by the enthusiastic desire of the survivors who had reached England to return to Belgium. I cannot recall the name of anyone who did not volunteer to face a second time the risk of torture and death, but some had to be turned down as unjustifiable security risks, especially when we had reason to believe they were known to the Germans. The final decision was Uncle Claude's and was usually expressed in the following words, 'I don't care a damn how keen they are or how well they are suited for the work. Nor am I much interested in their fate. All I am thinking of is the danger to the organization when they are arrested, as inevitably they will be. The Germans are not fools.' I have never had a moment's doubt that he was right.

Progress in overcoming the problems of Holland was less easily achieved but in August 1942 Airey Neave was able to recruit a young Dutch girl, Beatrix Terwindt (now Mrs Beatrix Schotte-Terwindt) a KLM air hostess who, on arriving in England, had volunteered to return to Holland. Once again we had to seek the help of SOE, who agreed that she could be parachuted to one of their organizations and on a cold January night in 1943 Trix, as she was code named, jumped through the parachute hatch of a converted Halifax bomber to land 'safely' into the hands of the Abwehr who had organized the reception committee.

There is no need to recount the terrible story of SOE's Dutch Section since it has been the subject of a number of books.* Suffice it to say that the organization in Holland had been penetrated by the Germans in June 1942 and until early 1944 was controlled by them. Trix simply disappeared and we did not learn of the horrors and privations she suffered until she was released from the concentration camp at Mathausen in 1945.

The second attempt, in Holland, when Dignus Kragt, code name Franz Hals, jumped blind in June 1943, was more successful, though he lost his wireless and most of his equipment due to being dropped into the town of Vasser rather than at the selected point in the open country. However, he succeeded in making contact with Comet in Brussels and sent through a number of airmen before the city was liberated.

All this work necessitated constant visits to 138 and 161 Squadrons which, based at Tempsford were respectively responsible for night landings and parachute operations, the former operating from Tangmere during the moon, or operational, periods.

Parachute operations from Tempsford tended to be

* Notably 'Inside SOE' by E. H. Cookridge.

somewhat soulless as one never met the pilot and crew of the Halifax and final arrangements for departure were made by the RAF liaison officer. The agents, or 'Joes' as they were called, were in excellent hands as during the last-minute check-up of their equipment this highly efficient officer could be relied on to produce anything they had forgotten from a revolver to a packet of contraceptives. He also saw to it that they were provided with any stimulant they might require to keep up their morale during the long cold journey to the dropping point, and for the plunge into the darkness at the end of the static line which would open their parachutes when they were clear of the Halifax's slip stream.

Generally I much preferred being the conducting officer for our 'Joes', taking off from Tangmere in a Lysander. Here one could say goodbye beside the aircraft and give the thumbs up sign as it taxied off into the darkness. All the pilots were friends – two, Flight-Lieutenant MacCairns and Squadron-Leader Guy Lockhart being PAO evaders – and there was the added excitement of waiting for the aircraft's return. If the operation was a success the pilot would send the single word 'Joy' over the wireless when he was clear of likely enemy intervention.

To stand at the dispersal control and watch the aircraft come sliding down to the dimly lit flare path was an unforgettable sight. It became a tradition that the reception committee gave the pilot a present, usually brandy or scent for his wife, and sent one for the officer in charge of the operation. It was a strange feeling to drink coffee and brandy with men or women who had only a few hours previously been in enemy-occupied territory and from a bottle that had come from the same place.

There were terrible moments, too, when the aircraft did not return or came back and reported no one at the landing field, or incorrect recognition signals. One evening of horror was when fog closed in and three aircraft crashed on landing, killing two pilots, three returning agents and one of the squadron pilots who was being brought home after being stranded in France the previous moon period.

The relationship between the Lysander pilots and the agents they trained in the technique of night landings was for the most part excellent but occasionally, when things went wrong, there would be furious rows and tempers would be lost. From the RAF side the trouble usually arose when the

field chosen for the operation did not meet their requirements. It might be too small, surrounded by trees, or unsuitable for a variety of other reasons, in which case the operation would be refused, or become abortive if the pilot judged the risk of landing to be too high. From the agent's point of view it was probably the only field in the area in any way suitable and he simply could not understand why the RAF were being difficult.

Another source of friction was the weather which might be all that was desired in the centre of France but a washout at Tangmere as far as flying was concerned. The final decision about whether an operation was 'on' or not rested with the Air Ministry, while the task of soothing an agent who had passed night after night gazing at a cloudless sky and brilliant moon was Airey's and mine. During one abnormally frustrating moon period a pilot wrote a poem in the mess scrap book, more in sorrow than in anger, high-lighting the failings of one of my agents. Alas I have no copy of it, nor of my reply, except that I remember the two first and last lines of the latter ran as follows:

'The moon is blazing in the sky
Will those buggers never fly?'

'The moon is dying in the sky
And still those bastards will not fly.'

The fact that no offence was given or taken says much for the splendid spirit of co-operation that existed between the pilots and the chair-borne officers in London.

Although the Air Ministry never reversed the general principle that Lysanders were not to be used to pick up RAF personnel, they did relax on specific occasions. Also the strict regulations that forbade any liaison between sabotage, intelligence and evasion networks were frequently disregarded, since the men and women in perpetual danger of their freedom took their own decisions. If it was easier to send an RAF evader back by air rather than go through the laborious business of contacting an evasion organization via London, then he was packed into the next Lysander that they had coming over. Equally the security risk of sending over a wireless operator to an organization which had lost theirs, through another network, was infinitely preferable to the long delays of sending him via Spain, during which time the organization might well disintegrate through lack of support. Uncle Claude and his colleagues of the old school might deplore the change but they could not stop it, though Uncle Claude did his best.

As a result evaders were occasionally rescued by night landings and in November 1943 five pilots were brought out in a Hudson aircraft, which was used when the number of 'passengers' was likely to exceed two, and earlier in the year due to the co-operation of one of the intelligence networks, we accomplished by the same means what I always referred to as the swiftest evasion of the war.

Dancing at the Savoy Hotel on a Saturday night a young pilot-officer got engaged to his girl friend and arranged a celebration party for the next Saturday. During a dawn sweep on the following Monday he was shot down but succeeded in parachuting safely, though he landed on a greenhouse in the garden of a large château where he was rescued and hidden by the gardener. The latter was under the impression that the owner, a French count, was collaborating with the Germans and he devoutly hoped that his ritual early morning walk would not take him near the greenhouse. However it did, and the gardener was forced to explain what had caused the large hole which was festooned with pieces of parachute and harness. The count was highly amused and gratified that even his gardener had no idea that he was working for us. By great luck the organization, of which he was a highly placed member, had a Lysander operation laid on for Thursday night, and the pilot celebrated a double event with his fiancée on Saturday.

The slowest evader was a squadron-leader who stayed nearly three years in a flat in Paris. We knew all about him and twice sent someone to dig him out. All was without avail as he refused to move, saying it was far too dangerous to leave the security of the flat and risk possible arrest. He and Paris were liberated together, and no disciplinary action could be taken despite rumours that he and his girl friend were frequent attenders at race meetings to watch his horse run.

In August 1943 Norman Crockatt warned me that I should be required for other duties in connection with 'Operation Overlord', the invasion of Normandy, and in September I handed over command to Airey and started building up Intelligence School Number 9, Western European Area, (not as it was often referred to by so-called witty colleagues 'Workers Employment Association') usually abbreviated to IS 9. I therefore played no direct part in the triumphant evacuation of large numbers of airmen in January 1944, from Brittany to Falmouth in motor torpedo boats manned by the Royal Navy. The collection, assembly and conveyance of these parties to the beaches was organized by Dumais and Labrosse who had gathered up and regrouped what was left of our earlier attempts in that area.

However, as the plans for IS 9's operation were to take over the evasion organizations as soon as the Normandy landing was successful I kept in very close touch with Room 900 which, at long last, had been considerably reinforced. In June 1943 Pat Wyndham Wright had joined us, soon to be followed by Ian Garrow and, as 'D' day approached, Donald Darling from Gibraltar and Brinsley-Ford from MI 9. Better late than never.

The selection and training of personnel for IS 9 meant giving up my lectures on evasion to intelligence officers from all three services and to key personnel taking part in Commando raids. I had much enjoyed this work but never more than when I briefed the crews of the 'Midget' submarines destined to attack the *Tirpitz* in Alten Fjord in Norway. Here I had also to subject them to simulated interrogation on capture. As a reprisal for the rough treatment I meted out to them, Lieutenant-Commander Donald Cameron, who commanded one of these 'X' craft, arranged for me to be 'kidnapped' and to spend two terrifying hours cruising about under water in one of the tiny submarines.

IV Z had had a good run for his money and I felt that I had not let my predecessor down. However, I damned nearly did do this by an act of stupid forgetfulness just before I left. When packing containers to be parachuted into France it was very difficult to assess the exact amount of the various requirements, food, clothing, money, cigarettes, whisky, forged ration and identity cards, and so on, which could be accommodated. Surpluses were returned to store but with money it was not so easy, as once signed for the War Office department concerned would not accept its return. Usually I managed to get it in but, once, the notes were of a smaller denomination than usual and I simply could not find a place for them all. I shoved some £500 in French francs into an envelope, labelled it 'Property of IV Z' with the name and date of the operation, and put it in a drawer in my desk for use next time supplies were sent in.

Months later the money was found and I was as near as no matter court-martialled on the charge of having 'expropriated funds of HM Government for my personal use'. As the Halifax carrying the container had been badly shot up and forced to dump the whole load in the English Channel I found myself wishing I had kept the lot and used it as charged.

My farewell to Uncle Claude was most cordial but I knew he regarded me as a rank amateur who would never become a professional. He had made this only too clear when Baron Jean Greindl, Nemo of Comet, and his colleagues had been condemned to death and Greindl's family had approached the Pope and General Mannerheim, the Swedish President, to intervene on their behalf. Inevitably Uncle Claude learnt of these approaches and was simply furious, not that he did not agree that Nemo had done wonderful work, but solely as a matter of principle. Nemo was, as he saw it, working for the British and it was not for Belgian outsiders to start meddling in other people's business. Further, he felt that when spies, agents, underground workers, patriots, call them what you may, got caught they paid the penalty and any talk of clemency or exchange would be creating a thoroughly undesirable precedent. For once I stood up to him and said that as we could not and would not do anything I did not see why his family should not try and save his life. 'What!' he exploded. 'Do you mean to say that every time an agent gets arrested we should run round to the Germans and Italians saying "he was not as naughty as you thought, please don't shoot him". We should be the laughing stock of Europe.'

In vain I pointed out we had done no such thing and it was the family who were taking action.

'And who put them up to it? You, I suppose. One of your failings is that you are too damned weak,' he replied with a gesture of dismissal. At the bottom of my heart I knew he was right but I just was not tough enough to equate the patriots in the occupied countries, who risked and frequently gave all to work for Britain and her Allies, with the pre-war spies who more often than not betrayed their country for money.

His final words of farewell recalled this incident – 'Your trouble is, Jimmy, that you love your agents.'

IV. ANOTHER DAY

14

Return Journey

The collapse of Italy, in the summer of 1943, had produced a fiasco for our POWs there. They had been ordered by radio not to leave their camps, in anticipation that these would be quickly over-run by the advancing Allied armies. Collection and repatriation would then have been easier 'en bloc' than if the inmates were scattered all over the countryside. But as it happened the Germans had recovered with astonishing rapidity, occupied most of the country and taken over the POW camps before the Allies could do much to intervene.

Even though this calamity was entirely due to a wildly over-optimistic assessment of the speed of the Allied advance, Norman Crockatt felt very deeply that if there had been an escape or evasion unit with the armies it might, under certain circumstances, have helped the camps. There were no POW camps in France, Belgium or Holland, but Crockatt was determined that there would be a unit with the invasion forces destined for Normandy, capable of aiding the several hundred evaders believed to be hidden in those countries. The War Office, together with the US War Department, consequently authorized the raising of IS 9 (WEA). It was composed half of British personnel and equipment, half of American, and had two rôles to perform.

The first was to set up, behind the advancing armies but as far forward as was feasible, centres for collecting, feeding, clothing, interrogating and ultimately repatriating all Allied military personnel who succeeded in escaping or evading from enemy-held territory, no matter by what means, or were over-run when in hiding by the advancing armies. It was not quite such a simple task as it might first appear since the intake could include deserters, traitors and enemy agents, or indeed anyone who initially claimed that he had at some time or other been a member of the armed forces of any of the nations fighting with the Allies.

The second task was to implement the actual rescue of evaders and escapers in enemy-occupied territory, bearing in mind the high possibility that, as Germany's situation deteriorated, Hitler was expected to give the order that all Allied personnel arrested in plain clothes were to be shot regardless of their status.

To carry out these tasks IS 9 was made up of two 'Jeep borne' Interrogation Teams and four Rescue Teams though all these could be subdivided or amalgamated as the situation required. Attached to the rescue teams were French or Dutch-speaking men and women called Retrievers, who, it was hoped, would be passed through enemy lines to pick up and conduct to safety evaders hiding in the immediate area. The unit which was commanded jointly by Lieutenant-Colonel Richard (Dick) Nelson of the US Army and myself, with a small mobile headquarters staff, was formed at Fulmer Hall near Beaconsfield. Airey Neave was appointed Officer-in-Charge of British rescue operations with an American opposite number, Major James Thornton. Airey was to remain in London directing and co-ordinating the work of the organization in the occupied countries only joining us in Normandy when a land link up with them became feasible.

Apart from routine training, the months preceding 'D'-Day were largely passed in getting to know our opposite numbers and formulating a 'modus vivendi' agreeable to all. Despite almost unlimited goodwill on both sides it was not easily accomplished. The time of meals was a constant source of irritation. Americans like to begin the day early with the result that by six in the evening they are ready for their last meal while, in the officers mess at least, the British were beginning to think of the pre-dinner glass of sherry or gin and tonic. Neither parties were willing to change the habits of a lifetime and after the dismal failure of an attempted compromise Dick and I were forced to accept American and

British meal sessions, the last thing we wanted when it was clear that much would depend on everyone working in the utmost harmony.

The Americans' higher rate of pay and use of this asset to attract English girls, which gave rise to the British dictum 'Over paid – over sexed – and over here', caused occasional trouble as did the American retort 'Give me a beer as quick as Tobruk fell.' However, by and large we managed to keep our difficulties under control, even when one of the senior British officers was knocked out cold in a local pub for having told his opposite number that he considered 'President Roosevelt the greatest President of all time.'

In common with most professional soldiers Norman Crockatt, now promoted to brigadier, had a strong dislike of private armies which he knew would be shared by SHAEF – Supreme Headquarters Allied Expeditionary Force – and the commanders of the subordinate fighting units in whose areas IS 9 would be operating. He therefore made it clear that all our plans must be approved by SHAEF or the Army Commander to whom the authority so to do was delegated and that he would not tolerate any action that might give rise to criticism by the higher command.

The work of the Interrogation Teams was relatively straightforward as it was entirely orthodox and meeting an obvious need. That the Germans would endeavour to send through trained agents in the guise of helpers was obvious; 50 evaders would be a small price to pay so that their 'guide' could be safely established behind our lines, perhaps in a safe hiding place and with a radio already prepared. Events were to show how justified these fears were.

The main difficulties lay with the Rescue Teams who would have to work in the closest possible liaison with the evasion organizations, which Airey and I had set up over the years, and any other clandestine organization or resistance army, whether known to us or created as the invasion progressed, harbouring evaders. We were certain that the movement of evaders would become increasingly difficult as the railways were bombed and the Germans forced to move their troops by road, but we were not so sure what instructions to give the organizations.

The simplest solution, the moment the invasion took place, was for all evaders to stay in their individual hiding places until they were over-run by the advancing armies or could be evacuated piecemeal by the Rescue Teams working with the organizations. The main disadvantages of this proposal were twofold. First, the organizations would regard it as a pusillanimous lack of initiative and probably act on their own, with God knows what results. Dumais I knew would be quite capable of arming his evaders and forming a resistance force; and, out of sheer desperation, the others might follow. This was the last thing we wanted as it would have given Hitler an excuse to shoot all the POWs in Germany. Secondly, the strict control of civilian traffic, which was bound to take place, would probably make the distribution of food and clothing to widely scattered evaders well nigh impossible. Hunger and the boredom of inaction would probably drive them to try and reach our lines, alone and in uniform.

Airey then put forward the proposal that the organizations should set up camps in sparsely populated areas, preferably forests, where the evaders could be collected and supplied with food and other necessities, by air, until the Rescue Teams could organize evacuation.

At first sight this appeared to be a hare-brained scheme with enormous hazards for, if anything went wrong, the Germans might well capture a hundred or more evaders at one go. However, there was a good chance that the camps would receive sufficient warning of impending German action to permit the members to scatter and try to reach our lines on their own, when they would be no worse off than if they had been forced out of hiding by lack of food or boredom. Reluctantly Norman Crockatt gave his approval to this scheme, and Airey was instructed to implement his plans for camps in France and Belgium; but I could see that Crockatt thought we were well on the road to setting up private armies.

Having received the 'go ahead' Airey wasted no time and

offered the job of organizing the first camp to Baron Jean de Blommaert, a brilliant and courageous Belgian officer who had just returned to England via Spain after a tour of duty with Comet. Airey had been forced to recall him early in 1944 as he had been betrayed to the Gestapo in Paris. Despite this he enthusiastically agreed to go back to set up a camp in the Forêt de Fréteval some 25 kilometres south of Châteaudun on the Chartres-Tours road. Plans were agreed to parachute in all the supplies he might need – food, clothing, tents, bedding, and so on – and in early April he and his radio operator 'jumped blind', to land safely near Issoudun in France and start their work.

Dumais was instructed to set up a camp in Brittany and tentative proposals were made for another in the Belgian Ardennes.

Such were the plans when IS 9 went to war with the Allied Expeditionary Force to Normandy in June 1944. As befitted staff officers Dick and I flew over in a Dakota which only a few days earlier had been dropping parachute troops but was now filled with senior American officers. In the hopes of some rabbit and pigeon shooting, possibly later partridges and pheasants, I had my ·20 bore shotgun with me in a brown canvas cover which I could see aroused the curiosity of an American major sitting next to me. As we were coming in to land he could contain himself no longer.

'Might I enquire, colonel, what you have in that case?'

'Yes,' I replied, 'my shotgun. I hope to get a little rabbit shooting.'

There was a short silence before he voiced his horrified indignation.

'Do you mean to say, colonel, that you have brought your scatter gun to do some hunting when our boys are dying on the beaches?'

There did not seem much to say so I kept silent.

'General,' he continued, addressing his companion, 'Don't you think this is going a little too far?'

The general gave me a slow smile. 'Major,' he retorted,

'in my view you are guilty of a very grave breach of security. I have reason to believe that the colonel is carrying the prototype of a new secret British weapon.'

As I was walking across the earthen runway to the reception tent the general came over to me and said, 'I'm mighty fond of rabbit myself. Good hunting!'

It was exhilarating to be back in France, as near as no matter four years after I had failed to get out via Dunkirk. But it was also strange for these were not the rolling plains of the north, which I had got to know so well, but more the kind of countryside I associated with Essex and Suffolk. I found the presence of the Americans unsettling, quite unjustifiably and illogically feeling that if anyone was going to liberate France it should be us, who had been chased out in 1940, and not our cousins from across the sea who had played no part in the tragedy. However, they were fun to work with and there were rarely any dull moments as was shown when one day a frantic American officer came into our headquarters and asked to use our field telephone.

I checked his identity and asked why. He hesitated, 'I don't think that's really your business, Colonel.'

'Maybe not but all the same I would like to know,' I replied.

'Well, if you insist I'll tell you. I have lost two tons of doughnuts and I want to find out if they are on your beaches.'

Doughnuts versus scatter guns I thought.

'Have they got jam in the middle,' I enquired. He was not amused.

A study of the order of battle maps on the British front indicated that the chances of any of our 'Retrievers' passing through the German lines without detection were very slim. I was finally convinced it would just be sending them to their deaths when I called on a French friend of mine who had been much decorated for his services to the Allied cause. His home and land had been liberated early on and as a further mark of appreciation his immediate return had been arranged. I anticipated a convivial reunion and was shocked when, as I was shown into his study, he looked up from his desk where he was writing and said, 'Get out, you bastard. I loathe all you and your friends stand for.'

I knew him well enough to reply, 'What the hell do you mean?'

'Exactly what I said. I suppose you have just come to commiserate.'

'I don't know what you are talking about.' He pulled himself together. 'You have heard nothing?'

'No,' I replied. 'I have only come to have that drink you promised me.'

There was a long silence before he spoke.

'I came back and as I expected I found my house requisitioned as a brigade headquarters which naturally gave me pleasure and I did my best to entertain the officers and make life as comfortable as possible for all concerned. I am a widower, as you know, but my only daughter was, of course, a great help; and yet I was appalled when she told me that an intelligence officer had asked her whether she would be prepared to cross over the lines and bring back all the information she could obtain about the Germans.

'I instantly contacted the officer and explained that she was all I had left and requested that, if only in view of my services to your country, the proposal be dropped. He was charming and immediately promised to take no further action. Nevertheless a day later she was sent over and this morning I learnt she had immediately been recognized, arrested and shot.

'I want that young officer court-martialled and, I hope, shot. All I have achieved so far is to knock out a senior officer who came to tell me no military offence had been committed as my daughter went of her own free will.'

I promised my help but all I achieved was a sharp reprimand from higher authority and instructions to mind my own business.

The lines in front of the Americans were more lightly held, but after a reconnaissance Dick and I agreed that even there the risks simply did not justify sending over a Retriever. It was all very frustrating but at least we were acceding to

Airey's urgent plea to hold all the Rescue Teams to liberate the camp in the Forêt de Frèteval, and the others near Rennes in Brittany, after a breakthrough took place. Before this occurred one interrogation unit was put to the first test.

Early one morning in July we were informed that a small party of evaders had landed behind the American lines, which now reached to the southern coast of the Normandy peninsula. Dick and I raced over to the Third American Army's headquarters where they were being interrogated for any information about local enemy activities.

The evaders were all American airmen and, other than the name of the fishing village from which they had sailed, they initially gave little information of interest and none about enemy activities. They had been hidden by helpers in farms, no names given, led down to the beach after dark, put into a small lobster boat with an engine and instructed to row out to sea until they were well clear of the coast. After that it was up to them to keep going in a north-westerly direction, parallel to the coast until they were past the battleline. They had some difficulty in identifying this, nevertheless dawn had found them safe and sound, well behind the American lines. But, and here came an unexpected crunch, if white paper could be dropped over an area some ten kilometres square, three kilometres inland from the village, between one and two o'clock in the afternoon, a second boatload would be despatched that night.

I glanced at my watch – it was already eight o'clock in the morning. I had visions of the time it had taken to arrange for any air operation, even dropping an agent blind, of the seemingly endless approvals that had to be given, of the questions about the value of the operation, of the availability of aircraft and priorities, of the weather and many other factors.

A pity, but just not on, I thought. I did not know my Americans.

'Waal,' broke in the American intelligence colonel. 'I don't see any real problems. You had better come and see the general. He likes to know what is going on.'

General George Patton's welcome was, to put it mildly, encouraging.

'I understand, colonel, you are pretty well up in this escaping game. Been through it yourself I'm told.' I nodded.

'Just give me your views and tell me what you advise. I think we might be able to help.'

My views at that moment were entirely swamped by admiration of him and the staff officers with him. Immaculately turned out, this was not the two-gun cowboy 'blood and guts' general – 'Your guts, our blood' as gossip had it one American sergeant had said – that I had visualized. This was a man of cold efficiency and awareness that took me by surprise. I pulled myself together.

'This, sir, is a local effort. It isn't the work of one of our organizations or they would have sent some form of recognition message. But from the evasion side I would welcome your agreement to their request.'

He smiled and turned to the colonel. 'OK Bert, get moving. Have the paper printed with a propaganda message. Arrange to have more dropped in adjacent areas from three to six o'clock. We don't want the Krauts to think we are just interested in one village.' He looked at me. 'We try to do our best, colonel.' He walked back to his tent as I saluted and muttered my thanks.

'A kinda paper snowstorm,' said one of the Americans from the second party when it safely reached the Allied beach-head. 'The French were delighted but seemed sorta surprised.' It was pleasant not to be the only one.

Dick and I considered the possibility of using the two lobster boats, which had rescued the Americans, to send in Retrievers, even though IS 9 had no naval experience – waterborne operations had not even been considered let alone discussed. As it was, events overtook us and the Allied armies broke out of the bridgehead, 21st Army Group making for the Seine, the Channel ports and ultimately Brussels and Antwerp, while the Americans, with the Free French Division under General Leclerc, made for Paris, Rheims, Sedan and Liège.

Airey had taken over command of the British Rescue Teams in Bayeux when it was evident that the breakout was imminent, leaving Donald Darling in charge in London. Dick generously put the American Rescue Teams at Airey's disposal, since he had reported that Blommaert had nearly 150 men hidden in the Forêt de Fréteval and Dumais around

100 men near Rennes. The operation to liberate these two 'camps' had been code-named 'Marathon' and early in August Airey launched and led it. Before he left we toasted the success of the operation in a glass of Calvados.

Its success has been brilliantly described in Airey's book 'Saturday at MI 9' and 'Mission Marathon' by the famous French Resistance hero Colonel Remy. Although the evaders in Rennes had dispersed before the teams arrived most of them were picked up by the advancing Americans and handed over to Dick's Interrogation Teams. In the Forêt de Fréteval the men had been hidden over six weeks, relying almost entirely on parachute drops for supplies, and evacuation was only achieved a few hours before the Germans sent fighting patrols into the forest. Their rescue was a very close run thing and a remarkable achievement, which reflected the highest credit on Jean de Blommaert who was awarded an immediate DSO.

With all the Rescue Teams committed and the Interrogation Teams moving forward behind the British and American armies IS 9 headquarters was like a nanny whose children have gone off to school. Worse still, all the teams were far beyond the range of the wirelesses on the jeeps even if they had had the time and inclination, which was highly doubtful, to inform nanny what they were up to. That headquarters must move was obvious, but where to? The advance was over a far wider area and at a much greater speed than we, and I think to be fair, most people had envisaged.

Dick and I had appreciated that if the advance was on a very wide front it would no longer be possible to exercise control from one headquarters. We had agreed that in this eventuality we would operate separately with his headquarters behind the American armies and mine behind the British. However, I was loath to divide headquarters as long as the British teams were operating in the American zone and they were now on the right flank of the southernmost American Army. For about six days we sat awaiting some stabilization of the front, the tension mounting hour by hour as the advance continued. I knew only too well that the general feeling was that 'the war has gone on too long for the old boy, he is just waffling – cannot take a decision'.

The decision was taken out of my hands one evening when a Retriever – we had gathered most of them at headquarters – rushed in from a local café with the news that Paris had been liberated. It was not true, but enough to push Dick to force me to act.

'I don't care a damn what you want. I am going to Paris tomorrow,' he announced.

Dick, as a young officer with the American Expeditionary Force in 1918, had frequently been on leave in Paris and I knew he longed to return. However I never thought he would be quite so outspoken. Apart from a brief message from Blommaert's radio, which had come via Room 900, announcing the success of 'Marathon' we had no idea of the whereabouts of the Rescue Teams. However there were a number of evaders hidden in Paris and it was also the headquarters of Dumais, so it was a fair guess that Airey and at least one of the teams would make for the capital.

Secretly delighted that Dick was so adamant I replied, 'OK. Let's go.'

For the first few miles there were relatively little signs of war but as we neared the area of Falaise we ran through all the sordid aftermath of victory and defeat and my thoughts turned back inevitably to the long road from Brussels to Dunkirk. This time, however, the burnt-out lorries, smashed guns and all the debris that littered the roads and fields were grey in colour; only the bloated evil-smelling horses and cows were similar to last time. For them it did not really matter which side won, they just got caught up in a battle and that was that. Not, I mused, that there was much we ourselves could do about it either.

However, the glorious August morning and the exhilaration of advancing soon banished melancholic memories, as hour after hour we drove through the rolling countryside with only the odd reminder that the war was not over. Three times we were stopped by small groups of German soldiers trying desperately to find someone who would accept their surrender. But with the jeeps loaded to capacity with food, petrol and some Retrievers, whom the Americans had recruited in Normandy, there was little we could do except direct them down the road in the hope that ultimately they would be picked up. Occasionally we heard distant machine-gun fire and once the familiar 'phut phut' of bullets passing overhead, indicating we might be the target. As no one else seemed to have noticed them I said nothing, consoling myself with the thought that at the speed we were driving the chances of being hit were small.

It was early in the evening when we decided to stop for the night in a small village near Rambouillet where, to my immense delight and, I may add, relief, we met up with Airey now in command of what was indubitably a private army. After making sure that all the evaders from 'Marathon' were safely en route to the Interrogation Teams he had ordered the Rescue Teams, accompanied by a heterogeneous collection of helpers and hangers on, to make for Paris.

Moving next day, 24 August, to Rambouillet itself, we planned to send into Paris all the Rescue Teams to search for evaders and, perhaps now more important, to try and save our numerous helpers known to be hiding there from any last minute reprisals by the Germans.

General Leclerc, commanding the Free French Division to which the Americans had, in their generosity, granted the honour of recapturing Paris, had given orders that no ancillary units were to enter until the Germans had been driven out. As a result the grounds of the great château at Rambouillet were packed with a wide assortment of intelligence units, private armies, press and radio men, all with only one immediate ambition – that of entering liberated Paris.

All through the long hot morning the tension rose as the wildest rumours circulated – 'The Germans are burning Paris' – 'General Leclerc has been driven back' – 'General Leclerc has taken the city and is advancing through the northern suburbs to Le Bourget' – 'The Germans are killing all civilians'. Finally in the late afternoon a despatch rider arrived with the news that the general had established his headquarters in the Metro station of Montparnasse, and that the city was rapidly being cleared.

This information proved too much for a group of Frenchmen whose jeeps and trucks were parked just inside the main gates, which were open though guarded by sentries with orders to shoot if anyone tried to leave. Shouting to the despatch rider to lead the way they charged for the gates.

Dick had used his influence, after all he was an American colonel in an American area, to park our jeeps a few yards behind theirs and I gave the order to go, calling to Dick who was standing a few feet away talking to the senior American officer. I knew the sentries would not shoot, they just looked on not even raising their rifles and as we roared through the gates I caught sight of the American officer raising both arms over his head as if pleading for some Divine intervention.

The French drove like maniacs and we had a hard job to keep up but as dusk fell we entered the outskirts of Paris and they were forced to slow down, to circumvent road blocks and mine craters. We had tied a large Union Jack and a Stars and Stripes to either side of the jeep's windscreen and we now lit these with torches in the vague hope it would help those behind to keep contact. It never occurred to us till afterwards that we also made an excellent target for any snipers! In the blackout I had no idea where we were until we crossed the Seine and turned left, when I recognized the Tuileries Gardens on our right. As we were about to enter the Place de la Concorde I shouted to Dick to stop.

'What the hell for,' he replied.

'If you don't I shall flood the jeep,' I said as I jumped out and relieved nature with the convoy thundering by.

'Now you have done it,' he grumbled. 'We shall never find them in the dark.'

'I have no intention of following. We are going where I know there will be a bottle of champagne on ice.'

The Place de la Concorde was lit up by burning lorries but we had no difficulty in going through it, unlike the Rue Royale which was almost completely blocked by a barricade and two disabled tanks, one blazing merrily. At last, however, we reached the Madeleine and turned left up the Boulevard Malesherbes, stopping at Number Twelve. There was a dim light in the concierge's room but I was slightly surprised when she let us in merely remarking, 'The family are at home.'

As I climbed the stairs my mind went back four years to

my last visit as a dirty dishevelled evader seeking help and a change of pus-soaked stinking bandages and I wondered how I could say 'Thank you'. 'Who is there,' a voice said in French as I knocked, but before I could answer another voice said, 'I will bet it is Jimmy. Get the champagne out.' The Droin family seemed to think the liberation of Paris was sufficient 'thank you', even justifying a second bottle of champagne. I was not so sure.

Due to Dick's guilty conscience at leaving the other officers and men to fend for themselves, and the intermittent firing through the night of a heavy machine gun on a nearby roof, at whom or by whom we never discovered, we were out at dawn to search for the unit. It was a glorious morning as we drove up the Champs Elyées already lined three deep with Parisians anxious not to miss any of the fun. We were the only vehicle on the move and I suppose the crowd seeing the flags mistook us for a brace of generals – anyhow we were cheered the whole way up, round the Arc de Triomphe, and back down to the Place de la Concorde. It was a splendid start to an unforgettable day.

We had no difficulty in finding our lost sheep who had bivouacked alongside the Champs Elysées or of locating Airey who had set up his headquarters in the Hôtel Windsor – now the Windsor Reynolds. He, and his private army were fully engaged in collecting evaders, contacting helpers and routing out suspected snipers and German collaborators. We left them at it and, after requisitioning the Hôtel Meurice in the Rue de Rivoli as our headquarters, went off to pick up the eldest son of 'my family' and his wife to view General de Gaulle's triumphant procession from the Arc de Triomphe to the Cathedral of Notre Dame.

During the next few days there were moments when Dick, Airey and I wondered if we would ever get all our problems sorted out and cursed the letters 'IS' in the unit's name since the French instantly assumed they stood for Intelligence Service and that we were the representatives of this renowned British organization. Useless to make clear our real rôle to the endless stream of French men and women who came with requests for awards, food, cigarettes, money or petrol, for services rendered – they merely dismissed our explanation as a clever cover story and became more insistent in their demands. We were also expected to search for collaborators, arrest suspects on the flimsiest of evidence and shoot out of hand those who admitted they had performed some service, however menial, for the enemy. Then there were the seemingly endless invitations to celebration lunches and dinners – refusal to attend caused affront to helpers, genuine or otherwise.

It was therefore with considerable relief that I received a high priority message from Norman Crockatt ordering me to report to Beaconsfield in person and without delay. Before leaving I co-ordinated plans with Dick and Airey for the unit's part in the liberation of Brussels, which was obviously imminent. No success had been achieved in setting up evasion camps in the Ardennes, so it was decided to instruct Comet to send all the evaders to the Hôtel Metropole in Brussels as soon as it was safe so to do.

Airey was to lead the Rescue Teams there and I was to follow with the British headquarters, leaving Dick in Paris. Once again the latter placed his Rescue Teams at Airey's disposal reasoning, correctly as it proved, that there were more American evaders in Belgium than in eastern France.

Back at Beaconsfield Norman Crockatt, as always, was most helpful and immediately arranged to set up an Awards Bureau in Paris under the command of Donald Darling, to check the bona fides of all 'helpers' – many of whom were, of course, unknown to us – and to make recommendations for awards and compensation. It was an appointment I would very much have liked to have had as I felt deeply my responsibility of ensuring that all the men and women who had worked for the organizations received full recognition for their courage and self sacrifice. I pleaded my case but Norman Crockatt was adamant.

'First, Jimmy, I am not changing horses in mid stream. Secondly, it is just possible that IS 9 may have a task to perform in Germany when it will be essential that it is commanded by an officer with fighting experience.'

In vain I pointed out that my fighting had consisted almost entirely of running away and that there were hundreds of officers with experience of advancing rather than retreating.

'Get up to Brussels as soon as you can and stand by for an order to meet me in Paris as soon as SHAEF is established at Versailles,' was his only comment.

All went well with our advance until we reached the outskirts of Mons which had just been liberated and we ran short of petrol. My efforts to obtain some resulted in an amusing interview with the general commanding the American division in the area, who was in very good spirits.

'What army do you belong to?' he asked. When I gave him the required information I could understand the reason for his enquiry as I was wearing service dress – Sam Browne and all.

'Ah,' he drawled 'Guards, different as usual from everybody else. Waal, this is certainly your stomping ground. What can I do for you?' I made my request.

'Out of gas,' he replied. 'Now isn't that just dandy. Well, so am I and my division. In fact my staff tell me we are five miles ahead of my fighting troops instead of ten miles behind as we should be. However, we have just captured a couple of hundred Krauts. Must be a record for a divisional headquarters. How much gas do you require?'

'Twenty-five gallons should be enough to get through to Brussels, sir.'

'OK. You can have it since that amount won't help us much.'

Mons was in an uproar and we had a great deal of difficulty in getting through the jubilant crowds to the Mairie, where some police were having violent arguments with a group of large and very menacing-looking Belgians, whose arm bands indicated they were members of the underground 'White Army' as it was called. Lying on the ground behind the police was a girl whose whole body was heaving with sobs.

The senior policeman saluted. 'These gentlemen say this

girl was a collaborator, who worked in the German Kommandantur and was the commandant's mistress. They want to take her away for punishment. She says she was working for the British, stealing German ration cards and passes to help pilots to go to Spain,' he said.

We had strict orders not to interfere in 'local politics' and several times I had watched with revulsion women and young girls having their heads shaved, and suffering other indignities, as collaborators, without being given a chance to refute the charges. However, here there was a good possibility that her story was true but also that she had been the commandant's mistress. It would not be the first time a woman had used her body to gain the confidence of the Germans in order to help the Allies.

'I believe her story,' I said to the policeman. 'So do I, but that is not going to help much with this lot,' he replied, glancing at the crowd who were in an ugly mood. 'We must get her into the barracks there,' he continued, pointing to a building some 100 yards away. 'They will never break down those doors.'

My appeal to the men of the 'White Army' was ill-received, not only were they balked of their prey, and to be fair they were convinced of her guilt, but also they were being made to look fools in the eyes of the crowd. However, it did give the policeman time to get the girl on her feet and explain our intention to her.

'If you will get her to the barracks, sir, as fast as possible, your men and mine will try and hold back the crowd.'

It was, I think, the speed of our departure that took the crowd by surprise. Commandant's mistress or not she was in excellent training and we all just made it, though as the policeman shouted above the yells of the crowd and the banging of the rifle butts on the stout doors, 'We have had good luck.' Her story proved to be true but it was a long time before she dared return to Mons.

Brussels had been liberated some three days before we arrived there and the celebrations were dying down, except in the Hôtel Metropole which had proved an excellent collecting centre for some 40 evaders, largely American airmen and their helpers. An American in uniform, who announced himself as a colonel from SHAEF, had authorized 'drinks on the US Government' and by the time I got there the bill was nearing the £200 mark. The hotel manager was no fool and appreciated, as I did when I saw it, that the written authorization for this expenditure was virtually valueless, being on hotel paper, undated and with a signature that looked suspiciously like 'Charlie Chaplin'! To ensure that he would receive more genuine evidence that payment would be forthcoming he had locked one of the Rescue Team officers in his room as a hostage, where he was raising hell.

It was comparatively easy to stop the flow of champagne but obtaining the release of the hostage necessitated pledging SHAEF or myself to pay. The American 'Colonel' was never identified – I think he was an exuberant war correspondent with a sense of humour – and there were a series of appalling rows before SHAEF finally paid up.

It was while I was placating the American evaders (who were vociferous in their complaints of what they considered very high-handed action by a British officer in closing down a good party), the helpers and hangers-on, the hotel manager and the Rescue Team officer, that an RAF sergeant evader asked if he could have a word with me in private.

We strolled over to a vacant table and called for two beers.

'Yes, sergeant,' I queried, 'what can I do for you.'

'Don't look around, please, sir,' he whispered. 'But that man in plain clothes over there is a German officer.' I choked over my beer. 'How the hell do you know?'

'Well, sir, I was a prisoner for a short time and he twice interrogated me.'

'Are you sure?'

'Certain, sir. Look out, he is getting up and walking out.'

'We will follow him,' I said. The street outside was full of people and it was obvious that he would be quickly lost in the crowd.

I came close up behind him, pulled out my loaded revolver and stuck the muzzle in his back.

'Stop,' I hissed nervously, 'you are a German spy.'

'No, no, no,' he quavered, 'I am a German officer trying to escape and I will prove it,' he continued, pulling a sheaf of papers out of his pocket only to drop them on the pavement at my feet.

It all seemed so natural at the time. 'Here, hold this,' I said, passing him my revolver and stooping down to pick up the papers with my one hand. A glance at the top one, his military identity card with a photograph was sufficient confirmation of his statement. I handed back his papers and received my revolver in return.

'The crowd will kill me if they learn who I am,' he muttered, glancing at one or two passers by who had stopped and were eyeing us with curiosity. Yes, I thought, they probably will but it is nothing to what Norman Crockatt will do to me when he learns I have handed an evading German officer a loaded revolver to help him on his way.

'You will be perfectly all right if you come along quietly with me,' I assured him. And so it proved as I handed him over to the nearest Military Police headquarters.

15

One More River to Cross

Our experiences in Paris stood us in good stead and it was not long before we had the situation in Brussels well in hand and the unit regrouped and ready to tackle whatever problems the winter might bring.

The regrouping was not achieved without a major internal row. Billets were very short and it was only after a lot of official and unofficial hard work that I was allocated a superb and luxurious 'Maison de Tolérance' for the use of the British Interrogation Team. Madame and the girls had, of course, been turned out and to my way of thinking it was just what we wanted. The small bar room made an excellent office for interrogations, while the café, the kitchen and another downstairs room were all that was required for a comfortable officers and other ranks mess and there was a surplus of beds for the evaders.

I knew the officer in command of the team was a Roman Catholic with deep religious feelings; I had already had trouble in Normandy when he had ordered one of his men to marry the girl the latter had seduced. But I was completely taken aback when he said the accommodation was not suitable since it was entirely unacceptable that he, his officers, men and evaders should have to sleep in beds recently occupied by girls of easy virtue. I pleaded, reasoned and cajoled without any success and finally gave him a direct order which he refused to obey. It was a farcical situation. He had fought with gallantry in the First World War – being wounded and taken prisoner – and to send him back in disgrace to England to face a possible court martial would do nobody any good.

There was nothing for it but to give in with the best grace I could summon and tell him to find his own billets. He won all along the line as he installed himself in a small comfortable hotel in Montaigu, close by the world-famous Basilique, passing a happy winter in the company of the monks and priests and sending out his interrogators by jeep to wherever they were required.

Meanwhile Airey Neave had sent one of our Rescue Teams to Antwerp and taken the rest northwards to Louvain and Holland in the hope of repeating the Brussels' success in Eindhoven and other Dutch cities. However, this was not to be as German resistance stiffened after the liberation of Belgium and it became evident that the war would probably go on throughout the winter of 1944. Furthermore the Rhine now lay across the path of our advance. My interest in the river dated back to the early days as a POW when I had asked a burly taciturn wounded sailor how he came to be in France. 'Mining the Rhine' was his astonishing reply. If it was big enough to justify mining it was going to be a fairly substantial defence line and a formidable obstacle for evaders.

Although Antwerp had fallen virtually without a shot being fired the German rearguard fought back strongly in the northern suburbs. In this fighting the Rescue Teams had given some help to the Belgian resistance army and when the Germans withdrew one of its members, a Dutchman, had expressed a wish to join IS 9. His offer was accepted, largely because we were very short of Dutch Retrievers, and he was given the code name of 'King Kong', a tribute to his physical size and gorilla-like appearance. Christiaan Antonius Lindemans was a boastful extrovert whom I disliked but that did not necessarily mean he would make a bad Retriever.

I reported his attachment to the Dutch authorities with 21st Army Group who immediately requested his transfer to their headquarters, for a period of rest and interrogation. I had perforce to acquiesce but a few days later he was back with us complaining about the boredom and lack of activity in the life at the Dutch headquarters which was not suited to a man with his talents. He asked to be sent through the lines near Eindhoven to collect evaders he was sure would be hiding with his resistance friends in that area.

The relevant Army Group intelligence section had already

checked King Kong's credentials and had reported 'nothing known against'. The Dutch army commander agreed to the mission but the head of their counter espionage section, Colonel Orestio Pinto, sent me a private warning that he believed it possible that King Kong was a German agent though as yet he had no proof.

For King Kong's subsequent action I must accept responsibility. Desperately anxious to establish land contact with the Dutch Resistance it never occurred to me that Colonel Pinto's suspicions might not have been passed to 21st Army Group, or if they had, that they might have been overlooked. In requesting a final security clearance I made no reference to these suspicions and received authorization for the mission to go ahead. Accompanied by a local guide King Kong successfully passed through the German lines. A week later he was back without any evaders, and claimed that his companion had been shot by a German patrol during the return journey.

On the liberation of Eindhoven he was named as a traitor of long standing by the underground there, the report adding, for good measure, that he had been seen going into the German headquarters a few days earlier. Arrested, he broke easily under interrrogation, admitting that after he had shot his companion he had reported to his German masters. Suffering from a nervous breakdown he was put in a prison hospital where he succeeded in committing suicide before his interrogation was complete.

It was the day after King Kong returned to us that the three great airborne landings in Holland were launched. The first two were successful when the 101st US Airborne Division captured the bridges at Grave over the river Maas, and at Nijmegen over the Waal. But the British 1st Airborne Division which landed at Arnhem – Operation 'Market Garden' – with the task of seizing the bridge over the Neder Rhine met entirely unexpected opposition and after a week of desperate fighting was overwhelmed. A considerable number of survivors were, however, able to evade capture and taken into hiding by the Dutch.

Did King Kong betray operation 'Market Garden'? If so where did he get the information from and, above all, who was the fool who sent him back to the Germans? These were the questions asked and the answer to the last was not difficult to find. I was officially exonerated due to the security clearances I had received from 21st Army Group but nonetheless felt I should have taken Colonel Pinto's warning more

seriously even though it was unsubstantiated. The answers to the first two questions were not so easily obtained and all I could say was that no one in IS 9 had any knowledge of the plans for operation 'Market Garden'.

Rightly and properly exhaustive enquiries were made into the activities of King Kong during the time he was behind Allied lines and the indications were that he had been in contact with individuals who knew of plans to use the British and American airborne divisions but that he could not possibly have discovered the actual dropping zones.

With this we had to be content until months later I was informed that the relevant German intelligence documents had been captured together with one of the officers who had 'worked' King Kong. The latter had reported plans for airborne landings but said that the targets were first Eindhoven and later possibly the bridges across the river Maas at Venlo and Roermond.

The German officer stated that King Kong was a very minor agent whose task it was to identify Allied units in the immediate battle area and they had not believed his report, putting it down to his boastful imagination. In fact, he added, King Kong had been sent away with a flea in his ear and told to adhere in future to his instructions. The officer was absolutely emphatic that all the airborne landings came as a complete surprise and the German evaluation of the written report of King Kong's interrogation confirmed that it had been dismissed as of no import. Nonetheless it was a narrow escape. Given a little more imaginative thinking about King Kong's information the Germans would almost certainly have ensured the complete failure of all three airborne landings before the parachute troops and gliders had even left England.

I was under no illusion that there was anybody more capable of organizing the rescue of the survivors of the Arnhem landing than Airey, who in fact was already in touch with the Dutch Resistance and knew where many of these evaders were hidden. I therefore had no difficulty in resisting the temptation to interfere, merely warning him to ensure we did not recruit another King Kong.

It was obviously going to be a tricky operation – code named 'Pegasus' – as the men had to be got over the Rhine, in occupied territory, with all the bridges guarded to forestall any such eventuality, and then the Waal which was the 'no man's water' between the enemy and our front line troops. Speed was essential and therefore Airey requested permission to send over a young British officer from the Rescue Teams and an American paratroop sergeant to work with the Dutch Resistance in setting up a chain of guides and to co-ordinate the crossing of the Waal in rubber boats. Both had volunteered but even then we knew we were on very dangerous ground. I only agreed to the mission, code name 'Harrier', when the British officer had personally promised both Airey and myself that under no circumstances would either of them ever put on civilian clothes or leave the 'safe' house during daylight hours.

On 14 October they arrived in the 'safe' house at Tiel but on 19 October a lone Dutchman rowed back across the Waal by night and reported that both the officer and the sergeant had been seen walking around in daylight in plain clothes, had been arrested by the Germans that night while in bed, and shot. The last piece of information proved incorrect. The Germans had found their uniforms and it was just possible they would accept the men's cover story that they were evaders from Arnhem and treat them as POWs, but the family hiding them were shot out of hand and their house burned to the ground. Rank disobedience and flagrant breaking of a promise had cost the lives of a brave Dutchman and his wife and there was naturally much bitterness within the Dutch Resistance.

We spent little time on discussing the pros and cons of rescue operations. Airey would give me the background and all the information necessary to obtain the 'go ahead' from 21st Army Group Operation Headquarters. It was rare that they had any comments though in the case of Pegasus* the clearance was accompanied by the message 'The Field Marshal hopes this will not be an Imperial Balls Up as if it is it will be the last IS 9 will make under its present Commanding Officer.'

The most serious consequences of the Harrier disaster was that it alerted the Germans to the evasion activities going on and vastly increased the risk of a successful evacuation of

* Code name 'Tokay' for 21st Army Group. All operations were re-coded when details were disseminated outside IS 9. We trusted no one.

what was now known to be between 200 and 300 officers and men. By sheer drive and determination Airey was able to make good the damage and on 22 October 'Operation Pegasus' was in every sense 'launched' and 138 men were safely conveyed back across the Waal under cover of darkness in boats rowed by Americans of the US 101st Airborne Division* helped by men from the Royal Canadian Engineers.

Meanwhile things were not going well with the 'Chairborne' side of IS 9. I had informed Norman Crockatt of the outcome of the Harrier mission, he had commiserated with me and accepted my report in full. All might have been well had not one of my senior officers, who was a friend of Harrier's father informed the latter that his son had been shot by the Gestapo while working in civilian clothes behind enemy lines. It was an act of gross disloyalty, since he neither informed Norman Crockatt, with whom he had been working since the outbreak of war, nor me of his action, and also a serious breach of security. Without checking the veracity of the information or the circumstances, the father referred the whole affair to his Member of Parliament and the fat was well in the fire. On security grounds Norman Crockatt was able to stop a Question in the House but there was a long time-wasting enquiry which engendered much recrimination before Airey and I were fully cleared, just prior to Harrier being reported safe and sound in a POW camp. The American sergeant was never heard of again.

As evaders from Pegasus reported that there were at least another 150 Arnhem survivors yet to be evacuated, a repeat was highly desirable. However, an appalling security break in London necessitated a long interchange of views between Norman Crockatt, Airey and myself. The facts were simple and their effects not difficult to assess.

One of our war correspondents had got wind of Pegasus; it was their job to smell out news and they were very good at it, and had somehow contrived to fly back to England with a party of the senior evading officers. Removing, or covering up his press badges, he had convinced them he was

* See Pegasus I and II – 'Saturday at MI 9'.

an intelligence officer fully 'au fait' with the operation and they had talked freely of their experiences. His article, which in some mysterious way by-passed the censors, was published in one London and several provincial newspapers and was, as near as no matter, a re-write of Airey's 'Top Secret' report. Through the neutral capitals, Dublin, Lisbon or Stockholm, the Germans received copies of all British newspapers in a matter of days.

There was one small consolation, we had not got to waste time on trying to guess how much the Germans knew about Pegasus. They had been handed all the facts on a plate and the increase of house to house searches and of patrols along the river banks indicated that they had correctly evaluated the information. The time that this large number of evaders could safely remain hidden and fed, however, was rapidly running out and it was decided to implement Pegasus II early in November.

Where possible, routes and crossing places were changed. But about 120 men were ambushed by the Germans as they moved stealthily by night along the Arnhem–Ede road. Several were killed or wounded, the rest forced to scatter, most of whom were subsequently caught and only three were rescued. It was a matter of general regret that the war correspondent was not among the captured; his report would have been studied by us with the same interest as the Germans had undoubtedly evinced in his earlier one.

It was a disaster, but the fact that 21st Army Group's comments were in the form of commiseration and encouragement to continue was ample evidence that they appreciated the splendid courage and determination displayed by the Dutch Resistance, the men of the American Airborne Division, who again manned the boats, the Royal Canadian Engineers and the Rescue Teams.

The bitter winter of 1944 with deep snow and treacherous ice covering the dykes, and sometimes extending into the rivers, put a stop to evasion in Holland and the time was passed training for further river-borne operations and building up radio communications with the Dutch Resistance.

Visiting the Rescue Teams which were occupying a series of isolated farms or houses in the small villages from Nijmegen along the Waal to the Biesbosch was always an exhilarating if occasionally nerve-racking experience. Both sides indulged in considerable routine shelling and sent patrols across the river. One commander of a small section assured me that they and the Germans drew their rations of tea, coffee, flour, tinned milk and meat, from a British dump which had been established earlier in the year and then left unguarded. 'We always go in the morning,' he commented, 'and the Germans in the afternoon. I don't think the poor bastards get much else to eat.'

It was with one of the teams that I passed the last New Year's Eve of the war. It was a hilarious and memorable evening, oysters from the beds on the island of Tholen where our small marine training school had been established, partridges I had shot, champagne, all spiced with the knowledge that only the Waal lay between us and the Germans who, dead on midnight, treated us to the finest firework display directed towards the heavens, not us, that I have ever watched. Much as I detested all the Germans then stood for I was deeply impressed and moved by the message of arrogance, pride, and courage, in certain defeat, which the bursting anti-aircraft shells, the stream of tracer bullets, the flares, and cascades of stars from the rockets, were so clearly sending us. As we exchanged 'Happy New Year' wishes in the cosy farm kitchen and drank a glass of hot punch, I found myself thinking, 'we have not seen the last of you yet, you devils', and I was not pondering on the year ahead but the 'fifties, 'sixties and 'seventies.

Thus IS 9 plunged into the year which was to see the end of the war in Europe.

During the first weeks of 1945 we were busy trying to help evaders in the Belgian Ardennes where General Von Runstedt had launched Hitler's last desperate offensive in the West. Early in December 21st Army Group Intelligence Headquarters had warned me officially that an attack was anticipated but in private had told me that there was a considerable difference of opinion between the British and Americans as to its likely timing, location and objective.

The British view was that it would be on a limited front, in very considerable strength, through the Ardennes, not long delayed and with the objective of driving a wedge between the British and American Armies – in other words a repeat of the May 1940 offensive. The Americans held altogether different views, maintaining that the winter conditions ruled out such a possibility and that any resumption of the offensive by the Germans would be in the early spring in a series of attacks designed to disrupt preparations for a continued advance into Germany. They added for good measure that they thought the British had got the wind up unnecessarily.

The Ardennes were in the American sector and I would have liked to have set up a number of 'safe' houses, each with a 'Retriever' and a radio set, to serve as collecting points for any evaders over-run in the advance. Dick was enthusiastic, pointing out with a grin that even if the God damn Limeys' appreciation was wrong nothing would be lost, while if they were by some miracle right, there was a good deal to be gained. He offered me the use of a Rescue Team and promised me his support but, and I fully understood, he was not prepared to invite the inevitable snub by taking the matter up with the American Army concerned.

I put the plan to 21st Army Group, the reply from whom was firm but kind. 'Be your age, Jimmy. If you were caught swanning around the Ardennes activating a plan based on the assumption of a retreat by the Americans there would be a most unholy row. At the best your dismissal would be demanded and we should have difficulty in refusing it. At the worst you would probably be shot out of hand as a German agent spreading defeatism.' I bowed to the inevitable and had to be content with making arrangements for the evacuation of certain Belgian helpers who would be shot should they ever be caught by the advancing Germans. I also sent a warning order to three Belgian Retrievers to stand by for a recall.

I was in Paris when the Von Rundstedt offensive, as it was

to be called, was launched and, after arranging with Dick where to send his Rescue and Interrogation teams, raced back to Brussels. The initial success and speed of the German advance made it imperative to finalize the plans for saving helpers which, if things got really bad, would necessitate the use of every vehicle that we could lay hands on. It was not until Christmas Eve that 21st Army Group, by that valuable 'old boy network', told me: 'Monty has the matter in hand; the advance will be contained', and I was able to cancel these plans and send an advance Rescue Team to the Ardennes to see what could be done.

There was little we could achieve other than set up a series of posts to collect American stragglers who somehow, occasionally with local help, had managed to get through the German lines after they had been cut off. The fighting was so confused that it was difficult to know where to send a 'Retriever' and as the Germans had infiltrated a number of sabotage teams dressed in American and British uniforms there was a justifiable tendency to shoot anyone whose accent indicated possible foreign connections; a fate which the 'Retriever' might well have suffered. Whether the setting up of 'safe' houses with 'Retrievers' would have helped must for all time remain a matter for conjecture and even now with all the hindsight available I still remain undecided.

With more than four years of experience of 'escape and evasion', both in theory and practice, I was beginning to think nothing would surprise me, but on returning to Brussels I was soon to be proved wrong. Early one morning, towards the end of January, a signal from one of the Interrogation Teams came in requesting my presence without delay as they had been warned to expect more than 100 evaders within the next few hours. Routine reports from Airey made no mention of any impending large-scale operation and I could not envisage a 'do it yourself' effort on this scale. The mystery only deepened when on arrival I was introduced to a senior staff officer in whose divisional area the interrogation team was operating. He wasted no time in coming to the point. 'I must first apologize, colonel, for dragging you over here, but a somewhat difficult situation has arisen. I must then request that you treat what I am about to tell you in complete confidence.' I agreed and that is why even today I feel the Division must remain anonymous.

He smiled somewhat grimly. 'Two days ago in the late afternoon, more than 100 men of a unit in the Division . . .' He paused and I could see he was making a difficult decision. 'I must be frank, and trust the discretion of you and your officers,' he continued. I nodded. '. . . walked over to the enemy waving white flags. There was no question of surrendering in battle, the Germans were completely quiescent, and voluntarily gave themselves up. Yesterday the Germans withdrew and left them to their own devices. More than half have already been picked up and as they claim to be 'escapers' are, in accordance with Standing Orders, being sent here for interrogation and . . .', he paused again, the implied enquiry was clear. 'For return to England, I suppose?'

Apart from the Ardennes we had from time to time been sent men who had claimed to have got away from behind the enemy lines but whom interrogation had quickly shown to have been temporarily cut off or simply lost. We had always sent them back to their units with a brief note of the circumstances, leaving their commanders to judge whether any desertion was involved. However, this case was very different – the men had been prisoners of war even if their claim to escape was somewhat weak.

'Are you absolutely certain, sir,' I enquired, 'of the circumstances under which they were captured?'

'Yes,' was the reply, 'two officers with them naturally refused to go over and their reports leave no room for doubts.'

For all I knew he was within his rights to order me to pass the men back to him without interrogation. On the other hand, I could refuse on the grounds that the men were, technically at least, not guilty of desertion until so proved by court martial.

'I think the best solution is for us to send you all the men who arrive here, without interrogation, on the understanding you get in touch with me personally should any factor come to light which radically changes the position. Further, I will do my best to ensure that the information you have given me is treated as highly confidential.'

He was profuse in his thanks and by the time I had returned to Brussels I had thought out a suitable answer to satisfy excited enquiries from those who had seen the message.

'Bloody signallers,' I said, 'who cannot distinguish between evaders and prisoners.'

Later I learnt that the divisional commander had been kind enough to make mention to 21st Army Group of what he called 'my tactful handling of a difficult situation'. This thoughtful action possibly saved me from a severe rocket the one and only time I met Field-Marshal Sir Bernard Montgomery.

An old friend of mine, Colonel Kit Dawnay, was the Field-Marshal's Military Assistant and it occurred to me that he and his colleagues might enjoy some oysters from the beds on the island of Tholen, where our training centre was located. Returning from a visit there I broke my journey at 21st Army Group Headquarters and sent a small barrel to his office. The message of thanks was accompanied by an invitation from the Field-Marshal for the 'Oyster King' to dine with him.

His welcome was most cordial but the faint smiles on the faces of the members of his personal staff alerted me that something was afoot.

'I have no doubt, colonel,' he casually remarked 'you read my Standing Orders and take all the necessary steps to see they are carried out?' Ah, there was the trap, but how to wriggle out of it as I knew we constantly infringed at least half a dozen orders, though not, I thought, seriously enough to warrant intervention by the Army Group Commander. However I must be wrong, and as I had only occasionally given them a casual glance when I had nothing better to do, a little quick thinking was obviously required.

'Of course, sir, though I occasionally get a bit behind when I am away from my headquarters.'

'You must be a very long way behind this time. Only last week I repeated the order that local oysters were not to be eaten due to the danger of typhoid, and now you drive gaily into my headquarters and present my personal staff with a barrel. As soon as you get back you had better catch up with your reading.'

His smile and the roar of laughter from the others assured me I was forgiven and I consoled myself with the thought that in a few weeks there would no longer be an 'R' in the month.

It was a memorable dinner in a relaxed and comfortable atmosphere with none of the austerity and aloofness I had been led to expect.

'Do you like fried eggs and bacon,' he said as he rose to go to bed.

'Yes, sir,' I replied.

'Well then join me at breakfast.' I did and it was with enthusiasm I delivered his farewell message.

'I know it sounds trite but please convey my genuine wishes to all your men and for the best of luck in the future.'

It was at the end of January that I made a quick trip to Paris to say goodbye to Dick, who was returning to America. However it was not the farewell party that made the visit a memorable one. My driver said there was some trouble with my jeep. 'Nothing serious, sir. If you could get the spare parts I think I could fix it myself.' We followed Dick's instructions and I reported my difficulties to the American officer responsible for meeting all the former's transportation needs. 'Go out and get yourself a coffee, colonel,' he said. 'Come back in an hour when everything will be O.K.'

I duly returned to find my driver transferring all our equipment to a brand new jeep.

'I don't want a new jeep,' I said to the American. 'Just those spare parts.'

'Sorry, colonel,' he retorted, 'my instructions are clear. Our boys are all set for the final drive into Germany and there is to be no messing around. I've got to give 'em all they want.'

My protests died away. 'What do I do with my old one?'

'Just take it away, colonel. Please don't leave it lying around here.'

I rang up a 'Retriever' who was on leave in Paris and we all arrived safely in Brussels without even having to tow my old jeep. Better still, I never signed for the new one.

Early in February the weather improved sufficiently to permit the launching of a series of brilliantly conceived and executed rescue operations in western Holland over the waterways, creeks and inlets that go to make up the low-lying polder land of the Biersbosch. Although during the next three months the number of men saved, all evaders from the Arnhem landings, were relatively small, about 50, each operation was a superb example of what could be done when the tools were available. The RAF loaned us two Mosquito aircraft which made possible ground to air radio communication with the Dutch Resistance. It cut out the inevitable delays in sending messages via London and also permitted 'in clear' verbal communication, since interception was only possible by an enemy plane flying at the same time, height and place. The Commando headquarters in London supplied us with electrically propelled canoes and a host of other gadgets to facilitate night water-borne operations.

The successes gained, however, did not stem entirely from the adequate provision of the sinews of evasion. The Dutch Resistance never lost heart during the long, bitter winter, while three officers of outstanding ability joined us. The first two, Hugh Fraser and Maurice Macmillan were both to become distinguished Members of Parliament; the latter also destined to rise to Cabinet rank. The third, Leo Heaps, had made a spectacular escape from Arnhem during which he swam across the Rhine.

It has always been a matter of personal regret that their successes did not receive the congratulations and rewards they undoubtedly merited and I must take most of the blame. In March, however, the Rhine was successfully crossed at a number of points and all eyes and thoughts turned east as the Allied armies advanced into the heart of Germany.

Long and careful consideration had been given to what the rôle of IS 9 should be in Germany and what part they should play in liberating the Allied POWs. It did not require much imagination to realize there was a very high chance that, when all was obviously lost, Hitler might issue an order that Allied prisoners were to be shot or otherwise liquidated.

There was no lack of suggestions as to action by the Allies, varying from threatened reprisals on the 'eye for an eye, tooth for a tooth' theme, to offering a reward or 'amnesty' to leading Nazis in exchange for the prisoners' lives. But most of these were utterly impracticable for a variety of reasons. The only one that merited careful examination was the possibility of dropping arms to the inmates of the camps, backed up by parachute troops from the SAS or airborne divisions. This possibility was discussed at a high-level meeting at SHAEF in Versailles early in February but unanimously turned down for one over-riding reason.

Prisoners of war who embark on armed resistance against their captors instantly lose all their rights under the Geneva Convention and it was quite impossible to guarantee that even the majority of the camps could be taken over and held against the inevitable counter attacks. There could be no half measures since an attempt, however successful, would to some extent justify any order Hitler might give and further might incite camp commandants to anticipate a possible armed rising by shooting those they considered potential leaders. We could only hope that camp commandants would not carry out any order Hitler might issue, either on humane grounds or for fear of their own skins.

It was frequently said that Hitler did give an order of this kind but I never saw a copy. If any of the camp commandants did receive such an order they never carried it out. In other words they justified our hopes of their going in for a little local skin saving.

The decision not to give any armed assistance to the POW camps in Germany, other than that which could be provided by the ground troops liberating them, and the instructions to the senior officers and NCOs to stay put until liberated, facilitated the planning of IS 9's rôle after the crossing of the Rhine and during the occupation of Germany. Apart from serving as collecting points for the last-minute escapers and evaders the unit's main duties were to undertake a preliminary short interrogation of the liberated POWs and to apprehend any of those suspected of collaborating with the enemy.

I viewed both tasks with considerable apprehension knowing only too well how much evaders, even though they were safely back in England, disliked interrogations. I could picture the reaction of the liberated POWs who would regard it as a frustrating and entirely unnecessary process further delaying their return home or at least to England. The evidence of collaboration was likely to be so nebulous as not to warrant arrest, and I felt any special treatment would alert the individual of trouble ahead, very possibly encouraging him to disappear before a case against him could be built up.

However, there was nothing for it but to make the best of what was obviously going to be a very difficult undertaking. The Interrogation Teams were sub-divided so that there were at least two representatives at the main staging camps at Rheims, Brussels and Antwerp and simple 'do it yourself' interrogation forms were printed and distributed. In theory these were to be handed out with a pencil to all returning POWs and to be collected when completed. A list of wanted men was also issued with instructions that when apprehended they were to be sent to IS 9 headquarters or to the Awards Bureaux in Paris or Brussels for further questioning.

I would have liked to have abandoned all rescue operations in Holland and sent the teams into Germany in the hopes that they might get into some of the POW camps immediately they were over-run and get some of the interrogation done before transport was available to send the inmates to the staging camps. However, we were too deeply committed with the Dutch underground so I left Airey with his rescue teams to deal with the evaders and helpers in northern Holland as soon as it was liberated and took the rest of the unit over the Rhine. After despatching a small section to see if they could give any help when the notorious concentration camp at Belsen was liberated, where it was possible some of our helpers might be, I followed the advancing British Army with the rest of my headquarters.

I was particularly anxious to reach the POW Camp, Marlag-Milag, near Hamburg, as soon as possible. It was the camp where most of the Royal Naval and Mercantile Marine prisoners were held and I knew that the survivors from the midget submarine attacks on the *Tirpitz* were amongst its inmates. Donald Cameron, who had 'kidnapped' me into his 'X' craft when I had briefed the crews on escape, evasion and interrogation, had survived and been awarded the Victoria Cross. I much looked forward to meeting him again and hearing his story.

The triumphant advance was my first real contact with the German people and I was shocked at the abjectness of their surrender. Most of the houses had white sheets hanging from their windows and even the chicken houses, pig sties and stables were liberally decked with white flags. There was little evidence of dignity in defeat though one old lady ran out of her house and spat at me, but only succeeded in hitting my jeep's windscreen. When my driver asked me if he should box her ears to teach her more respect I replied 'No, give her a packet of cigarettes and a clean handkerchief, if you've got one, as a token of my respect for her courage.'

Occupying was a sordid and distasteful experience, made worse by the order 'No fraternization'. How anyone expected to stop the British soldier from fraternizing with little children and pretty girls and cripples was beyond my comprehension. I soon turned a blind eye to the furtive handing out of chocolates, sweets and cigarettes, and comforted myself with the thought that I was obviously not cut out to be a victor. The girl friend problem was rapidly reduced to the absurd by the slogan, said to have been the unofficial instructions by General Patton, to his Army, 'Fornication is NOT fraternization unless you say thank you afterwards.'

The entry into Marlag-Milag behind the leading troops was one of my highlights of the war. Shouting 'Interpreter,

interpreter' in German at the top of my voice – it was one of the few words I knew – I ordered a German officer who responded to lead me to Donald Cameron's room.

Donald was sitting on the edge of his bunk and his face lit up when he saw me.

'Heartiest congratulations on your Victoria Cross,' I said. 'Few moments have given me more pleasure than to be the first from outside to congratulate you.' He grinned, stood up and saluted. 'May I congratulate you on your splendid simulated German interrogation. The real thing was so similar that I felt I was reacting a part I had already played.' I remembered somewhat shamefacedly that I had smacked his face when he had given an insolent reply to one of my questions. 'May I add,' he continued 'that your slap was harder than the one I received from the German interrogating officer.' We both laughed and I felt a glow of inward pleasure at having achieved something, however small.

During the next few hours, when it became clear that there would be a long delay before the lorries arrived to collect the freed prisoners, discipline began to break down. Inevitably some of the inmates got hold of drink and I had to display my revolver to enforce my orders that the German officers were not to be stripped of their watches and cigarette cases, as they were loaded into trucks en route for their POW camp. I had no compunction in so doing – I had been fairly treated when captured and I saw no reason for not repaying in kind.

Our efforts at interrogation met with little success, partly due to the men's unexpected refusal to answer questions originating from soldiers – or bloody Pongos as we were occasionally called by the more bellicose. The Navy in most cases did their best to co-operate and the trouble usually came from the Mercantile Marine personnel who resented any form of control. As we were far too few to be effective I discontinued our forlorn efforts since we were doing more harm than good.

Our experiences at Marlag-Milag were a taste of things to come and I spent the next three months doing the rounds of the interrogation sections, congratulating them on doing their best in impossible circumstances and giving them the encouragement they badly needed. The truth was that most of the returning POWs were not amenable to interrogation however brief and were prepared to go to considerable lengths to avoid it. Ultimately we ran out of pencils and reverted to helping in the administration of the staging camps and interrogating the odd individual who was bursting to tell everyone how well he had behaved in prison and of his legendary attempts to escape.

I would have liked to have helped the Awards Bureaux in Paris, Brussels and the Hague to welcome the pitifully few helpers and agents who were saved from the concentration camps but this was not to be and I had to be content with brief visits to some of them in hospital. However, I did have the consolation of getting hold of Pat O'Leary, who had been liberated in Dachau, and taking him to my home in Suffolk where I hoped he would recuperate. I planned a week but after sleeping for one day, eating almost continuously for two, he said it was time he went back to France to find out what had happened to the rest of his colleagues.

It was not until the end of June that the last POWs were rounded up. Quite a number had decided to take some self-allocated leave with friends, new or old, in France or Belgium.

IS 9 was now concentrated at Bad Salzuflen prior to being disbanded, and I was given the uncongenial task of compiling a report of the unit's activities since 'D'-Day. 'And no witty cracks,' said Norman Crockatt. 'You are writing official history.' The Rescue Teams working with the organization had saved some 400 evaders who otherwise would have fallen into enemy hands and I shall always regard Pegasus I as the finest evasion operation of the whole war in western Europe, if only because the route out was through an area held in great strength by the German fighting troops, who were not in the habit of going to sleep when in contact with the enemy.

The Interrogation Teams' task was less glamorous but they obtained much information of value, notably from an RAF pilot who had escaped in Normandy before he could be sent to Germany. His German interrogator had told him that the best way to deal with V1's, the flying bombs, was to fly a fighter in front of them. The fighter's slipstream would affect the V1's stability and it would plunge earthwards before reaching its target.

IS 9, the brainchild of Norman Crockatt, was a brilliant conception, not too big so as to give rise to the criticism that it was an unnecessary appendage to the invading forces, not too little so as to be ineffective. It met and solved the problems as they arose and carried the saga of escape and evasion to a triumphant conclusion. However, in keeping with its tradition, disbandonment raised the last unforeseen problem.

In the spring of 1940 in France I had been fined £2 by a court of enquiry for losing an army bicycle. My spirited defence that I was only on charge because I happened to be the junior officer present in the mess when it disappeared from a stack of some six others outside was not accepted. In January 1945, in my capacity of officer commanding, I was found guilty of gross negligence and fined 10 shillings when a brand new three-ton lorry was stolen from outside our headquarters in Brussels. This despite the removal every night of all four wheels and part of the ignition system; a fact which I considered a more than adequate defence. It was therefore with considerable pride that on handing in all our transport I was able to report that I was one jeep to the good.

'You cannot be, old boy,' said authority.

'I am,' I replied, 'it was a present from the Americans.'

'Well, get rid of the damn thing,' came the retort. 'Losses we can deal with. Surpluses, no. If you insist you will be court-martialled for stealing Government property. Bury it.' We did, by driving it over the edge of a disused sandpit full of water.

It had been a long war but not long enough for me to grasp the intricacies of the Military Mind.

16

The End of the Day

If I found difficulty in understanding the 'Military Mind' I was in goodly company when the plans for demobilization were announced. To many they made little sense as they appeared to be based largely on age, making little allowance for length of service which aroused, not unnaturally, widespread criticism. In July 1945 when IS 9 was disbanded and I had said goodbye I found I had another seven months to serve before my release date came round. The regiment had little to offer other than a posting to Pirbright with the prospect of endless drill parades and field training. MI 9 was also being disbanded, while IV Z had already been returned to store, presumably until the next war. There was nothing for it but to find employment in western Europe and I was offered and accepted the post of Town Major in Antwerp. Before taking this on, however, I revisited some of the places that had been so much part of my life in the early years of the war and sought out my 'helpers' in Lille and Paris.

Around Bachy and Pont à Marc there was little left of the defence lines built during the 'phoney war', since during the years of occupation the industrious French peasants had filled in or flattened all the trenches and breastworks and removed the miles of barbed-wire entanglements. However, all the Pill Boxes had survived and in the anti-tank ditches I was pleased to see that some of the willows we had planted were doing well; while the welcome by the farmers and villagers left nothing to be desired. Even today, after more than 30 years, I exchange Christmas or New Year cards with my hosts in Bachy.

The areas where we had stood and fought during the retreat to Dunkirk had changed little, but it was somewhat of a shock to find my grave, or at least a white cross with black lettering giving my name, rank, number, regiment and date of death, in the grounds of the Chapeau Rouge near Dunkirk where the CCS (Casualty Clearing Station) had been located in June 1940. How the error had occurred I was never able to discover, but in due course the occupant of the grave was disinterred and identified. Much to my regret I was unable to get possession of the cross, which would have made a fine family heirloom.

My reunion with Madame Caron, my 'war godmother' whose daily food parcels had done so much to save my life in the prison hospital in Lille, was most moving. I had brought her a silver coffee pot as a small token of my gratitude which with difficulty I persuaded her to accept. Then her eyes flooded with tears and she said, 'I have kept these until you returned,' showing me two brass Coldstream badges of rank which I had cut off my battledress and given her. 'Would you let me keep them, they have meant so much to me during all the years we have been occupied by the Germans?' It was my turn to wipe the tears from my eyes.

I nodded and in true French fashion she became practical. 'I learn that you are still rationed in England, how sad as the victors.' she said, dragging forward a huge brown paper parcel, 'I have been saving these knowing you would come back.' Tea, coffee, sugar, tinned butter, ham, more than I could carry. How, I thought, can one ever say 'thank you' to people like these.

It was much the same when I called on the Carpentiers, the family of dentists who had hidden me during my first night of freedom in Lille. 'It was an honour and a privilege to help you, the least we could do,' they all said. 'We have had our reward, we are liberated. Now we know you love French food and wine, we are arranging a special dinner tonight – let's call it a "thank you" celebration.'

In Paris, first in my mind was the Institut Mozart, members of which had organized my onward journey to Unoccupied France, but despite an intensive search, much helped by the

Awards Bureau, I was never able to trace it. The trail finished in Lille, where Madame Samiez had disappeared, the only person who probably could have named the man she sent down to Paris and whom I fortuitously sat down next to on the bench in the Champs Elysées that lovely October evening.

It was in the course of my visits to the Awards Bureaux in Paris and Brussels that I became increasingly aware how swiftly the human frailties of greed and ambition rise to the fore when the dangers of death or imprisonment recede. The great leaders, Dédée of Comet, Pat O'Leary of PAO, Dumais of Shelburne, Mary Lindell and those of their colleagues and close associates who survived, continued to work for others. They were unceasing in their efforts to ensure that awards were justly made and, when help was required to mitigate suffering, that it was swiftly forthcoming.

However there were countless cases of individuals who, as soon as there was no fear of German reprisals, were vociferous in their claims to have hidden and helped Allied evaders. To prove or disprove these claims was not an easy task. Some were genuine helpers who were only known under the 'nom de guerre' they had given to evaders and whose link with an organization had been broken when the Germans arrested their contact. Others had merely helped an evader on his way with food and a night's shelter. Since even doing this risked being shot they naturally felt they should receive some award. Then there were those who were known to have had dealings with the Germans but who claimed that any collaboration had been solely to obtain ration cards, food and false papers for evaders. And so it went on down to the sheer impostors who hoped that the British or Americans would substantiate their stories when they could claim to be 'Heroes of the Resistance', and flaunt their foreign awards in the face of their disbelieving fellow countrymen.

The Awards Bureaux did magnificent work in proving or disproving all the claims and of assessing their relative merit for awards. Miscarriages of justice were few but nonetheless there are men and women today still basking in the glory of deeds of heroism in the field of evasion which were figments of a lively imagination but could not be totally disproved. During the years since the war I have met several of these individuals but have done no more than think of President Lincoln's famous saying, 'You can fool some of the people all of the time . . .'

Then there were the traitors, the men and women who helped the Germans to destroy the evasion organizations and who knew that their work would result in hundreds of people being tortured, then shot or sent to concentration camps. Most of them paid the penalty for their treachery in front of a firing squad,* but not always.

Roger the Legionnaire (Roger le Neveu) who personally arrested Pat O'Leary and betrayed a number of others in his organization, was reported to have been liquidated by the French 'maquis' in the south of France after the liberation. I was not the only one to doubt the veracity of this report and I believe it very probable that he took refuge in Spain.

Prosper Desitter and Jacques Desoubrie, of Belgian origin, who were largely responsible for the disasters suffered by Comet in 1943 and 1944 were tried and shot.

But there is no doubt that a number of minor traitors, of whose activities we had reports but whose real identity was not established, escaped justice. Nor were any of the 'agents provocateurs', Germans in British or American uniforms posing as evaders, ever caught. One of them I would very much have liked to interrogate to find out why he had failed to 'die' as arranged. He had parachuted by night from a German aircraft over northern France and had made contact at dawn with a farmer and his wife who had hidden him in their cellar. Claiming to be from a bomber squadron which at this time was not operational, his true identity had been swiftly established, but the farming family shrank from killing him in cold blood as instructed and demanded some poison pills, such as were carried by agents for use when arrested by

* As a final act of denigration they were not permitted to face death but were strapped to the posts with their backs towards the firing squad.

the Gestapo. These were duly despatched and administered, though quite how this was done I never discovered. Guaranteed to kill in a matter of minutes, the only result in this case was, in the words of the farmer 'extreme constipation and intense headaches'. Still unable to nerve themselves to kill by other methods, they drove him some 40 miles by night and dumped him in a wood, hoping he would be unable to relocate their farm. Their luck held, but I would have liked to know what went wrong with the pills.

The task of dealing with British traitors and the like was made the responsibility of Scotland Yard, but the Awards Bureaux were naturally actively involved as far as Paul Cole was concerned, and it was from Donald Darling and Pat O'Leary that I heard what became of him.

The full extent of his treachery during the years 1941–45 will never be known, but he certainly denounced more than 150 French helpers, a large number of whom were either shot or died in concentration camps. Nor was it ever possible to ascertain how many evaders he handed over to the Germans during 1943 when posing as the head of an evasion organization. That the Germans appreciated his work was clear as he was seen leaving Paris in August 1944 a few days before the liberation dressed as a German officer and riding in a staff car.

Nothing further is known of his activities until in the spring of 1945 he contacted an American unit in the south of Germany, posing as Captain Mason of the British Intelligence Service. He immediately gained the confidence of the Americans by denouncing a number of erstwhile colleagues in the Gestapo and Abwehr and his credentials were not checked. However he must have known that sooner or later his identity would be questioned and it was presumably with the idea of returning to France that he sent a postcard to a girl friend in Paris. She, convinced that he was a genuine British agent working on evasion, showed it to Donald Darling at the Awards Bureaux.

Cole was arrested and brought to Paris under guard where he succeeded in escaping from the SHAEF Military Prison wearing a stolen American sergeant's uniform jacket. He might well have got clean away had not the landlady of the room over Billy's Bar in the Rue de Grenelle, where he was hiding, told the police she suspected he was a deserter. He was killed while shooting it out with the two gendarmes who came to arrest him, and Pat O'Leary identified his body.

As Town Major in Antwerp, Bourg Leopold and finally in the small market town of Turnhout in the north of Belgium, I had ample time to ruminate over the successes and failures of Escape and Evasion in western Europe 1940–45, as indeed I have done over the years that followed.

'Figures,' said the Professor at Harvard Business School, opening his final lecture on Company Finance and Accounting, and pinning up a brassiere on the blackboard, 'can be made to mean anything,' a statement with which I cordially agreed. More than 3000 members of Allied aircrews shot down over France, Belgium and Holland before the Normandy landings successfully evaded and returned to England. To this impressive figure must be added 200 or so soldiers from the retreat to Dunkirk, the gallant stand of the 51st Highland Division at St Valery en Caux and the Commando raids such as Dieppe and St Nazaire.

The number of people who were shot, died under torture or in concentration camps to achieve these successes will never be known, but I believe it to be far in excess of 500 recorded names. In all three countries hundreds of men and women were arrested and condemned to death under the charge of having helped the Allied cause, with no specific details given. That for every successful evader a Belgian, Dutch or French helper gave his or her life would, I think, be a fairer estimate of the price paid.

The value to the war effort of a successful evader is equally hard to assess, being virtually zero in the case of some survivors of the BEF, who had undoubtedly deserted during the fighting in May 1940, but very great where fighter pilots, bomber aircrews, commandos and other highly trained personnel were concerned. It was on this latter fact that Norman

Crockatt based his fight for recognition. What was not foreseen was the incredible boost to morale given by an RAF evader's return to the station from which he had gone missing. Initially, and very naturally, the RAF were sceptical as to the practical value of lectures on escape and evasion, the issue of 'escape packs', foreign currency, compasses and maps: but when the end product walked into the mess with a cheery, 'Well chaps, I'm back,' everything changed.

In the 1914–18 war the issue of parachutes to the RFC was long delayed due to the view of the High Command that their use would encourage pilots to abandon their aircraft on the first pretext and not fight it out to the end. The same muddled thinking was applied to escape and evasion during the first two years of the last war, and the only epitaph I can find for the work of Norman Crockatt, Airey Neave, Donald Darling and myself is 'Too little and too late'.

It is because of this feeling that I rarely attend re-unions of the survivors of the organizations, though hardly any have ever hinted that our efforts were not as helpful as might have been expected. They are far too great people to indulge in recriminations; in fact I find their obvious pleasure in seeing me and their expression of appreciation for what little we did do most embarrassing.

I do not blame any individual for our shortcomings, least of all Uncle Claude, whose task of building up an intelligence network in France, Belgium and Holland was overriding and to the fulfilment of which he justifiably allowed no obstacles to come in his way. No, the fault lay in the inability of anyone to see that the apparently impossible was possible. It was accepted that the odd fighter pilot or bomber crew, baling out over enemy-occupied territory in uniform, might be lucky enough to get back to England but that this would become almost routine and that there were thousands of men and women prepared to risk their lives to this end was not appreciated as quickly as it should have been.

The results of the failure to grasp the immense potentials of organized escape and evasion are self evident and it suffices to say that had it been granted the same sinews of of war as SOE, and similar status, I am convinced much more would have been achieved and that the lives of many of the major organizers would have been saved. Far too frequently they were arrested simply because they had continued working long after their activities were known to the Germans and they should have been pulled out for rest and training, but we had no replacements.

If I look back in sorrow and sometimes in anger at the frustrations, failures and cost in lives that marked the years 1941–43, I also take pride in remembering what was achieved and in having worked with men and women whose devotion to a cause was so whole-hearted and unswerving, even in the face of death.

Dédée de Jongh survived the years in the concentration camp of Ravensbruck and still works at her self-appointed task of helping others as the matron in a leper hospital in Addis Ababa. Pat O'Leary has just retired as the general commanding the Belgian Medical Corps; all the horrors of Dachau never broke him. While Jean de Blommaert lives in Belgium and Dumais in Paris.

Norman Crockatt died a few years ago not, however, before he had the satisfaction of meeting and congratulating most of the survivors from the organizations. Airey Neave, who as the first British officer to escape from Colditz, is perhaps the greatest living expert on escape and evasion, is MP for Abingdon, while Donald Darling, after many years in Brazil, lives in London and Ian Garrow in Scotland.

It was shortly after the end of the war that Uncle Claude, by then Sir Claude, died – even he could not wriggle out of that one.

Apart from the 3000 or so escapers and evaders who returned to fight on and the beneficial effect on morale at the fighter and bomber stations, there were some very important ancillary rewards. The information brought back by the survivors from the Dieppe Raid and the attack on the shipping at St Nazaire by the cockleshell heroes was of immense value, as were reports on how and why an aircraft had been shot down. But perhaps the greatest achievement of all was rescuing an individual who was shot down knowing all the plans for 'D'-Day. The recovery orders issued to the organizations: 'Alive if possible: kill if he looks like falling into German hands', were a fair indication of his value.

Demobilized in 1946, I thought I would see what the Officers' Employment Bureau had to offer. 'Just the job for you,' said the officer who interviewed me, 'You have all the necessary qualifications though I am afraid I don't know what the work is – highly secret I believe. I'll send you round in my car.' Over the laughter that greeted my reappearance at Broadway Buildings I could hear Uncle Claude saying from the great beyond, 'Not suitable, he loves his agents.'

Well, if ever people deserved to be loved it is those brave men and women whose courage and self-sacrifice enabled so many to live and fight another day.